# Involvements

# Colman McCarthy

# Involvements

## One Journalist's Place
in the World

ACROPOLIS BOOKS LTD.
WASHINGTON, D.C.

*Other books by Colman McCarthy*
## Disturbers of the Peace
## Inner Companions
## Pleasures of the Game

**ACROPOLIS BOOKS, LTD.**
Colortone Building, 2400 17th Street, N.W
Washington, D.C 20009

**Printed in the United States of America by**
COLORTONE PRESS
Creative Graphics, Inc.
Washington, D.C 20009

**Attention: Schools and Corporations**
ACROPOLIS books are available at quantity discounts with bulk purchase for educational, business, or sales promotional use. For further information, please write to: SPECIAL SALES DEPARTMENT, ACROPOLIS BOOKS, LTD., 2400 17th ST., N.W., WASHINGTON, D.C 20009.

**Are there Acropolis Books you want but cannot find in your local store?**
You can get any Acropolis book title in print Simply send title and retail price, plus 50 cents for postage and handling costs for each book desired District of Columbia residents add applicable sales tax. Enclose check or money order only, no cash please, to: ACROPOLIS BOOKS LTD., 2400 17th St., N.W., WASHINGTON, D.C 20009

**Library of Congress Cataloging in Publication Data**

McCarthy, Colman.
   Involvements: a journalist's place in the world.

   Includes index.
   1. McCarthy, Colman—Addresses, essays, lectures.
   2. Journalists—United States—Biography—
Addresses, essays, lectures. I. Title.
PN4874.M48394A34   1984   070'.92'4 [B]   84-14441
ISBN 0-87491-757-3

*Thanks to the Washington Post Writers Group and *The Washington Post* for permission to include several Washington Post copyrighted articles in this collection.

For Justin, Denis and John McCarthy:
good men and loyal brothers

## Acknowledgments

Grateful acknowledgments are made to the following magazines, whose editors first took the pieces. Some titles have been changed, along with deletions or additions where needed.

Newsweek, *"The Mugging of Liberalism;"* The Nation, *"On Chicago's Margin,"* *"The Outsider;"* The Washington Monthly, *"Sargent Shriver;"* The National Catholic Reporter, *"New Shoots for Peace,"* *"Whose Church Is It?"* and Notre Dame Magazine, *"Daniel Berrigan,"* The Runner, *"Meeting At the Wall,"* and *"Press Runs."*

Most else is from The Washington Post, with much of the copy first passing through the hand of Anna Karavangelos, a world-class editor and first class friend. My thanks also to Al Hackl, owner of Acropolis Books. I like him for staying in the game for 38 years against the might of the New York publishing conglomerates. More, he respects the unions in his plant and the writers in his care.

# Contents

## 1. Teaching to Learn, Learning to Teach    19

New Shoots for Peace
Children Who Disagree
Elementary Détente
My Best Student
Two Who Didn't Burn Out
Letter to a Haitian Boy
Backstage with Joan Baez
Where Have All the Idealists Gone?
Dear Director of Admissions
Who Needs Accreditation?

## 2. Wives and Children: Take Time    53

Fathers, Father Figures
Together for the Long Run
Winging It
An Innocent Looks Right, Turns Left
What Mothers Silently Know
Becoming a Man by Tending Children
Sharing the Faith With Children
Confessions Of a Halloween Wierdo
A Father's Day

# Foreword

There are very few columnists whose pieces I often clip. Most columnists are all too perishable. They just read other columnists and watch television, just as we do, so they're literally quite useless. Oh, a few do have "interview opportunities" with Presidents and Senate leaders and barons of the Pentagon, but all they pick up and disseminate that way is official lies. Again, they're quite useless for future reference.

I mean, think about the biggest "names" among columnists. Would you buy a book of their collected pieces, even at the remainder counter? Even in the same year in which they've been published?

Colman McCarthy is another matter. First of all, he is a reporter first, so his columns bring you information—and most important, actual people—first-hand. Second, he goes places most columnists have no interest in. Schoolrooms, for instance. He not only goes there, he sometimes teaches there, which is a much better way of learning about learning than just observing. (If public television had any imagination, which it clearly does not, except for how to raise money, McCarthy's classes in nonviolence for schoolkids would have been a series. A series worth repeating as a corollary to the history of the war in Vietnam.)

McCarthy also goes among the homeless and brings back their news. I would pay dearly to see Bill Buckley or Joe Kraft among the homeless, but that's a wicked thought and probably has no place in an introduction to the work of the least wicked—and yet most believable—man I know.

So, I clip a lot of McCarthy's columns, and show them around. But I mainly clip them for myself. Sometimes for reference—like the pieces of Joann Newak here which became the base for a series of my own on that brave and innocent young woman. And I also clip for sustenance. Spiritual sustenance, if an atheist may use that term.

Let me tell you why. Years ago, Tom Wicker said of I. F. Stone—who, like George Seldes, has been a mentor to me just by being and not giving up—that the thing about Izzy is he never lost his sense of rage. McCarthy too. The man will not adjust to injustice of any kind. This makes him rare among all kinds of citizens, certainly including journalists. But there is another part to that. As with Izzy Stone, McCarthy does not sup on rage along. He keeps showing his readers, but first himself, that it can't go on like this forever. (Whatever "it" is at the time.) Reagan and all his cruel, crabbed works, for example. And McCarthy shows us that possibility is possible by—again—going out and reporting. Finding people who also are not accepting injustice and instead are *doing* the right and just thing. Some are teachers, some are Maryknoll missioners, some are in the A. J. Muste-Martin Luther King tradition of direct nonviolent civil disobedience, heathen though a number of them may be.

I turn back to those McCarthy columns, then, when I need something more than Scotch in the night. In some of them, I've just circled a line or two. Like these in a piece about a day when McCarthy went to talk to 4th and 5th graders in a Washington public school about writing:

"To ask children to disagree if they like is to give the message they hunger for: You matter."

They'll not inscribe that in marble anywhere, but you'd be surprised how few adults know what children hunger for, and the harm that comes from adults not knowing it. And I figure maybe one or even a few parents and teachers may have happened on that column, and McCarthy's line may have taken root and some kids, at home or at school, may owe Colman one for that sooner or later.

Not that he'd ever want to collect. He's like Izzy Stone that way. Izzy once said to a group of young journalists that he's forever surprised that he gets paid for what he does because he has so much fun doing it.

Another time, when McCarthy went to a schoolroom—this was a storefront community learning center in Baltimore—he mentioned Willa Cather's belief that "handiwork is a beautiful education in itself, and something real ... The one education which amounts to anything is how to do something well, whether it is to make a bookcase or write a book."

Or to write a column twice a week, and other pieces from time to time, that are so real and so well-made that they provide a continuing record, for anyone who wants to look, of where we are (quicksand and all), where we ought to be going, and even how we might get there.

That is some piece of work, week after week, and that's why this is no ordinary collection. You'll want to keep it around for your grandchildren. And you'll want it around for yourself, if you ever feel you're losing your sense of rage—and your sense of possibility. This McCarthy will not let people doze.                    *Nat Hentoff*

# Preface

In the summer of 1968 I spent some time interviewing families in Mound Bayou, Mississippi, an all-black community in the Delta flatlands. The citizens lived in what was then the poorest county in what is still the nation's poorest state. The news that summer was medical. Nurses and doctors from Boston had begun a health clinic to care for hungry black people whom nearly everyone else had forgotten. Drugs were dispensed, all of them the latest on the market. Not a virus, germ or wheeze would be unattacked. But soon it was learned that the most effective medicine was not the newest pharmaceutical miracle. It was food. The local epidemic of malnutrition could be controlled, and possibly cured, by vegetables and fruits grown in the community.

I wrote the story of modern medicine's arrival in Mound Bayou and sent the 2,000 word article, unsolicited, to The Washington Post. A few days later, Howard Simons, then an editor of the Sunday Outlook section and later The Post's managing editor, phoned to say that he liked the article and would run it. I was ecstatic. The deeper joy was when Simons, an instinctively friendly and go-for-it fellow, suggested cheerily that I write again for The Post.

I did. The pieces ran, and a few months later I was invited by Philip Geyelin to join the paper's editorial page staff. I have been at The Post since.

It was Mark Twain—it usually is—who said that "work is what you do when you'd rather be doing something else." By that durable definition, I've never worked. It's been play these 15 years of writing for what I think is the country's most readable and vibrant daily newspaper. The Post is a writer's paper. A scrambler's too. In 15 years, unwalled, I have been free to write for all of its sections, beyond what I was contributing on a regular basis to the editorial and op-ed pages. This has included book reviews, page one news stories, metropolitan reporting, sportswriting, obituaries, Sunday magazine essays, Style section profiles, Outlook analyses and religion page commentary. Editors at The Post, I learned early and have rejoiced about since, are not people to cut off possibilities. Such managerialism occurs at other papers where freedom of the press, it seems, doesn't always extend to letting the writers enjoy the freedom of the newspaper.

In addition to relishing the company of some of the country's most inspired and honest journalists—Morton Mintz, Herb Block, Mary McGrory, to start the list—I have admired the paper for its institutional support of community organizations. The Post has faults, but aloofness isn't one of them.

In this atmosphere, I have enjoyed what Henry James called "accessibility to experience." Why bother to be a writer unless you can engage your soul and emotions—and not only your head—with the best of the ideas, events or persons you are writing about? From this, I have had involvements. This is a collection of them, my own favorites and ones that I remember as pleasing to my family and others I care about. The communion between a writer and reader is part of the pay that is the true compensation of journalism. The other part is the coalition of caring that can occur when there is a purpose in the writing beyond getting it into print and, tally-ho, onto the next fox of a subject. The purpose is no mystery. Everyone is attracted to what she or he thinks is beautiful. All the philosophers, or at least the grounded ones, have said that. I've become convinced that many of this world's most intensely alive people— those with souls intact, minds unbought—are to be found at the bottom or on the fringes. This is not to romanticize poverty or eccentricity. It means that when I get a chance to write about some idealists who run a shelter for homeless people or a prisoner unjustly sentenced or a family that's being stripmined off its land in Mingo County, W. Va., or a fourth grader who wonders why the adult world is so violent—from all of that, a chance exists to elevate myself a little by being aligned with values that are enduring.

These are no more than the common aspirings of each person wanting a share of the world's bounty—a home, some food, a chance for a job, and perhaps some conversation with an understanding person. Writing, even daily journalism, can on good days for a lucky few be a way of proclaiming that the beauty we hunger for—justice in people's lives, a chance to love and be loved—is findable, and can be jotted down in a reporter's notebook and brought back to the typewriter to be shared with others.

In the end, the sharing becomes the beautiful that we've been seeking all along. It doesn't matter what or how much we give, as long as the generosity is pure. When Ernest Hemingway won the Nobel Prize for Literature, he gave away his medal to a Cuban fisherman. An astonished friend asked why he did that. Hemingway replied that you don't really own anything until you can give it away. Every person knows this to be true, however agonizingly hard it is to practice most of the time.

The sharers are the ones with whom I have sought involvements. They are the people of action I want to be aligned with. In 15 years of writing for a living and another 15 getting ready for it by writing in grade school, high school and college, I have met many more than the half-dozen—my "kindly mentors"—whom I have included here. I have had to limit also the pieces on ideas and events that have been my personal or professional involvements. A collection shouldn't be an amassment.

Most of the columns and longer magazine articles here allowed me to get beyond spectatorship and put something of myself—my beliefs, ideals—to the test. I live a comfortable easygoing life, made so by God's blessings of good health and the delights of a marriage to a woman who practices a command of the heart that only a faithful few ever obey for the duration: be of love a little more careful than of everything. My deviations are benign: I am a pacifist, a vegetarian, a Catholic trying to become a Christian, a bicyclist and runner. I am a union member who is grateful to the brothers and sisters who won a 37½ hour work week, which is about all the time I think is fair to take away from my wife and three sons. All four are owners of my heart.

These are small risk-free protests from the established way. I should do more. If it is not enough, it still takes me beyond what I'd be doing if I didn't agree with what I think are the most beautiful words Carl Jung ever wrote: "My family and my neighbors are my life—the only thing I can experience. What lies beyond is newspaper mythology. It is not of vast importance that I make a career or achieve great things for myself. What is important and meaningful to my life is that I shall live as fully as possible to fulfil the divine will within me. This task gives me so much to do that I have no time for any other. Let me point out that if we were all to live in that way we would need no armies, no police, no diplomacy, no politics, no banks. We would have a meaningful life and not what we have now—madness."

Each of us should try to interpret Jung's word "neighbor" to mean more than the people on the block. Neighborhood should mean any place that needs our compassion and time, any place that shelters common life and allows a writer to enter its impersonality to transform it to the personal and knowable. How can involvements not occur? Why should they not be celebrated?

All of us, if we paused and noticed in what directions our hearts are traveling, would be proud of a few involvements and ashamed of some others. Walter Lippmann said that "many a time I have wanted to stop talking and find out what I really believed." This collection of columns and longer pieces is such a stop—a mid-career mid-40s look at what I believe in and how those beliefs might be better put into practice. I share them with numberless others, so this book is least of all about me. I just happen to be lucky enough to have a typewriter, and be part of a great newspaper and some equally worthy magazines that want the copy coming out of it.

If there is any collective fault with what the media are doing in the United States, it lies in what Saul Bellow said: "Here we write well when we expose frauds and hypocrites. We are great at couting warts and blemishes and weighing feet of clay. In expressing love, we belong among the undeveloped countries." I think that's changing. I visit a fair amount of newsrooms when I travel. Where else to find local color? More and more, I am noticing younger editors and reporters who, though not comfortable with using a word like love, are in fact expressing it in the choices of subjects they write about. Many are beginning to realize that "media neutrality" can be a cover for the fear of choosing sides. Choicelessness is in itself a choice. When a newspaper assigns a reporter to cover the local beauty contest rather than investigate the filthy conditions of the county jail, the power of the press is on display. Power is squandered. The paper went with fluff, not life. Choices are present everyday for publishers, editors, reporters, columnists.

Do we write about political games or political prisoners? Do we give the victims a shot in the arm or a shot in the head?

We have excuses. All of us suffer from outrage overload. Our circuits can take only so many crises, so much governmental violence, corporate crimes, or personal affronts. It is crucial not to be overcome, to stay balanced. My own imperfect solution is to try to be professionally angry and personally gentle. To stay angry, there are the obvious questions: how does public policy affect the powerless, how accountable are the powerful? To be gentle, there is the second question: if everyone does as I do would the world, beginning with the person next to me, have less violence or more?

I have no plans to be discouraged by the flawed answers that are either served to me or I serve to myself. I cling to my involvements out of necessity as much as nourishment. Journalism regularly fails, but through the example of giants like George Seldes, I. F. Stone and Tom Gish, and the many unknown Timermans now in prison in countries where the press is silenced or stoned, the strengths prevail. I expect to keep drawing on them. I expect to keep reporting about education, because as I have written in several pieces collected here, I am uplifted whenever I visit classrooms to teach and learn with children. I will keep writing about politics because I have been honored to know men like Phil Hart, Sargent Shriver and Andy Jacobs, and women like Mary Rose Oakar who understand that government, on its good days, deals in guaranteeing citizens their potentials. I will write more about social justice, religion, peacemaking, sports, animals and—most important—families.

These are involvements imbedded in my heart. Amid the pestilences of the 20th century and the dangerous war decrees of our latest pharoah, East or West, I couldn't survive without them. What I have learned from my involvements is the truth that wise friends have told me they have learned from theirs: forget about being successful, just be faithful.

*Colman McCarthy*

I think it's a citizen's duty—and a journalist's duty—to fight.. You never can tell, sometimes you win. A friend once gave me a word of hope. He said, 'You know, Izzy, if you keep on pissing on a boulder for about a thousand years, you'd be surprised what an impression you make.' I never thought, at the time of the witchhunts, that I would live to see the day when J. Edgar Hoover would be recognized as the kind of jerk he really was, and when guys like me would find a certain kind of acceptance, if not applause. I never thought that would happen. Who would have thought that a Senate committee would expose the dealings of the CIA, the attempts to kill Fidel Castro, the dirty work against Salvador Allende? That was wonderful. It's still a free society, but it'll become less so if people don't have the courage to utilize it.

*I. F. Stone*

*Chapter 1*

# Teaching to Learn, Learning to Teach

Think about the kind of world you want to live and work in. What do you need to build that world? Demand that your teachers teach you that.
—*Peter Kropotkin*

## New Shoots for Peace 1983

As demands go, the one made on me by 25 high school sophomores, juniors and seniors did not vibrate with the militancy of a clamorous student protest. It was soft, respectful. These were children of the '80s, not the '60s. The demand was that I teach a 10 week course on the techniques, history and philosophy of nonviolence and pacifism.

This was at the School Without Walls, the stroke of educational genius begun 12 years ago by some creative District of Columbia educators. The school is housed in the Grant Building, a bulky structure at 21st and G Streets NW on the campus of George Washington University. The walls that are happily done without by 17 teachers and 180 students are those which confine the mind by taking the excitement out of learning with too much structure and too little innovation.

At the School Without Walls, the teacher of zoology has the odd idea that classes at the National Zoo are as necessary to mastering the subject as reading the textbooks. The art history teacher believes the city's art galleries are where learning best takes place. The Shakespeare teacher brings the children to the Elizabethan

19

theater at the Folger Shakespeare Library, where they dress in 17th century costumes to stage Hamlet and Lear. They get Shakespeare into their heads by getting him into their bones.

From the school's view, I was on the premises as an expression of innovation. About a year ago, I met Phyllis Weiss, an English teacher in the District's schools for 17 years and at the School Without Walls since 1975. We had common feelings about education. It was the shame of American schools, I said, that the young are not taught even the basics about nonviolence and pacifism: We raise our children in a culture saturated with violence and then wonder why individuals, groups and nations keep opting for violence—fists, guns, bombs, nukes—as the way to settle their differences.

Weiss agreed. She wondered how peace can be built if the schools do nothing about teaching the ways it has been achieved in the past and can be achieved in the future.

This would have remained another God-ain't-it-awful conversation except that Weiss, with a low tolerance for the glooms, cut it short. Quit griping, she said to me, and come teach a course: If you want to get back to the basics, get basic with a personal commitment.

Put that way, with bluff-calling directness, I said yes.

In late winter, my course was offered as an elective. Weiss had talked among the students and believed interest was present. She was surprised, as was I, that 25 signed for the course. Comparatively, she said, that is a large turnout. Another elective offered the same 10 weeks was on military careers, to be taught by visiting military personnel. Only two people enlisted. One was my oldest son, a sophomore at the school. He announced at dinner one evening that it was time he heard the other side. I cheered the lad on. But the principal dropped the course for lack of interest.

In one of the first classes, we read an excerpt from "All Quiet on The Western Front" by Erich Maria Remarque. Several students said they had "heard" of the book, but only one—a girl who had transferred the year before from private school—had read it.

I kept my comments about the book to a minimum, and especially avoided saying that it had stirred something in me when I read it one summer in college. I wanted my students to feel the impact of the words themselves, free of any pushing from me about what they should or must feel. The excerpt, which a student read aloud, told of the killing of the soldier Gerard Duval, fighting for France in World War I. Paul, fighting for Germany, has just knifed Duval and is in the trench with him, trapped by bullets passing overhead:

"The silence spreads. I talk and must talk. So I speak to him and say to him: 'Comrade, I did not want to kill you. If you jumped in here again, I would not do it, if you would be sensible too. But you were only an idea to me before, an abstraction that lived in my mind and called forth its appropriate response. It was that abstraction that I stabbed. But now, for the first time, I see you are a man like me. I thought of your hand-grenades, of your bayonet, of your rifle; now I see your wife and your face and our fellowship. Forgive me, comrade. We always see it too late. Why do they never tell us that you are just poor devils like us, that your mothers are just as anxious as ours, and that we have the same fear of death, and the same dying and the same agony—Forgive me, comrade; how could you be my enemy? If we threw away these rifles and this uniform you could be my brother just like Kat and Albert. Take twenty years of my life, comrade, and stand up—take more, for I do not know what I can even attempt to do with it now.'

"It is quiet, the front is still except for the crackling of rifle-fire ... 'I will write to your wife,' I say hastily to the dead man, 'I will write to her, she must hear it from me, I will tell her everything I have told you, she will not suffer. I will help her, and your parents too, and your child—'

"His tunic is half open. The pocketbook is easy to find. But I hesitate to open it. In it is the book with his name. So long as I do not know his name perhaps I may still forget him, time will obliterate it, this picture. But his name, it is a nail that will be hammered into me and never come out again. It has the power to recall this for ever, it will always come back and stand before me."

The excerpt ran for another page. It ended with the German soldier pledging to live—"in order to save myself"—for the slain French soldier. "Deep down in me lies the hope that I may buy myself off in this way and perhaps even get out of this; it is a little strategem; if only I am allowed to escape, then I will see to it ... I have killed the printer, Gerard Duval. I must be a printer, I think confusedly, be a printer, printer, printer."

During the reading, the class was grippingly still. No shuffling in the seats. No yawns, no note-passing. When we finished, I didn't want to risk dissipating the power of the trench scene by a mere class discussion. Instead, I tried to keep the stillness going by having the students write their impressions of what they had just read.

A girl, black and from a family stationed at Bolling Air Force base, wrote this: "I am 16 and a senior. My plans after graduation are the military. I have thought a lot about the military and if that's what I really want to do. Deep in my heart I know I want to go into the military and serve my country. This excerpt and also this class has shown me another side—a side I believe the soldier in the story has never even realized before then. And that is the actual fact of killing not just 'Russians' but 'people' very much like ourselves." This girl had had a change not in heart but direction. "I'm no longer sure if I will or can kill for my country. I ask myself why I've suddenly changed. Maybe I'm growing or maybe I'm must learning to be a nonviolent person."

Another girl—16, a transfer student from the private National Cathedral School for Girls and the daughter of a senior official in the Reagan administration—was more analytical than confessional. She called the excerpt "strong. It shows us a horror we have never known before. This excerpt also should help us understand the plight of many of the Vietnam vets. They went through the same thing the German boy is experiencing. Most people assume that the military is not bad and they are overcome with the pride and glory of a battle. What they don't realize is that they're no longer going to be watching it on a silver screen or playing with plastic soldiers. They will be out there burning just like them, young boys who joined the military, told to hate the 'enemy,' and with many people at home waiting for their safe return."

A third student—a quiet, reserved boy who sat in the back of the class in a corner—wrote: "Personally, after having read this with the class, it gave me a fairly good feeling about what war is basically about . . . . Even in today's modern warfare tactics, the people are still basically the same, with different surroundings and culture. The fact that war can be basically a remote-control war where all a country has to do to wipe out another country is push a button, does not change the fact that it is very personal, even though all has an illusion of impersonality . . . . War is just an inhuman extension of misunderstanding."

At the School Without Walls one of the enlightened practices is class scheduling. Each student attends one class in the morning—from 9 to 11:30—and, with an hour for lunch, another in the afternoon, from 12:30 to 3. With two daily classes of two and a half hours duration, the opportunity for depth is present. The conventional high school is flawed with six or seven daily periods. Students waste their time shifting their bodies from class to class. They fragment their minds by going from math to science to literature to gym to this to that. Learning is made as difficult as possible.

At the School Without Walls, I relished the two and a half hour periods. (Ten minute breaks were provided.) Not once did the class seem tired or bored. On the days when I was out of town or had a writing deadline, Phyllis Weiss took over. In addition, she was present for all the classes that I taught. When she sat among the students, I found myself thinking of several teachers of my own: a composition teacher in grammar school, an English teacher in high school and a creative writing teacher in college. Each was in love with language and writing, and each propelled me to find out for myself the reasons why such a love is possible. Now, three decades later, I am still coming upon newer reasons. So are they, I would bet. None has left the classroom.

In my first class at the School Without Walls, I needed to know what the students knew about both historical and contemporary teachers of nonviolence. Their education, it turned out, had been neglected. I gave them a list of six peacemakers—Henry David Thoreau, Dorothy Day, Martin Luther King, St. Francis, Joan Baez and Isaiah—and asked that they be identified. All knew of Martin Luther King. About half were familiar with Thoreau. No one could identify Dorothy Day, the pacifist who co-founded the Catholic Worker and fed and housed the poor for nearly 50 years in the Bowery. Some guessed that she was an actress. Many knew nothing about St. Francis nor Isaiah. Joan Baez was another forgotten ancient, far back in the mists of time. She was, said one safe-guesser, "a woman who fought for peace."

The basics, then, it would be, with the simplest of wrappings. Each class, I stuck with the same structure: a lecture of about 20 minutes on the life and thought of a practitioner of nonviolence, the reading aloud of an excerpt from his work, an essay written in class about that work, a discussion of a topical event involving nonviolence, an

essay on that event, and, finally, another excerpt and another essay
to evoke their thoughts on the workability of pacifism. I went heavy
on writing because I know too many college teachers who lament
the wooden prose that even the brightest of their students turn in.
High school students don't write enough. Mine would. I wanted to
make writing primeval, their second nature. As it turned out, nearly
all of the 25 thrived on writing. It was as though they hadn't been
asked before.

The two texts I relied on were "America Without Violence" by
Michael Nagler, a Gandhian scholar and a professor of the classics
at the University of California at Berkeley, and "The Disarmament
Catalogue" (Pilgrim Press) edited by Murray Polner. The excerpts
included: "On the Duty of Civil Disobedience" by Henry David
Thoreau, "No Bars To Manhood" by Daniel Berrigan, "The
Doctrine of the Sword" by Mohandas Gandhi, "What Would You
Do If?" by Joan Baez, "Why Destroy Draft Cards?" by Dwight
Macdonald, the Bible (Isaiah, St. Matthew's version of the Sermon
on the Mount), "Pilgrimage to Nonviolence" by Martin Luther
King, "The Long Loneliness" by Dorothy Day, a speech by A. J.
Munte, and an essay on vegetarianism by Isaac Bashevis Singer.

No matter what excerpt we read, I emphasized one theme
common to them all: that alternatives to violent solutions exist and
that, if individuals and nations organize themselves properly, moral
force is stronger than physical force. The force of sharing wealth is
stronger than hoarding it. The force of organized resistance is
stronger than that of disorganized terror. The risk of defeat or
death from the use of moral force is large but it is still much less
than the risks run by using instruments of hate or war.

Some students opened their minds to this immediately. Others
couldn't. Among the latter was a senior. In class, after reading from
Gandhi, I gave this writing assignment: "If Gandhi were alive today
and were visiting America, what do you think he would tell us?
Would we listen?" The student wrote that he himself would listen
"and most likely agree. But most folks would still be against him,
i.e., Ronald Reagan, Shultz, Kissinger. There is not much we can do
about violence and war in terms of defense. If someone tries to hit
us, we just cannot stop and try to be rational. The same is true for
the USSR. They don't want to talk peace. I must admit the nuclear
war game is stupid, but we must protect ourselves. If it cannot be

done verbally, there are no alternatives than fighting in defense. I don't know if Gandhi had any solutions. It rather annoys me to just hear the problems."

The student's paper reflected the argument most often thrown up against the teachers of nonviolence that we were studying. Pacifism is mistakenly equated with passivity. In class, we read Gandhi: Nonviolence "does not mean meek submission to the will of the evil-doer, but it means the putting of ones whole soul against the will of the tyrant. Working under this law of our being, it is possible for a single individual to defy the whole might of an unjust empire to save his honor." But I had the sense that Gandhi was too culturally distant to be understood by the students. He was up against the "civilized" British, not the "evil empire" Russians. In class discussions, which I kept closely focused because with only a veering they would have become rank bull sessions, one refrain was heard: nonviolence and pacifism are beautiful theories but in the real world . . . .

This was in the early classes. We went to more reading and more writing. We spent an hour one day on the essay of Joan Baez, "What Would You Do If?" The clarity of the piece is in its form: a dialogue between an explainer of pacifism and a skeptic. The two talk about whether it is natural to kill. It is, says the skeptic. "It's something you can't change."

"If it's natural to kill," the pacifist replies, "why do men have to go into training to learn how? There's violence in human nature, but there's also decency, love, kindness. Man organizes, buys, sells, pushes violence. The nonviolenter wants to organize the opposite. That's all nonviolence is—organized love."

"Your crazy."

"Tell me that violence has been a great success for the past 5,000 years, that the world is in fine shape, that wars have brought peace, understanding, brotherhood, democracy and freedom to mankind and that killing each other has created an atmosphere of trust and hope . . ."

"I'm doing O.K."

"Consider it a lucky accident."

"I believe I should defend America and all that she stands for. Don't you believe in self-defense?"

"No, that's how the Mafia got started. A little band of people who got together to protect peasants. I'll take Gandhi's nonviolent resistance."

"I still don't get the point of nonviolence."

"The point of nonviolence is to build a floor, a strong new floor, beneath which we can no longer sink. A platform which stands a few feet above napalm, torture, exploitation, poison gas, A and H bombs, the works. Give man a decent place to stand. He's been wallowing around in human blood and vomit and burnt flesh screaming how it's going to bring peace to the world...

"From the ground up. By studying, learning about, experimenting with every possible alternative to violence on every level. By learning how to say no to the nation-state, no to war taxes, 'NO' to the draft, 'NO' to killing in general, 'YES' to the brotherhood of man, by starting new institutions which are based on the assumption that murder in any form is ruled out...

"It sounds real nice, but I just don't think it can work."

"You are probably right. We probably don't have enough time. So far we've been a glorious flop. The only thing that's been a worse flop than the organization of nonviolence has been the organization of violence."

Some in the class thought this was the most persuasive piece they had read on pacifism. In a class writing assignment, I asked for a discussion of the strong points and the weak points in Baez' essay. One of the most critical minds in the class was a senior boy from a military family. I was extra aware of his presence throughout the course, because, first, he was articulate and, second, he was ready to sound the alert should I stray from teaching to indoctrination. In his paper this day, he went for exactly the weak point that I myself detected. He wrote: "The main weakness was the pacifist's disbelief in self-defense. Nonviolent resistance is not going to stop Communist tanks, troops, planes or nuclear weapons. If no one defends them in this instance, soon there will be no pacifists. The Communists won't allow behavior like that, and anyone preaching that would soon find themselves digging trenches and breaking rocks in a concentration camp somewhere.... It is my personal belief that a military will always be needed until such time as enough people in the world can come to follow the path of peace.

Don't set down your knife until your antagonist is willing to do the same."

The student hit the core of the issue: who makes the first plough-share. The answer is always personal: I do. It is always national: my country. And then global: my planet. Intellectually, the choice has to be made that the risks of nonviolence and organized resistance are less than the risks of violence. If Gandhi and Martin Luther King were remote, there is the current example of Lech Walesa. Few lives have been lost to date by the Polish workers. They are winning—slowly and not spectacularly, but winning nevertheless.

A few of the student's were wits. They brought laughter to the class. Sometimes it would come out in the class papers. We were talking one day about Gandhi's belief that "poverty is the worst form of violence." For a writing assignment, I asked this question: "If, after school today, a homeless person—not as sweet-smelling or as presentable as perhaps we'd like—came up to you on the sidewalk and asked, 'Can I spend the night at your house, I'm hungry and cold,' what would you answer? And why would you answer the way you did?"

Among the papers were these:

"I would explain my situation at home, being a minor under the care of her parents who own the house and most of what is in it, and tell the man that I was very sorry. And I would be. If I brought a street person home with me after school one day, the chain of events at my home would go something like this:

(1) the registered nurse who takes care of my grandmother would flip and either quit or immediately call my mother, probably both.

(2) My parents would come rushing home.

(3) They would kick my newly acquired friend out of the house.

(4) My mother would attempt suicide because of her worthless life, failure at raising a child and prejudice.

(5) My father would yell at my mother for attempting suicide and raising me badly.

(6) My little sister would yell at me for being tacky.

(7) I would leave.

The second paper: "If a street person came up to me and asked for help, I would help them even if it meant being demeaned by my father. I say this because I know that what I was doing would not only be a fantastic learning experience for me but because I would be helping someone and that person would be my best teacher yet to come."

In an early class, I talked about the baggage of problems I brought in with me. The first was that I came to them as an amateur teacher, not a professional and that as an amateur—one who loves and with no thought of money as payment—I didn't believe in what many of the professionals of the teaching trade believed in: homework, tests or grades. If you are here to make an A, I said, or be certified by me that you are worthy of four years in a bright-kids-only college, then this is the wrong course. Homework, tests and grades have nothing to do with pure learning, and everything to do with adults lording it over the powerless young: Be smart or else.

Not here, I said. If you learn something through me, it will be because of your own desire to learn. Desire is the essence of education, not brains.

The students let me know that the absence of homework, tests and grades was a hardship they could bear. One student's face brightened as if a beautific vision had passed before him. Others contained themselves. They were skeptics who would believe when more proof was in. At the end of the ten weeks, I believe they trusted me. I hadn't pulled anything on them. The only concession I was forced to make was on grades. A few students wanted them for their records. Phyllis Weiss suggested pass/fail grades, a compromise that I agreed to. Everyone passed. What they passed with—perhaps a desire to begin a lifelong study of nonviolence, or a feeling that a ten week course was enough, or loathsome regrets that they wasted their time—was for them to decide.

In the last class, I asked for one final paper—a course evaluation. By now, most of the writing was expressive and unconstrained. The pressure of grades being removed meant that the students were writing with confidence: I wasn't another adult about to pounce in judgment on them. I wrote the question I wanted them, in frankness, to answer: "It's your school, your five hours a week in this class. Has the course been worthwhile and enervating or merely another ho-hummer high on the boredom chart? Could any of us—me, you, the guest lecturers—have done better? What are you taking with you from the course?"

The response of the son of the military family was of special interest to me. If I had been alienating him all along, it would have been a bust for me. He was spunky to the end. He corrected the Woodrow Wilson quote, which I had written on the top of the assignment papers:

"The purpose of education is to make the young as unlike adults as possible."

In place of "as unlike" he wrote "much better than." Then he wrote: "I first decided to join the class because I felt my presence would add an air of diversity. As a supporter of the military, I thought that I would help to portray both sides of the argument. It has been said that opposition provides drive, and I hope I made my points felt. I see now that I have benefitted by being shown both sides and the middle-ground of the argument: violence or non-violence.... I learned a great deal about other means of settling differences, be they between individuals or nations. I came in here ignorant of the accomplishments of Gandhi in particular and non-violence in general. It has been a very rewarding, enriching experience."

A senior girl who had transferred—as had a fair number of School Without Walls students—from a private school wrote: "Whenever my relatives come over for dinner (like last night) they always say, 'so what are you doing in school these days?' And they are always most interested in this class. My Dad used to laugh when I told him I was taking [in gym] bowling and frisbee on Mondays, but when I told him all the neat things we talk about and do in here, he's really impressed. And all my old classmates from Georgetown Day School wonder why they're paying $4,000 a year and not having courses as interesting as this.

"I have learned to appreciate things more from this class, like [Vietnam] veterans and bums. I don't think anything could have been improved. I loved it."

From a senior boy: "This course was pretty good. It's the type of course that makes you think about yourself and about your own views on matters you never thought about or paid attention to before. The class itself could have been a little more exciting, not that I'm saying it was a total bore, but it could use some pep so to speak.

"I'm taking with me from the course the thought that you don't have to use violence to get a response or to get through to people. That there are nonviolent means that can very well be receptive by people."

A fourth, from a senior girl with a developed and critical mind and whose papers were always fired by gut-feelings. "Unfortunately it is not really *my* school, and not really *my* five hours a week in each class—at least not in the eyes of most teachers and administrators. But I know that you honestly do feel that way, and so for this one class, I do too. It has truly been a joy to have a class where I leave and continue to talk about what was said in the past 2½ hours, and I have. I've talked to my friends, and my family, and what would be classified as strangers. Energy—true energy to this education experience. I have never, and would never speak out against education—just the means by which it is administered. But this class has been great. And if nothing else, I've learned more of how I feel about all sorts of things."

The evaluations were touching. I had come to have affection for the class as a whole, and warm feelings for the ten or so students I was able to get to know personally. I'm not posturing with false modesty, but with the same material, anyone could have gone to the School Without Walls to teach this course and evoked a similar positive response. With a line-up that runs from Christ, Gandhi and King to Dan Berrigan, Joan Baez and A. J. Muste, nobody could blow it.

Then too, 1983 is the year when peace studies courses have begun to flower in all parts of the country. The National Education Association and the Union for Concerned Scientists recently released a teachers' guide called "Choices: A Unit on Conflict and Nuclear War." They are swamped with orders from schools in all parts of the country for the book. This year, more than 80 colleges are offering degree programs in peace studies. In 1970, the number was two.

Teachers, though, even parttimers like me, should proceed at their own risk. In the White House, the Commander in Chief thinks ill of the trend. In a recent war preparation speech calling for more money for weapons, Ronald Reagan said that "the most upsetting letters I receive are from schoolchildren who write to me as a class assignment. It's evident they've discussed the most nightmarish aspects of a nuclear holocaust in their classrooms. Their letters are often full of terror. This should not be so.... Our children should not grow up frightened." With 50,000 nukes in the world, they should grow up blissfully?

In my childhood, the way the fear of bombs was dealt with in schools was by drills: the bell rang, the teacher called out "air raid practice" and we dove under the desks for five minutes. Then "the planes" passed and we went back to arithmetic. Nothing was discussed. The fears were held inside.

This generation wants a healthier approach. They want to read, talk and write about the alternatives. From what I have been told, and from what I discussed myself, the teachers are amazed at the ardency of the students. They share it. The teachers want to learn. Old trees can also get new buds. We can all be new shoots for peace.


# Children Who Disagree                               1983

A break from filling blank pages presented itself: an invitation to speak to fourth- and fifth-grade classes in a neighborhood public school. Except for a midday bicycle jaunt on the Mall between the Capitol and the Washington Monument, no rejuvenation is more relaxing for me than stealing off to talk with children about writing.

Children at this age are feeling for the first time the elation of forming their own opinions. They are questioning. They are moving into discernment. They are taking our messages about rules, goals and values and saying to themselves deep inside, "I wonder now..."

This process is one of the thrills of childhood, and to be on hand when it begins—in a classroom among beginning questioners—is for me a thrill of adulthood. On this morning at Somerset Elementary, I encouraged the children to exercise their right to independent thinking: disagree with me as openly and candidly as you wish. I will talk for 20 minutes, I said, and then we'll have a free-for-all of the mind. I wanted to hear their thoughts about my thoughts.

This was a school in which teachers were comfortable with children who spoke their minds. Many teachers aren't. How can kids learn, they seem to ask, if they waste their time thinking? Besides, who cares what kids think?

This shut-up-and-learn curriculum is reflected in many of the education reports that have been issued of late. Teachers, principals, boards of education, parents and the authors of the reports have chalked the blackboards with solutions to education's problems. Why aren't children asked for their ideas?

A few weeks after my talk, 39 letters arrived. They were as lively as the exchange we had that morning. "I really appreciate you taking your time to give us a good idea of what a news reporter does," began one letter. "At the beginning of your speech you said you liked people who disagreed with you. Well, there were quite a few things that I disagree with. I don't want to hurt your feelings but it's true."

Another said: "I liked some of your ideas but some were so unusual that I couldn't stand it." A third wrote: "Thank you for coming. I do feel that you had some unusual ideas about the world though."

These three disagreers, like others in the class, had trouble with the SOS (Standard Outrageous Shockers) that I sent: boxing and football are not sports, armies are useless, animals have rights and owning them as pets is slavery, poets know more than politicians, prisons should be abolished.

In the class discussion, we wrestled these out. We could have gone all morning. The hour passed like 10 minutes. Every child wanted to say something. Ideas were straining to be released.

The children wanted to be there. I wasn't the attraction. Their own enthusiasm was. I was a newspaperman talking about journalism and some of the issues I write about. I could have been a bus driver or a plumber, provided I invited the children to give me their independent views. If kids at this age are reaching intellectual independence, why not take advantage of it?

When I leave schools after giving talks like this, I always wonder why so many teachers burn out or get bored. How can anyone be wearied by children's minds? I know it is easy for me, a one-shot visitor, to tell teachers how to practice their craft. Don't I understand, teachers can ask, how the school system beats down even the most creative educators?

I do understand that, but the school world is first of all a world of children. Why enter it unless you are willing to be co-equals with the young? And why make that world colorless with only the grays of textbook knowledge, while leaving out the bright reds, greens and yellows of life to be found in the openable minds of children?

To ask children to disagree if they like is to give the message they hunger for: You matter. That should be the first function of a school. One child wrote to me: "I think it was good for you to come. You made us think about everything you said. Were you just trying to make us think or do you believe what you told us?"

Both. After loving, all we have is thinking and believing.

# Elementary Détente                                          1982

Some of the wittier children in my neighborhood are talking these days about their class's recent field trip to "the little red school-house." It's about a mile away: the Soviet Embassy school, where children of Russian diplomats posted in Washington are educated.

The visit was part of a successful and well-regarded cultural appreciation program that is federally funded under the Emergency School Aid Act. The children I've been hearing from—including 10-year-old Eddie McCarthy, who sits to my left at the dinner table and is on the left, too, on such political issues as allowances, bedtime hours and haircuts—are students up the street at the Janney elementary public school. Each of my boys—James, John and Edward—has gone to Janney, and from there to public junior and senior high schools. At Janney, teachers like Ursula Cossel practice a craft rarely found at the expensive private schools of Washington. Through an embassy adoption program—more than 40 embassies are involved—fifth- and sixth-graders from Janney have been exchanging classroom visits with Russian boys and girls.

Détente may be dead between the leaders of the children's governments, but the interaction created by the exchange program—as fleeting as the three or four get-togethers were—appears to have been beneficial to the American kids. One wrote in a classroom essay: "Due to this trip, I found out Russian people are not different except for their beliefs. They are friendly, humble people who, like us, want to enjoy life peacefully."

Another child, more introspective, wrote that her new friends were "open and fun to talk with. I learned a lot about the Russian children, but it confuses me because all the articles in books and magazines tell me a whole different story."

As a parent and a citizen, I am overjoyed that federal money is being spent to counter in at least one American school the strident irrationality that undergirds the prevailing attitude toward both Russia's government and people. It has become so mindless that diatribes against Soviet leaders are vented with no apparent factual or diplomatic restraints. Ronald Reagan needed only his first press conference to lay into the Soviets: they "reserve unto themselves the right to commit any crime, to lie, to cheat, in order to attain" their goals.

The vilification of Russians reflects a type of nationalism found in the global historical pattern. Tribes and nations project evil onto other tribes and nations as a way of avoiding the painful task of correcting "the crimes, lies and cheating" within their own borders and hearts. But America's hostility toward Russia deviates from the pattern because as a nation we seem to be deliberately denying the obligation even to understand the culture, politics and language of this supposed demon enemy.

Rep. Paul Simon (D-Ill.) reports in his book, "The Tongue-Tied Americans," that from 1975 to 1979, "52 colleges and universities in the United States dropped the teaching of Russian." In the schools resisting the trend, "Russian language classes are fewer and poorly attended, and Soviet study programs are suffering." Simon tells of a 1979 study that reported "a total of 4,943 positions in the federal government [that] require Russian proficiency, but there are only 3,206 persons who can fill that need."

With our hostility growing like a mold on ignorance, anyone who seeks to understand Russia by studying, say, Marxism, runs risks. In 1980, when right-wing ideologues learned that Maryknoll seminarians routinely took courses in Marxist-Leninist theory, they said, aha, this proves the order has gone communist. Seeking to understand the Soviet system was equated with espousing it. Journalists who dare to write a benign word on Marxist theory can be assured of hearing from readers screaming the epithet, not "go to hell," but "go to Russia."

Russia's history, politics and culture are complexities that could absorb any American's intellectual energies for a lifetime. That Russia's current leaders are brutal despots of narrow vision and that hardly a one of the country's 262 million doesn't suffer because of it is no excuse not to make a passing effort to understand the Russian people.

Many Russians are as ill-informed about the United States as we are about them. In the recently published "Russian Journal," Andrea Lee, writing of a year she spent in Moscow and Leningrad, recalls the comment of a young Communist student she came to know: "We're studying American yellow journalism, propaganda and how your government controls newspapers like The New York Times and The Washington Post."

Ignorance and fear—and its poisonous byproduct, hate—exist in plenty on both sides. But as this academic year closes, both America and Russia can look at two schools—Janney elementary and the Soviet Embassy school—and say happily that at least a few children there remain unpoisoned.

# My Best Student 1983

On a playground midway between the State Department and the White House is a small, clapboard, one-story, single-room building. It is owned by the District of Columbia's recreation department. With wooden planks supporting the roof over the porch, it looks like a sharecropper's home in the rural South. On the brim of the playground are the back entrances of about a dozen residences. Closer still is the School Without Walls where I have been teaching.

The students dubbed the building Smoke House. It was the hanging-out place for a few of the kids who fraternized on the porch to smoke.

In early September 1983, Lexie Tillotson, 16, who graduated from the school in June but was still in the area as a George Washington University freshman, believed that some homeless people had more need of the building than the student smoking club. From a well-off family, Lexie is a young woman with the rare blend of a searching mind and feeling soul. She was in my class on nonviolence. I recall during a discussion period of Gandhi's line that "poverty is the worst form of violence" that here was a child alive to the possibilities of her own compassion. She understood that the essence of nonviolence is to be active, to ask Simone Weil's question, "The love of our neighbor means in all its fullness simply being able to say to him, 'what are you going through?'"

At first, getting to know some of the street people provided a touch of adventure for Lexie. Society's untouchables are meant to be off-limits for schoolgirls. But she chose to push through the stereotypes and see the street people as human beings. To bring some peace into their lives, Lexie, aided by another student, jimmied open a steel-screen window on the front of Smoke House. From within, the front door was jarred loose. She passed word to some neighborhood people that squatter's rights were theirs if they wanted them. They did.

From September to December 1, the heatless building served as a shelter for five men and a woman. On that morning, a policeman appeared and ordered the group to leave. The next day, when I asked the officer for a reason, he told me that some local residents had complained.

The story of the Smoke House Six reveals the unceasing tenuousness of life on the streets, the poor being treated with kindness by a compassionate student one day and the next finding themselves displaced by suspicious neighbors. It isn't only the cold wind of winter that can whip up anytime. The chill of middle-class fear—that the unknown poor might be criminals, might be hazards to property values—also blows with killing bite.

A few minutes after the police evicted the six poor people, Lexie, with an instinct for news, phoned me to ask if I could come over to report on what was happening. I went over immediately. When I interviewed the group, they told me that they were clean, orderly and quiet. The principal of the high school confirmed this. So did a chaplain at George Washington University across the street. He had befriended the six. He was surprised to learn that two of the six had jobs. They were not total dropouts as he believed all of the homeless were. The woman was a cleaning lady for the federal government. She moved into Smoke House with her husband. The couple had had an apartment, but couldn't keep up with the rent and other debts on only her salary.

Lexie Tillotson, whose father is a Washington attorney, understood that going through the Smoke House windows to help poor people wasn't the same as going through channels. Officialdom itself—the policeman, the director of the recreation department—hesitated before removing the six. They were not heartless. But the city must function. The officer, who often finds corpses of homeless men after being fished from the Potomac River, offered them a list of city-run shelters that might take them in. One of the men, instinctively seeing the illogic of the gesture, protested: "But you're putting us out of a shelter now."

The six have scattered. The husband and wife resisted going to public shelters. They had some pride left. As well as some questions: What had they done wrong by living at Smoke House? Who complained to the police. When will they next be kicked around?

While I discussed these and other things with two who were the husband and wife, I didn't feel right about walking away from them cold. I would have a hard story and they would have a hard night. I had some money that I needed to get rid of. I took the couple to a nearby hotel and gave them enough funds to spend a week there. Later the husband phoned for more money. I gave it to him. On handing in the story of Smoke House, I mentioned to the editor that I had given a few dollars to the couple. The next day, she told me the story was killed. The editor over her said there was a conflict of interest, reporters aren't supposed to get financially involved with people they are writing about. I suppose if I were a better newspaperman I would not have given the couple hotel money and let them risk freezing. Then, of course, when the police found them stiff and dead in an alley, I could have written the definitive ain't-it-a-shame-society-doesn't-do-something story.

Lexie Tillotson caught all the angles of the Smoke House tragedy. I wondered, did it make her cynical? Or more determined to give of herself the next time? The answers aren't to be known right away. In time, I will find out. The best students have a way of staying in touch.

# Letter To a Haitian Boy                              *1982*

A letter came from a fourth-grade boy. Days before, I had been invited to speak to his class in a public school in my neighborhood. All the children sent letters. I was surprised at how well they wrote. Even at this age, for some children, the gift of writing shows itself.

The letter from Anthony Jean-Claude was brief: "I enjoyed your visit to John Eaton School. My mother wishes that she was there to meet you. I am Haitian. Do you know where Haiti is? Well, if you don't, here is a map. If you plan to take a boat, this is how you get there." The boy crayoned a map of Florida, Cuba, Jamaica and Haiti.

He drew a boat sailing over blue water to Haiti. Beneath it, he had a final sentence: "Do you believe the earth is going to vanish?

I am sending this reply:

Dear Anthony Jean-Claude:

Yes I do believe the earth is going to vanish, unless you and I, your classmates and our earthmates do more to reduce the violence and preparations for war that surround us.

That may not sound hopeful to you, but compared with large numbers of people, I am an optimist. I think that each of us can brake our lunges toward earth-destruction. Those who have given up agree with Bertrand Russell, a philosopher who lived to an old age: 'Mankind collectively is engaged in the great task of preparing its own extermination.'

Our earth is small. We have the bombs to make it vanish—and if we could get the bombs into space, as our leaders are panting to do, we could finish off the moon, too. Before this century, we thought our earth was large. Now we know even our solar system is tiny. We send contraptions to take pictures of distant planets, looking for life. Our search prompted Helen Bevington, a retired English teacher at Duke University, to write in a book: 'We go on hoping we're not alone in the universe, while we prepare to destroy the only planet we've got.'

We talked about war and peace when I came to your class. Perhaps I should have spent the time telling you how journalists write about burning buildings and interview fire chiefs. But I saw that you are old enough, and fearful enough, to be leveled with. It's a burning earth we need to think about. We have political leaders, in this nation and others, ready to turn our bodies pink and our skies red in the name of keeping the peace. In January 1981 we had a general who, while getting ready to run the State Department, claimed that 'there are more important things' than peace.

In class, I didn't mention General Haig. He is unworthy of any child's admiration. Instead I referred to men and women who gave their lives to finding saner ways to find peace than building, testing and storing nuclear bombs. One of these was A. J. Muste. He said something every fourth-grader, and even first-graders at your school, can understand: "There is no way to peace. Peace is the way.'

That thought is powerful enough to base your life on. You are not too young to become a peacemaker. You can begin by writing about it. Ask your teacher to help you and your classmates start your own newspaper. We need newspapers that pay attention to the progress being made by ordinary people to make America a less military and less violent country. With your school newspaper, you can create your own peace beat.

Go interview people in your neighborhood who volunteer time to care for the elderly, or teach English to people with reading problems, or gather clothes for the homeless poor.

As you can figure out, what I'm saying is that the works of peace are all around us—in your school, at home, in the neighborhood. Why not write about it, if that's what you have a skill for? From the letters I've received, your class does have the skill.

After that, get involved personally. Perhaps your class could join Amnesty International and write letters to dictators demanding that political prisoners be freed. Or you can offer to make home visits to the elderly in your neighborhood. Come up with your own ideas for peace.

If the earth does vanish because the nukes explode, the desire for peace will have had to have disappeared first. You and your class can start today to prevent that. Keep me informed.

# Two Who Didn't Burn Out 1979

People who love their jobs—really love them and think of their paychecks as the least of the rewards—are as rare as they are valuable. But the other afternoon, when I was visiting Long Island for some reunions with old friends and haunts, I had two of them before me. They were teachers—my teachers, when I was in grammar school some 30 years ago.

At first, talking with Edna Ashley—who is now 80 and retired and who was my first-grade teacher—and Marye Picone, who taught me in the third, fourth, seventh and eighth grades, was like looking out of a bay window into the past. A panorama of three decades spread out before us.

We hadn't seen each other all these years, though I have remembered both women in the enduring image I formed of them as a child at the Glen Head grammar school.

At the front of the class, Mrs. Ashley was a maternal presence. She had children of her own, she told us on the opening day of school. I remember feeling good about that. She would be as much a mother as a teacher, with the roles not being much different. She believed that each child had gifts of the mind and spirit waiting to be discovered in the schoolhouse. It was her calling to help this discovery happen.

Mrs. Picone shared this view, though 33 years ago, when I was in the first class she taught, she was not much more than a schoolgirl herself. She had been out of college only a few months.

Her idea of an exciting Saturday afternoon was to marshal her bouncing energies and gather about five or six neighborhood children to go into New York City to a museum in the morning and an afternoon at Madison Square Garden for a Knicks game. She was telling us, like Mentor urging on Telemachus, that a world was out there: learn to tie your shoelaces and leap into it.

After a sharing of stories and updates the other day, we began talking about the art of teaching. As one who believes that teachers are among the earth's most undervalued and overextended citizens, I tried to learn from both Mrs. Ashley and Mrs. Picone how they had avoided teacher burnout all this time.

It was a topical question. Every September when teachers take to the picket lines in one city after another, I find myself wondering how they can absorb the foul treatment heaped on them. Instead of honoring teachers and freeing them from school board hassling about salaries, curriculums and paper work, we seem driven to give them as little support as possible—and then get angry that our children aren't learning.

Mrs. Picone, who currently teaches in a junior high school in Huntington, N.Y., confessed that teaching was becoming harder of late. A few times, she has come close to burning out. She couldn't point to one lone pressure and say that everything came from that. Perhaps it isn't even pressures at all, she seemed to be saying, but rather evaporations. She would try to touch a student's mind, only to find less and less to grip.

The formlessness means that students show little interest not only about the traditional subjects like history and English, but even in learning about their own culture. Some of this, Mrs. Picone believed, was merely a reflection of the children's coming from homes where books and learning aren't valued. Except that that has always been the case. What's alarming now is that large numbers of the young are confident that they can wing it. They think they can forget learning how to tie their shoelaces. Just leap, the world can be bluffed.

It was too pleasant and breezy a summer day to get into the heaviness of student passivity. Besides, burnout was the question. Mrs. Picone's method of resistance was to keep her spirit of independence intact. A couple of days a year, when the bell of the last period rings, she bolts for the door and tells everyone that the workday is over: no afternoon faculty conferences, no meetings with the principal, no cleaning out her desk. It's time now to go to a museum or to see how the Knicks are doing.

Mrs. Ashley never burned out because she was too busy being fascinated by children. "I have always been an advocate of an individualized approach to learning," she told me, "both in the classroom and at home. I tried to have each child read to me alone for a few minutes each day, just as I spent a little part of the day with each of my own children at home."

As the current teacher strikes plague the country and as teachers find themselves out of jobs because of budget cutbacks, the life and times of women like Edna Ashley and Marye Picone may seem too peaceful to be real. But if we looked closely, we would find that every school has two or three teachers like them—exceptional educators whose kindly ways with the young are making all the difference.

# Backstage With Joan Baez                                        1983

"I can't tell you how boring it would be for me," said Joan Baez, "to give a concert and not have it be connected with people's lives and people's suffering and real issues. There's no music for me outside of that."

For two hours, Joan had performed for 3,000 people at Constitution Hall, one of 27 singing dates in her seven-week tour just
completed. Her soprano voice remains unaffectedly pure. Now,
though, the concert was over, and Joan was in a backstage reception
room with 25 high-school students. Last spring they were in my
pacifism class at School Without Walls. We had studied an essay on
peace that Joan wrote in 1966, when, as today, she was in a fierce
hurry to get on with it.

A few weeks before she came to Washington, Joan, a woman of
generosity, gave an emphatic yes when I asked if she would meet
with my students. I had come to know her years before when she
would pass on information about political prisoners. She had a
moral firmness that I have known in few others.

Bring your kids to the concert, she said, and we can talk and relax
after. That was a large gift in itself, but Joan then gave them $240
worth of front-row tickets.

The students loved her singing, and backstage they connected
quickly with her mind. She was not a star now. She was a constell-
ation of ideas, questions, opinions and reconsiderations. During the
concert, Joan surprised many in the audience by dedicating a song,
"Goodnight Saigon," to the Marines in Lebanon and their families:
"That may sound strange coming from me but I really am a person
who is committed to the sanctity of all human life, especially young
men who need not have died in their prime."

In spirals of anecdotes and theories, she built a case that gradually
peaked into the high ideal that radical nonviolence is the best and
only answer worth offering to children. "I understand any kid who
looks at the news in the morning and says, "I wanna smoke dope for
the rest of my life.' It's so huge what we're facing, so scary." Joan
said it was her commitment to offer to young people alternatives to
despair.

Briefly into her talk Joan, who sat atop a dressing table, asked for
questions. Draft registration was first. "The draft has no right to
exist," she answered. "Nobody has the right to tell you how you are
going to live your life. What they'll tell you is, you have to preserve
democracy around the world. But you can't bring democracy into an
undemocratic setup. And the least democratic setup I can think of,
offhand, besides possibly the U.S.S.R., is an army." She advised the
students to study the alternative options to the draft, including jail
if that's what it comes to.

As a pacifist, was she ever afraid of violence? The fear is always there, she said. She told stories of being in Hanoi during the Vietnam War and taking to the shelters to avoid being killed by American pilots dropping bombs on the city. She had had bomb threats in Belfast, police-state threats in Argentina and Chile, billy-club threats in Mississippi. "You learn to pray," she said.

One student wondered what Joan believed "U.S. interests" means, considering that the phrase is used repeatedly in foreign policy discussions. "What do you think they are?" she asked the student. He said they were so "ambiguous and vague" that "I have no idea." Joan replied, "I agree with you. I don't know what they mean."

On tax resistance as a way of protesting the government's military policies, Joan said that she refused to cooperate with the IRS in the 1960s and that it may be time to say no again. "It may be much more of a risk this time. I also have to decide that if I end up in jail, is that worth it? Probably yes. It's probably the best thing I can do."

None of this was too heavy for the students. Joan's radical non-violence was not irrelevant to their lives. Some let her know that in their gut they felt the same revulsion to the world's violence that Joan felt when she was a teen-ager going to Quaker meeting houses. She sensed then that only pacifism and organized resistance to violence was the answer. She has given her life, and her talent, to it.

When she was last in Washington, Joan had called. We met and spent time talking about her just completed trips to Latin America. There, she had been seeking to renew the energy of her folksinging with its only strength, the folk. In Argentina, she sang at a Mass for the mothers of citizens who have disappeared. In Brazil, she met with labor leaders who have been punished for striking. In Chile, she sang in a free concert for a Santiago human rights group.

The primitivist governments in each of these countries found Baez and her music too threatening. She was denied permission to give commercial concerts. Banned in public, she sang in private—in churches, homes and anyplace else where people gathered to ease their anguish about the systematic violence that is crushing them daily. Joan sang their own songs of hope to them, as well as those that have risen up from the repressed in other countries.

Amid the torturing and silencing that is standard equipment in these countries, Joan, even if she weren't a glowing artist of independent mind, would have still been a worrisome figure for the governments. She is the president of Humanitas International, a human rights organization. Based in Menlo Park, Calif., it already has 5,000 paying members. It is different from similar groups because Joan is an activist, not a theoretician. She will turn up in a Chile or a Northern Ireland, just as she went in 1979 to the refugee camps in southeast Asia. She has denounced the "Stalinist leadership" in Vietnam as vehemently as the oligarchy in El Salvador.

Humanitas International, she says, is "quite simply, for the right to life. We recognize that Somali refugees, Salvadoran peasants and Cambodian children are not concerned with the fine points of Marxism or capitalism—they are struggling for their survival. And if what we can do in our small way aids in that struggle, then all our efforts are worthwhile."

Those words have meaning. Aside from her persistent idealism and her commitment to nonviolence, Joan is matched by few performing artists for using talent on behalf of the world's poor.

Backstage at Constitution Hall, Joan spoke to the students not as children but as adults with crucial choices to make. They were grateful. They didn't want prolix philosophizing or another there-are-no-easy-answers lecture. Joan gave them what they wanted: a call to action, a call to conscience.

# Where Have the Idealists Gone? 1982

BERKELEY, Calif.—At first, it seemed like old times at Sproul Plaza. It was at this storm center on the University of California campus where student radicalism peaked in the free-speech movement of the mid-1960s and the antiwar protests shortly after. On the announcement board at Sproul Plaza was a poster that looked to be a definite summoning to purpose.

"In Defense of Marxism," read the top line in bold letters. Underneath was a quote from the master himself, "Marx on the party." "A party? You call this a party? The beer is warm, the women are cold and I'm hot under the collar."

The Marx being quoted at Sproul 1982 was Groucho, not Karl. The last line, also in bold letters, called out: "Smirkers of the World Unite."

One goof-off poster hardly represents a Sociological Shift of Large Import. Nor are my eyes much given to student watching. But in the 15 years since my last visit to Berkeley, the difference between students then and now is like the night and day between the Marxes, Groucho and Karl.

In 1967, the tumult on the Berkeley campus was against the government's war policies in Vietnam. Now the anti-government protest is against the Berkeley town council for passing a municipal noise ordinance. The campus Interfraternity Council, it seems, believes that the new anti-noise policy means the end of frat house parties on Friday and Saturday nights.

Elsewhere on this campus that generated so much of the nation's anti-war feeling just when that was needed, the military's ROTC program is flourishing. Business courses are popular, and a professor in the journalism department says he is regularly challenged by students who see nothing disturbing—as does the professor—in the increasing control of the daily press by news-paper chains. Reading The Wall Street Journal has replaced reading the Berkeley Barb, now defunct.

"Our students are getting further and further away from Vietnam," a teacher of military science told me. He was explaining one of the reasons for the increasing number of undergraduates enrolling in the Reserve Officer Training Corps (ROTC). "They don't remember Westmoreland, Rusk or Calley."

That, to the military man, was pleasing. On this University of California campus, the students who were babies or children when the mistakes and horrors of the Vietnam War were in full view, are now saluting military values in such surges that the ROTC is back in fashion. Enrollment for Army, Air Force and Navy ROTC programs is up 25 percent from 1977. Nationally, the new glow is even rosier. For the Army ROTC, 1,315 schools are now on the rolls—up from 679 in 1973. The student enrollment is 72,000, against 33,000 in 1973.

Unfamiliarity with Vietnam is only part of the ROTC resurgence. Another is economic need. With student loans and federal aid for higher education drying up, ROTC money is tempting for both undergraduates and administrators. To a student, ROTC means an untaxed $100 stipend a month on a tuition scholarship that can mean as much as $10,000 a year at some schools. On graduation, there is "a job." A college administration does well financially because the Pentagon provides and pays the instructors, while through the scholarships, the school can be assured of large sums in tuitions.

In 1982, the Army is paying out $26 million in scholarships and $7.5 million in monthly stipends.

For both students and faculty, a final appeal is the aura of patriotism. With the Reagan administration pushing the dubiety that America is militarily weak, academia can take pride in doing its bit to supply the officers and gentlemen.

But America isn't weak and its armed services are in no manpower crisis. Instead, the ROTC revival means that once again the schools, instead of being centers of resistance against the war-preparation mentality, are centers of recruitment. The merger of the academe with the military contradicts one of the ideals of education, that the learned person knows better ways of both creating peace and effective self-defense than by relying on armed might.

With more money going to more military programs and less to the arts and sciences, the imbalance is likely to lead to still more ROTC growth. But it isn't a total rout for the military. On the Berkeley campus, classics professor Michael Nagler is organizing opposition to the ROTC by setting up a peace studies program. Nagler, author of "American Without Violence," believes that the new peace program "will in the long run—if we have a long run— erode the ideological basis for the ROTC and the pro-war, war-accepting framework. Rather than marching down the street and shouting to the ROTC, 'hell no, get out,' we're going to slowly help people understand what peace is and how to get it."

Teachers of nonviolence like Nagler find themselves confronted by opponents who see the presence of ROTC on campus as an academic freedom issue. No one is forced to join, it is said. And besides, it offers money and jobs to students so inclined.

One who has often heard this argument is Rev. Richard McSorely, a professor of theology and director of the Center for Peace Studies at Georgetown University. McSorely tells of the reply he once gave to a student. Suppose "an international prostitution ring offered me $500,000 provided I would help get a department of prostitution into the university. All the teachers would be chosen by the ring and the courses would be controlled by it ... the courses would be taught by only recognized and certified pimps. What would you think of me, if I (endorsed) that as a course offering for students on the ground that the university needed the money, and after all, no one was forced to take it?"

The student replied that McSorely had turned an academic issue into a moral one. "I do consider it a moral question," he replied, "and if anyone thinks it is unfair to the military to compare them to prostitutes, I reply that it may be unfair to the prostitutes. Prostitution does not threaten the survival of the world. Prostitution is not supported by taxpayers' money and the power of the Pentagon."

Despite years of fine effort, McSorely has yet to rid Georgetown University of ROTC. And Nagler, just beginning at Berkeley, is likely to find similar frustration. But if their work persuades only a few students to think twice about the lures of campus militarism, they will be serving their schools well.

The sharp contrasts here at Berkeley help focus what I've seen in more muted regressions on the dozen or so other campuses I've visited in the past two years: the phasing out of idealism. It is still present in many students, but they keep it quiet. Nursing students, for example, don't dare say that they are studying medicine to help people by easing their suffering. Instead, they express individual career hopes of being supervisors by the time they are 35. Why can't they say they want to be nurses because they love people?

Students don't talk of service to others, but of benefits to themselves. Personal growth is out, intellectual self-grooming for corporate recruiters is in. Courses are taken to get a marketable skill, not to acquire skills for reasoning or for human understanding.

The tension between idealism and careerism isn't new, or unnecessary. But seldom has it seemed this one-sided. The students aren't to blame. They are trapped. As the colleges and universities have less and less resources to devote to the humanities and liberal arts, where a sensitivity toward social advancement has traditionally been nurtured, they are forced to look to private industry for money. Edward E. David Jr., president of Exxon Research and Engineering Company, reports in Change magazine that corporations are becoming the big men on campus. In the 1980s, he projects a tripling of industry support for academic research, from $200 million a year to about $600 million a year. He emphasizes that this is not mere industrial philanthropy; the money goes to research "consistent with a commercial 'mission.'"

The main industry objective is to ensure a supply of "excellent people" among the graduates. David cited a study that "showed that the disciplines most aligned with conservative political ideas and favorable to the private sector are engineering, medicine, physics and mathematics."

Among the most horrified at how students have fewer altern-atives as the campuses become military and corporate annexes are the faculty members in their 40s who themselves were idealists in the 1960s. At every college I've visited, I've met professors who speak of their frustration. They want to pass on their ideals about public service to their students. But they can't. The imbalance now favors military and corporate recruiters who have the economic might to tell the students, "Serve us."

# Dear Director of Admissions...        *1980*

Among the minors on the move in my neighborhood, word has been spreading that I'm an okay recommender. For college. For graduate school. For law school. And this year, in what is a happy first, for kindergarten.

This being the end of the letters-of-recommendation season, I believe I'm one of the league leaders in the production of letters to admissions offices. I sent off my eighth last week—to the University of Wisconsin Law School on behalf of an American University graduate who came here wanting to be a teacher. But now, after four years in the hemisphere's most lawyer-layered city, her head has been turned.

I write my letters on the assumption that admissions staffs are as unmoved by the puffery in these letters as book reviewers are by blurbs on dust jackets. I assume, too, that other recommenders will be writing on and on about the applicant's academic brilliance, high moral quality and straight teeth.

So it's brevity first, three paragraphs at most. That alone must lift the admissions board into a kindly mood. Then I play to the Long

Shot Quota, the slots reserved for the unselect who have too many C's and too few extracurricular brightnesses on their records but who have one flickering sparkle of mind or soul that hints of potential excellence.

The long shots can be the surest shots. So many boards are burdened with must acceptances—the well-connected children of corporate givers, children of tenured professors, the seven-foot basketball players—that the admissions tedium surely is broken when a candidate of no connections turns up.

Deciding the fate of these odds-buckers may be the sole merriment of the day. Frank Brownlow of the English department at Mount Holyoke College, South Hadley, Mass., writes in a recent bulletin of the Portsmouth (R.I.) Abbey School that these days the keepers of the academic gate are a down group. "To begin with," he writes, "secondary school education is so poor and standards are so low that admissions boards find it all but impossible, once they have weeded out the few applicants at the extreme top and bottom of the list, to make any significant academic distinctions at all. For awhile they trusted the 'scores.' But 'scores' tell little about the candidate's actual knowledge, and as the quality of secondary education worsens even scores become unreliable guides to a student's promise."

This increases the pressure on us recommenders. My toughest letter this year was for a 5-year-old who lives a few streets away. His parents had their eyes on a private kindergarten that cost two times the college tuition I once slaved summers to help pay. I told the admissions board that although my acquaintance with the candidate went back only as far as 1977 and it was only recently that I had had the chance to discuss his philosophy with him, I did recall one exceptional quality. On the many occasions I took him and his friends to the ice cream shop he seemed to enjoy singing in the car the most. I can see him at Yale as a lead tenor for The Whiffenpoofs.

With the professor from Mount Holyoke saying that education is worsening by the minute, the other pressure on us recommenders is that we are no more than oilers for the treadmill. In Carol Tinzler's recent book, "Your Adolescent: An Owner's Manual," little Kimerbly asks her parents: "If they tell you in nursery school that you have to work hard so that you'll do well in kindergarten, and if they tell you in kindergarten that you have to work hard so you'll do well in high school, and if they tell you in high school that you'll have to work hard so you'll get into a good college, and assuming that they tell you in college that you have to work hard so you'll get into a good graduate school, what do they tell you in graduate school that you have to work hard for?" Kimberly's parents answered: "To get a good job so you can make enough money to send your children to a good nursery school."

For the treadmill bunch, my policy is not to write letters to admissions boards. Instead, I write to the kids: Take a year or two off, you'll learn more out of school.

# Who Needs Accreditation? 1983

BALTIMORE—Do not tell Tom Culotta, as he is told all the time, that he should get a college degree before he dares go into the classroom to teach. Culotta, 29, is the president and one of three faculty members of the Community School, a storefront learning center for 25 students in a neighborhood of displaced and poor white Appalachians. The public school dropout rate in the eight-block-by-five-block enclave in north-central Baltimore ranges from 65 to 85 percent.

College degrees, teaching certificates and doctorates in education are not needed to reach the trammeled kind of young people who find their last-chance way to the alternative Community School. All that matters is that a natural teacher such as Tom Culotta be there to share his time and knowledge. He is an instinctual encourager and inspirer. He has given his uncredentialed skills for the past three years in a setting where little that is beautiful—least of all education—is thriving.

"We've had a good year," Culotta told me the other afternoon in the Community School's book-lined basement, which doubles as a classroom. "We haven't had a single rat day." A rat day occurs when school is closed so the students can trap, drive out or kill the rats that occasionally infest the building, which is attached to a liquor store on one side and a pawn shop on the other.

There were no rats during the past school year because Culotta, dozens of community people and some of his students renovated their once-ramshackle three-story structure. The school received a $30,000 HUD grant through a city housing agency. Only $100 went for labor. Culotta and the community volunteered the rest:

the designing, carpentry, wiring, plumbing and painting. They put into action Willa Cather's belief that "handiwork is a beautiful education in itself, and something real.... The one education which amounts to anything is learning how to do something well, whether it is to make a bookcase or write a book."

The bookcases at the Community School are heavy with the basic texts in English, math, science and social studies. In the nearby junior high school, the teacher-student ratio is one to 36. At the Community School, it is one to 12. The difference is between chaos and calm. Culotta knows the names, families and personalities of each student. He has been to their homes. A small room on the third floor of the school is his own home. He isn't just a teacher; he is a community presence. With an exuberance bordering on rapture, he has persuaded a poor working-class white neighborhood in which 85 percent of the residents lack a high school diploma that education is crucial.

Culotta has had the conventional academic successes that are a mark of unconventional schools: Students getting up to grade level after three or four months of classes, attendance rates rising sharply, high morale. No one sleeps in class. Fighting is rare. A community-service program has been started.

Most of the alternative high schools now operating in the United States report these kinds of breakthroughs. They are the natural results when learning is individualized, students are respected and teachers are unstinting in their drives to educate kids whom everyone else has given up on.

Among alternative school teachers, Culotta is forced to be doubly creative. He has no large budget. In 1983, the Best Products Foundation came through with a $22,000 grant, enough to hire two certified teachers. Because his operation is small and only three years old, it is not accredited. "The main reason the kids come here," he explains, "is to get an education, not diplomas or a piece of paper. We would like to give them that, but for now we are satisfied that at least the major need is taken care of—a genuine education."

Culotta believes in discipline, but it is not a posturing toughness that so often means an incompetent teacher humiliating a child. Part of the Community School's rigor is asking the students for tuition: $2.50 a week. This is nickel and dime compared with yearly tuitions of $4,000 and $5,000 at elite private schools. "The $2.50 is collected," Culotta explains, "because we want the kids to know that education isn't easy and it's something they are going to have to want and go after. We work them hard. They learn at an incredibly fast pace."

Tom Culotta and the Community School emit a sense of warmth. Students and teachers trust each other. The recent run of commission reports on education had little to say about self-educated teachers in unaccredited schools in scruffy neighborhoods. Next time around, the commissions should drop by this Baltimore school. They will learn something.

# Chapter 2

# Wives and Children: Take Time

**I**'ve yet to meet anyone who chose family over career and regretted it. No one on his deathbed ever said 'I didn't spend enough time with my business.'

*Paul Tsongas, on leaving the U.S. Senate*

## Fathers, Father Figures 1974

My three children and a threesome of their friends climbed into the car and, without a headcount, we drove away. We had been feasting like emperors at an ice cream place and affixing our eyes on spatial single-dip pleasures. Arriving home, it became clear by counting and by the soft acoustics, that one of the troupe had been left behind. It was my three-year-old. The child experts might argue that he should have had a case of "anxiety separation," but he was actually only separated from his parents and brothers, not the ice cream cones the manager kept spooning. After a successful rescue I asked one of his befrienders how the little one had held up. No problems, I was told. "I asked him his name," said the kind stranger, "and he said 'Eddie.' I asked for his father's name. He knew that, too: McCarthy. Then I asked for his father's full name. He said 'Daddy McCarthy.'"

I have told this story several times to other parents, and with every retelling I am moved a few inches further along to a truth I had always seen, squinting, off in the distance: that one must be not only a father but a father figure. I have been looking into this dear baby's eyes since his birth, always thinking that I know well what he sees. But all along his vision of me has not been as a person, with a name and identity, but as a figure, a common daddy, farmed from the same rows and rows where all other reproducing males rise from the earth and bloom to fatherhood. Standing on our land, all of know well enough what it is to be a father. We take chesty strides into the jungle, dig at the bacon and bring it home. But are we ready to come home and be not only fathers but fatherly?

That is largely what the three-year-olds in our lives demand when they see us as father figures. They ask, have you the bravery to be fatherly? Can you come out of the shade of that safe masculine world, from under the clouds of easy male choices having to do with excessive work during the week and weekends with adults, and stand in the sunny innocence in which children live? This can be the demand of more than the youngest: it comes also from the 10-, 15- and 20-year-olds. We know that the need for fatherliness may be constant well into adulthood. We hear of women marrying older men because they seek the fathering their real fathers never gave. Even among athletes, the relationship between coach and player can be of a father and son. Leo Durocher, in his book, "Nice Guys Finish Last," says that "I think it has been pretty well established by now that between Huggins, Weil, Landis and Ricky, I had more fathers in my baseball career than Shirley Temple used to have in those pictures of hers."

Leo, whether on the basepaths or in the dugout, was ever the little devil, and his deep need for father figures was hardly a coincidence. It is often the supposedly worst children—the scrappy, restless ones—who seek fathers, and for whom natural fathers often find it so hard to provide gentleness and understanding. Unlike mothers, who give love to their children unconditionally, paternal affection leads the heart in a different path. In "Social Character in a Mexican Village," Erich Fromm and Michael Maccoby write: "The nature of fatherly love is that he makes demands, establishes principles and laws, and that his love for the son depends on the obedience of the latter to these demands. He likes best the son who is most like him, who is most obedient and who is best fitted to become his successor, as the inheritor of his possessions."

The list is long of sons whose behavior didn't "earn" final affection, forcing their fathers to retreat from fatherliness: Francis of Assisi who shared none of his father's glee about marketplace profits, William Penn, the pacifist son of a warlord in the British navy, John Stuart Mill, pushed by his father to read Latin at age three and later suffering a mental breakdown because of the strain to excel. Daughters also leave father's knee and bounce off to disapproved trails. Jung noted that "every father is given the opportunity to corrupt his daughter's nature, and the educator, husband or psychiatrist then has to face the music. For what has been spoiled by the father can only be made good by a father."

The absence of fatherliness often runs through the generations, passed along as surely as skin or hair color. A father who has gone through life searching for father figures will likely pass on the compass to his children; they too will become searchers. In the horror stories about child abuse, case histories usually reveal that the father who maims his children was also beaten in his own childhood. Runaways do not flee merely to sightsee among Greyhound stations, as Ogden Nash knew in his verse:

> One would be in less danger
> From the wiles of the stranger
> If one's own kin and kith
> Were more fun to be with.

Can the family tree be grafted so that at some point in the generations a branch shoots out and a father becomes also a father figure? It happens occasionally, when forgetting and foreseeing come together. What a father needs to forget is the life that he could have lived. Middle-aged men get done in less by taking up with whiskey or women than by the greater threat of their imagination, of dreaming too much about the unfulfilled. The father's failures are imposed as goals on the child. Demands are made, rather than an offering of gradual freedom; the latter is what children unconsciously ask of their fathers. If denied it, they will seek it in father figures.

Foresight involves seeing ahead to the moment when a son or daughter may also become a parent and another co-creator of the race. It is rare to hear grown men and women deride their fathers in the lippy manner of, say, an adolescent knocking the old man's failures. Grown-ups have felt a few of the world's kicks and they know that surviving the bruises is not easy. Chesterton believed the family has value "because it is uncongenial. The men and women who, for good reasons and bad, revolt against the family, are, for good reasons and bad, revolting against mankind. Aunt Elizabeth is unreasonable, like mankind. Papa is excitable, like mankind. Our younger brother is mischievous, like mankind. Grandpapa is stupid, like the world; he is old, like the world."

Who is the better father: one who spends six hours a day with his kids but with his mind adrift elsewhere or one who spends only 20 minutes but in full paternal concentration? The question has no formula answer; children have turned out well or badly in both environments. What is often decisive is not the amount or quality of time in the relationship but whether a force so simple as a spirit of companionship is present. Does the father live with his children or merely alongside them? Does he watch passively while his young grow up, like an onlooker at a rite, or does the father understand that his own life should still be growing and now there is a child that has joined the process. F. Scott Fitzgerald once wrote a bitter letter to his daughter complaining that she seemed to be an "idler," that in her early womanhood she had appeared to stop growing and had become dead weight. "My reforming days are over," he wrote, "and if you are that way I don't want to change you. But I don't want to be upset by idlers inside my family or out. I want my energies and my earnings for people who talk my language. I have begun to fear that you don't."

Fitzgerald doubtlessly saw himself as a responsive father. Such a self-image is crucial. All fathers want their children to honor them, but it is another question whether the fathers are using their lives to earn that honor. Children don't automatically offer respect unless something is present to be respected. For a father, the difficulty is that winning honor from one's children makes different demands than being honored elsewhere—in the factory, office or the success ladder. The larger world is all too often easily fooled by appearances, words and other devices of social bluff, but in the smaller theater of the family such stage props deceive no one.

One father who thought about this was the late Rabbi Heschel. In an NBC-TV interview shortly before his death, Heschel said: "I have a daughter. I would like her to revere me as her father. And I ask my self again and again, "What is there about me that would be worth her reverence?" Unless I live a life that deserves her reverence, I make it impossible for her to live a life of Judaism . . . If the children complain about the father, maybe they are right, and maybe they are wrong. If I saw my father speak in a way that could evoke my contempt and my distrust, I would have a tough time revering him. But I would say to young people that in spite of the negative qualities they may discover in their fathers, they should remember that the most important thing is to ponder the mystery of their own existence. The people who represent the mystery of my existence: father and mother. And if I have no reverence for the mystery of my existence: father and mother. And if I have no reverence for the mystery of my existence, regardless of the special faults of my parents, I'm simply not human."

This is a hard truth for many sons and daughters, learning tolerance of their father's flaws. How many tough-talking sons aged 20 criticize the old man's weaknesses only to sink under the weight of the same weaknesses on reaching their own adulthood? The only time a child has a fair right to say his father failed is when he reaches the same age and meets the same trial but succeeds. Probably if he does succeed, he will be sufficiently humble—humility, the rarest of modern virtues—to know that only through Providence or luck did he not repeat his father's errors.

Literature has many examples of children realizing that finding flaws in one's father may be the worst flaw of all. In "The Master of Hestviken," Sigrid Undset's saga of 14th century Norwegian life, we hear the children of Olav—in one of the novel's many powerful scenes—talk of their father who lay dying. "You are right, brother—father was more of a man than we guessed. And yet . . . for half his lifetime he bore the guilt of an unpardoned slaying. And when he would make amends for it at last, God took judgment into his own hand." The brother replies: "We may not inquire into such things—God's hidden counsels. But never will I believe it fell upon him because father's sin was worse than most men's. Perhaps it was done to show forth an example—the rest of us take so little heed of our misdeeds. And God made choice of father to do full penance, since He knew his heart—stronger and more faithful than we poor wretches who would not be able to swallow one drop of His justice."

Just as these are unsettled days for many mothers, it is true also for fathers, except that camouflaging may be easier for them. Fathers receive little support from each other; some high schools and colleges have "fathers clubs" but these mostly gather as cheer-leading squads for the athletic program or fundraising efforts. Institutional support is rare; the Wall Street Journal recently told of a report to a symposium on the future of the family. It said: "the more the family goes downhill, the more the power of the institution increases." Television programs commonly portray fathers who are witless buffoons, just the kind of fools the sponsors want real-life fathers to be, in order to believe the inane commercials.

It all seems as if forces conspire to cut us off from our past, from union with the events and emotions that shaped our fathers and their fathers. That is the illusion from which modern fathers need deliverance—that they are not alone in their fatherhood. Confused and tired, perhaps, even unrevered, but not alone. The past line of fathers goes back too far for that, and the future line—sons becoming fathers—will stretch out even further. There is comfort in continuity.

For fathers to be fatherly—to become a figure when one bargained only on becoming a parent—involves responding to a call that often seems intolerable. "Love can be hard service, giving your all," wrote Florida Scott-Maxwell in her journal. But she added: "It may be finding your all."

Going back to the ice cream place for a lost baby may be going back for a lost part of the self.

# Together for the Long Run                          1979

They are lovers. On St. Valentine's Day, when carved hearts shape our boxes of chocolate and clue feelings that we lazily shape into squares and cubes the rest of the year, they are perennial romantics. I see them at the track where I run. They are sensible walkers. They keep to the outer lane, which for them is lovers' lane.

She is thin, her hair bobs as she walks in soft legerity and her face is femininely soft in its calm. He is angular. He has granite in his bearing. It is a moveable love feast when they take their laps, because what they exude is exquisite tenderness. Arm in arm, body to body, these are old lovers, not young ones: they look to be at least 80 years old.

I confess to a bias. Any couple married 25 years can be assured of applause from me. For 30 years—or 40 or 50—I give them standing ovations. They have conquered the momentary. They have oozed beyond the primordial. There is genealogy to their love: in the beginning was attraction, which fathered friendship, which fathered devotion, which fathered eros, which fathered fidelity.

I know that I sometimes read too much into the beauty of long marriages. Maybe it is time I stopped letting my switch be tripped by the aura of romance that engulfs couples like the one I see at the track. These are times, after all, when neo-pornography passes for music in songs like "Let's Get Physical" and hedging the marriage bet is shrewdly caught in the New Yorker cartoon with the young man leaning across the table and proposing to his girlfriend, "Will you be my first wife?"

If the times are passing me by, as are all those six-minutes-a-mile runners at the track, I take comfort in the archaeology of long marriages. Dig beneath the levels of rocktop, and the emotions that flowered in youth are perfectly preserved. The lovable that each saw in the other decades ago has not been crumbled by time. What lovers give to each other in the early years of their marriage become, as Eliot wrote in "Four Quartets," "the gifts reserved for age."

Successful long marriages are rare in America because we are trained to seek democratic individualism. The phrase "marriage partner" seems quaint to ears dinned by messages urging us to "do it your way." Young women are told that they betray feminism if they let themselves become dependent on a man; marriage, it seems, is an admission of dependency. To be a partner means you don't have what it takes to go it alone.

The word "lover" has been watered, too. It has come to mean the illicit, not the stable. Lovers have affairs, while married people have mortgages. Actually, lovers were once correctly seen as the dull ones. In "The Psychology of Marriage," Balzac wrote: "It is easier to be a lover than a husband for the simple reason that it is more difficult to be witty every day than to say pretty things from time to time."

Synchronicity—a man and woman marrying not merely to be together but to grow together—is the eventual achievement of a long marriage. For the newly married, the delusion of the institution is that everything ahead will be struggle-free, even though no one—not even while walking up the aisle to the wedding altar—disagrees intellectually with Jung's belief: "Seldom or never does a marriage develop into an individual relationship smoothly and without crises. There is no birth of consciousness without pain."

One of these years we ought to set aside a St. Valentine's Day for Old Marrieds. In the 1970s, we had plenty of couples of longevity who were known to be as in love after 40 years as 40 days: Will and Ariel Durant, Linus and Ava Pauling, Claude and Irene Pepper. Every community and neighborhood has couples like them.

If a problem remains, it is that Old Marrieds tend to use Old Phrases in explaining their happiness. We always talked out our troubles, we knew how to forgive, we never went to sleep mad.

Those are yawners when "How to Make Love to a Man" is on the bestseller list for 22 weeks, and Sally Field is telling us how macho a guy is Burt Reynolds. But if that's the choice, then I'm for some yawning.

# Winging It                                                    *1979*

It isn't often that I discover I have anything in common with Tolstoy, one of my heroes. But the other day, a friend convinced me that I did: "Your children ignore you when you preach that vegetarian line. So did Tolstoy's."

With Thanksgiving at hand, and the three McCarthy boys happily playing the annual blood sport of turkey eating, I will sit at the head of the table and feel as the great Count Leo must have felt among the flesh-eaters at his table: loved but misunderstood, heard but not heeded.

The exits and entrances of my vegetarian arguments have been revolving doors through which my boys pass in separate compartments of personal taste. Turkeys are flavorful, they say; let's eat 'em. That holds for cows, pigs, chickens and other cooked corpses served up by the cadaver lobby known as the American meat industry.

I don't talk like that at table. George Bernard Shaw, another vegetarian and another hero, regularly did, only to end up being described by Oscar Wilde: he "has no enemies but is intensely disliked by all his friends."

I have been told by a number of vegetarians that I do the cause no good at all, much less the moral and physical health of my children, by allowing meat into my house, however much I keep it from entering my mouth. I considered that ham-handed approach once, but on the day that the boys leave the nest I'd like it to be for grander reasons than rushing off for the forbidden pleasures of Burger King.

According to a recent whimsical essay on vegetarianism in Time magazine, I am not part of the sociological pattern. "The conflict between beef and greens," said Time, is caused by vegetarian adolescents using their bloodless diet to rebel against their carnivore parents. The essayist didn't say where he did his research, but I can't believe that large numbers of the young are renouncing chicken breasts for chickpeas, or hamburger for Limburger.

Even if the children do come to their senses about the horrors of meat, the assault on the rest of the kitchen can be terrifying. Dick Gregory—the final hero I will cite—reports that after he "gave up meat and became a vegetarian, my weight went from 130 pounds up to 288 pounds. It was because of fear: by not knowing how healthy I was, I really thought I was endangering my life. But I was willing to make that sacrifice from a moral standpoint.... I was even drinking, smoking four packs of cigarettes a day. Anything that didn't have to be killed, I ate."

Gluttony in the name of morality has yet to entrap the McCarthy boys. But when I see them chomping into a breast of turkey, a leg of lamb or shank of cow, it is hard to hold back. What a moment, I think, for making the strong pitch for vegetables and fruits: the economic argument in the immense wastefulness caused by using animals for food, the health issue that links meat consumption with diseases and the ethics that give value to animal life.

But hold back I do. Mealtime with children is better given over to examples than debate, and it's wise to keep it light. It is a moment to talk about Amby Burfoot, the distance runner who won at Boston in 1968 and runs marathons on vegetables and fruits. Or Marty Feldman, the British comedian-actor whose wife is from a family of butchers. Feldman has said that "it was not the idea of their Catholic daughter marrying a Jew that shocked them. It was the idea that the daughter of a family of butchers was marrying a vegetarian.... I mean, how would a butcher understand a vegetarian?"

At Thanksgiving, the hope of peaceful relations between men and turkeys seems dim. But glimmers of progress do appear. Last month, the Associated Press reported that the U.S. Army once considered turkey feathers as a weapon in biological warfare. Tests showed that turkey feathers, when dusted with cereal rust spores and dropped from planes, are excellent contaminants of farmland.

I give full support to defending America and stopping communism with turkey feathers. First, we have more turkeys than Russia, as the CIA could confirm. Second, I volunteer the McCarthy boys to be in charge of the program.

I recall their Great Living Room War—my wife and I were at the movies—when they cut open pillows to blindside each other with goose feathers. With briefings from a few generals at the Pentagon's Turkey Command Center, the boys could easily make the transition from goose feathers to turkey feathers.

And I'd be happy because the defense budget would be lowered, gobble-gobble turkeys being cheaper than C5A and MX missile turkeys.

# An Innocent Looks Right                               1978

Even before I took my 11-year-old son to hear Ronald Reagan stir the believers at a 1978 banquet sponsored by the American Conservative Union and the Young Americans for Freedom, I was being criticized for child abuse.

"You're a typical wishy-washy liberal," said a right-wing friend who is a lionizer of Reagan. "You want to expose the kid to all viewpoints, so you take him among the conservatives. That's not how I do it. In my house, my kids don't even know that liberalism exists. I'm a conservative. I tell my kids what's true, and that's that."

Perhaps my liberalism did lead me to still another moral lapse, but exposing Jimmy McCarthy to Ronald Reagan fulfilled a promise made some months ago. I had taken the boy to hear George McGovern at a dinner of the Americans for Democratic Action. An evening with the Left deserves an evening with the Right.

Eleven-year-olds, with minds shaped more by impressions than facts or arguments, notice the behavior differences between conservatives and liberals much more clearly than adults. For us, politics is a blur. For kids, confronting it fresh for the first time, they can't help see that:

—Conservatives whine a lot. Reagan, a boring man reading a tiresome speech, cheerlessly went through his list of look-how-bad-

Washington-has-gotten alarmisms. OSHA is beyond control, big government is a mess, taxes are too high, regulations too strict, free enterprise too maligned, everything too this or too that.

—Liberal big shots are more accessible than conservative big shots. The dais at the ADA dinner held mostly workers in for the weekend from the field offices. Leaders like George McGovern, John Kenneth Galbraith, Patsy Mink and guest speaker Jesse Jackson took their places at floor tables among the faithful. They welcomed 11-year-old table-hoppers. At the ACU-YAF banquet, a 150-foot-long head table, raised off the floor, separated the elite like Strom Thurmond and Jesse Helms from the masses.

—Conservatives are more obsessed with the Left than the liberals are with the Right. In his warm-up speech for Reagan, Rep. Robert Bauman, R-Md., a YAF alumnus who has plenty of wit in him if he would only let it out, fumed that "liberalism has become a hard-core slum that is beyond renovation. We need bulldozers." He railed about "the decrepit structure of liberalism." Conservatives have a mission "to bury the rigid corpse of dead liberalism." This could have been the annual convention of the Funeral Directors Association.

ADA speakers, having passed beyond the belief that if you hate something hard enough it will go away, spoke factually rather than metaphorically about the Right. Both its war chest and ambitions are fearsomely large.

—The old days for the conservatives really are old, while for liberals the ancient times of happiest memory are the 1960s. Reagan, promising the millennium to anyone who thinks ill of the federal bureaucracy, said a new day is here: "The people are marching to a different drummer, and it's Yankee Doodle." Bauman, with younger and sharper ears, heard the music *and* the gunfire: Conservatives "are mounting the most serious challenge to tyranny since Bunker Hill."

McGovern, Jackson, Mink—the Hawaiian who is the president of the ADA—were content to recall the second American revolution, as led by such patriots as Martin Luther King and Robert Kennedy. If I were a more alert parent during these two dinners, I would have taken the pulse of Jimmy McCarthy to learn whether the ADA or ACU had his heart beating faster. But I do know which got him on its membership list: the ADA.

It wasn't all the message. A waiter at the ADA meeting gave Jimmy an extra dessert—ice cream and strawberries. At the ACU banquet, Jimmy asked for a second dessert. No, he was told. Even at their banquets, the right wing opposes handouts. If there are no free lunches, good God, there are definitely no free desserts!

After dinner, Barney Frank, the improper Bostonian, took the microphone to raise funds. Pledge cards at the table could be filled out, and passed up front to be read aloud. After hearing the applause for each fat cat, Jimmy McCarthy chose to be a thin cat by pledging a dollar. His card, listing the amount and his age, evoked a hearty cheer, far louder than the one given Galbraith for his $500. Upstaging Galbraith is a cosmic achievement the gods give to few mortal men, not to mention mortal boys. But to date, it's the best dollar I've seen this lad spend.

# What Mothers Silently Know                1971

Why are so many mothers feeling restless, isolated and dissatisfied? Among women who have young children, it is rare to meet one who is not planning ahead to a project next year, or five years from now, to a goal that can be fulfilled only when "the kids are finally in school." It is always life in the future, carom shots forever bouncing between one kind of tomorrow or another. Among older women, with children who are leaving or have left home, it is the opposite, the reference usually being to the past. Before I married, they say, I studied voice, or had a future in business, or had options for several careers; any number of spirited purposes could have been completed, though none ever was—except motherhood.

Among both groupings, lives seem to be sunk in a trap of inevitability. Existence as a mother is a dry diet, but it wasn't that way yesterday and it won't be tomorrow. Yet why must today be suffered through, as if all its light is dimmed in clouds hanging too low? One possible answer for the discontent of mothers is that at the time of marriage so few knew what they were in for. We send girls through grammar and high school, and many through college, exposing them to subjects they will never use, and then ask them as mothers and adults, to master skills they were never taught. It is the shock of a woman's life to have the first baby and discover that the baby does not fit into the mother's life but the mother fits into the baby's life. A woman can pass 16 years of exquisite education and never hear a classroom syllable about that astounding fact. Schools are hot to teach young women the heavy sociological data about birth control and their abortion "rights" but presumably the responsibilities of raising a child are meant to be learned the hard way.

Small wonder that mothers of young children feel restless and isolated. The sudden shock of children's total dependence—which directly cuts into the woman's independence—means that motherhood is endlessly contending against opposite forces. The woman is at once a short-order cook, dishwasher, maid, chauffeur, medical expert and psychologist, all this enforced versatility with never even a few moments to be free of a deadline. There is not only that but something else: the same mothers who have no time for their own needs are often surrounded by household technology, the main feature—and costliness—of which is time-saving convenience. At a moment when a woman needs reinforcement of her personality, she gets the opposite—depersonalization caused by being an extension of plastic and electric gadgets, by being a secretarial service to machines ever requesting dictation.

It is true that mothers in earlier cultures had similar responsibilities in raising their children. But they also had what many of today's mothers do not have: emotional and educational preparation for their vocation before they went into it and communal support after. In America of 100 years ago, it was common for a girl of 10 or 12, or early teens, to be put in charge—for long hours—of either her younger brothers and sisters or the neighbors' children. The exposure to the wear and tear of infants and young ones did not make later motherhood easier, but at least a continuity existed. Caring for one's own this year was not much different from caring for another's children last year. Today's women cannot enjoy this continuity. There is no flow between girlhood and motherhood. If a young woman is taught anything, it is not that children she will bear will make enormous demands on her physical and emotional strength but that her future husband will have his demands, so learn how to make yourself compliant to men. Thus, the unmarried young woman, unless she has the perceptiveness to resist conventional guff, falls for this line and goes into marriage believing it is only a relationship with a male. It is, of course, but if children come, it is much and often overwhelmingly more: a relationship with people whose behavior is unexpected and whose dependency is total. It is worth wondering how many divorces in marriages under five years occur not because the husband and wife were unprepared for each other but because both were unprepared for the little house guest padding around.

One who has wondered is Shirley Radl, whose book is "Mother's Day is Over." She writes: "When I was five months pregnant with my first child, my husband and I celebrated our eighth wedding anniversary. He gave me an exquisite bracelet, made of thousands of tiny seed pearls. It was elegant, feminine and provocative— everything he believed me to be. Six years later, I was picking up the pearls in my vacuum cleaner and by hand whenever I spotted one of them on the floor. The torn and twisted bracelet is a sad symbol of the effect two children have had on a once beautiful relationship. My young and very beloved son destroyed that token of my husband's devotion, and to some extent the affection and devotion itself slipped away in the complicated and demanding process of caring for small children."

There is no going back—except until divorce do us part—when such a slipping away occurs. Many in the women's movement rightly are trying to involve husbands in the challenge of raising children. But too often trying to move the inert male can be as emotionally draining as constantly being rubbed raw by the children. The husband becomes another baby, forever asking why and, when the tensions come, running for such pacifiers as working overtime, evenings with the boys or with the even more reliable friend, television sports. Far from wanting a beauty queen wife, the demand of many American males is for the kind of woman described by Milovan Djilas in "Land Without Justice." "This was my mother. She devoted her whole being to that which she regarded as natural and inevitable—begetting and rearing children, being good to her husband, and working slavishly. Apart from that no joy or thought existed for her."

The difference between a father and a mother, when they discover their lack of preparation for children, is that the man can run for cover and have it appear normal, even be applauded because he is "rising in the world," but if the woman tries such a fast one she is made to appear strange. "You mean you don't love children?" we ask. The question is unfair, as many mothers silently know. They love their children all right, and they can even sweat out the inequalities of motherhood, but there is a resentment at never having been told or shown what it would be like.

Much of this is another result of forces constantly at work in our country to reduce contact among persons; we even use bubble umbrellas now, ensuring protection for only one person, the owner, and all others keep out in the storm. Mothers may think it tactless to reflect on such heavy thoughts today, amid May's lightness, and perhaps they deserve the day off. If so, the reflection needs to be done by nonmothers, by those who, despite their hushed respect for the Institution of Motherhood, have forgotten or don't want to know that mothers are first of all human beings in search of completeness. Or, as poet Michele Murray notes, in answer to Freud's sly question of what do women want: "The same as men want—the unattainable."

# Becoming a Man by Tending Children        1971

By the nature of things, no one is allowed to know the exact moment when the seasons change, nor the precise time when a friendship becomes a relationship, nor when a commitment to a life's vocation is made. Change is a mystery, and all of us are only pebbles in the stream of reality that carries it along in a rushing flow. Occasionally, though, however predoomed we are to getting the brush-off at great moments, the shadows of an event are sharp enough to suggest the general outline of when a change is happening. The event whose shadows I was lucky enough to see happened during the last 12 months, from April to April. I saw a boy become a man. My eye is not trained for this sight, but no corrective lens was needed to guarantee the accuracy of my vision.

When Joe Hunton, a 15-year-old in the neighborhood near American University came to work at my home last April he was a boy: when he left last week to take a job at Johnson's Florist on Wisconsin Avenue, he was into manhood. His job at our home was taking care of the two older boys in our family, ages four and three, for some six to eight hours a week during the school year, and every weekday morning during the summer and holidays. The work was neither hard or highly specialized, and anyone over 10 could hardly help being over-qualified. The job—at $.75 an hour to start—meant coming over Saturday mornings at 9, getting the kids out, walking to the playground, playing with them, back for lunch and then putting them down for a nap. The job was babysitting. I thought of streamlining the term, perhaps calling it "childhood management" or "infant development" the way bureaucrats go wild over their Form 57 adjectives under job-description. But Joe accepted the title of babysitter as evenly as he took on the assignment. Some of his friends ribbed him about this kind of employment, calling it girls' work. Joe got a laugh out of that. For one thing, he had only to look at his ungirlish frame—180 pounds on it, full of glandular growth, and already moved about with a trudging step. As for his friends' concern about masculinity, Joe easily knocked them out of the ballpark with his reply that at least he had a job. They didn't. Oddly, some of the younger boys in the neighborhood—11 and 12—not yet misled by the he-man cult, saw Joe's babysitting as classy stuff. One has applied for the job this year, now that word is out that Joe's number has been retired.

When we first talked with him about working for us on a regular basis, Joe's mother, who only a few years before was hiring baby-sitters for Joe, insisted in fairness that we be told that reliability was not his major life-force. In fact, supplying us with the official resume, she said he seldom rose before noon on weekends, he had trouble listening to people, he had taken the garbage out only twice in three years and even then it was on the way to someplace else, he habitually left the water running in the sink and he set indoor records for television watching. Joe was a normal and fine boy, his mother allowed, but if it was a bottle of reliability we wanted to pour our babysitting money into, well, perhaps we should shop on other shelves.

In the year's time between Aprils, Joe was never late for one Saturday. He showed equal activism about getting the kids dressed and out, as though, like a wrestler, he kept his muscles tight for special occasions. He came on strongest with his eye for freshness, seeing old things for the first time: at the playground, for example, he often took turns on the slides and swings himself. Why not? A few mothers looked twice at this but why shouldn't a member of the community use the community playground? One skill he had was keeping the kids moving. This is the rarest talent among Western hemisphere babysitters. Most take their work in the literal meaning—sitting the baby, with so much emphasis on sitting that

that is all it is. Sometimes I would see the happy threesome coming back from a walk, the two boys bobbing along the street like corks, floating in the sea of Joe's guidance. Joe had learned the oldest lesson of being with children: wear them out or they wear you out. Persuasion was seldom needed for them to take naps after an outing with Joe Hunton. By the end of last fall, Joe earned a raise to $1 an hour. The 11 and 12-year-olds had even more respect for Joe, now that he made big money and parked overtime on Easy Street.

His father, mother and sisters were amazed at our positive reports. "Our Joe?" they would ask, stuck in the old gear. They were not only surprised that he had persevered through the summer and all the run of fall and winter Saturdays, but were amazed to learn that at our house he often took out the garbage (and came back), hung up his own coat and brought his own dirty dishes to the sink. On the latter extras, this was not apple polishing; first, we were too busy to notice the shine and, second, it was done routinely.

What delivered Joe from childhood to manhood? The guidance counselors would ascribe it to some vague notion like "character development." My view is that Joe's first crack at responsibility came exactly when his emotions were ready for it. Like the odd salmon out, he lit upstream when he, not the pack, felt right. A person's first job is crucial. If forced and pushed into it, he will try to push out ot if, rebelling inside where all the bad rebellion happens. If allowed to loaf about though, even set laziness records, and pick how own time to get passionate about something, the average young person will grow in ways the parents never imagined. He is into new territory, exploring on his own and caring about things that matter to him in his own unshared privacy.

It is a pity that many adults push youngsters into work when the latter aren't ready, and it is sad also that so many of the young have shallow notions of what it means to achieve manhood or woman-hood. There is the "Summer of '42" vision, a strange thesis that says you aren't a male until you can bed a female. Another masquerade which easily tricks youngsters is that you aren't an adult until you can get drunk the first time or get into a good cigarette habit. Tooling a car past 100 mph is also big stuff. Here and there, you meet someone under 20 who rejects this nonsense, knowing that at best they only mean you've become big physically, not that you have grown up emotionally. Responding to other people's needs is what makes you grow, not responding to your own.

Joe's mother tells us that of late he's been different around their house also, not only ours. His room is clean, he shuts off water drips, he listens better. He learned recently of a job—harder hours but better pay—at Johnson's Florist and we encouraged him to take it; we'll recoup our gains, we said. For now, my only thought about Joe Hunton is: Johnson's Florist, you have a good man.

*Joe Hunton is now 28, a carpenter and using all the skills he learned with my boys on his own baby, a girl age two.*

# Sharing the Faith With Children          *1976*

When the four parents talked during lunch about their Easter plans, the four children with them listened. Then one of the adults realized the youngest child, age 6, might not have known the meaning of Easter. So a quiz began, a test of faith for the three older children who were 12, 10 and 9.

The next few minutes were not among the inspiring moments of Christendom. None of the children knew what occurred on Good Friday. None knew who denied Christ three times. The guesses were several miles wide of the mark: St. Patrick, St. Paul and Christopher Columbus. Those were among the more intelligent answers. Asked to name the disciple who betrayed Christ, the group thought it was "Jupiter." No, said the 6-year-old, "It was Mars."

That brought some laughs. But later, the parents, as though in a group grope at Esalen, began feeling blindly for mutual support from each other. They realized that these were children who had had some exposure to organized religion, because the parents had been hauling them to church for years. They knew also that religion was talked about in the home. But as keepers of the faith, the parents wondered exactly whom they were keeping it for. Not their children, if the lunch table test scores meant anything.

It is probably true that we are raising a generation of children who know more about Charlie's Angels than God's angels. But it has to be asekd: What exactly do parents want from religion for their children? If they think that churchgoing is crucial, the examples of Jacques Maritain, Thomas Merton and Dorothy Day ought to be considered. These are three of the towering figures of Western spirituality in the 20th century, yet none of them went near a church service until age 25. Not only did their churchless childhoods not stifle their souls, but perhaps those periods were actually a boon to spiritual growth. How many parents dutifully march their young off to religious services every week, only to see them become devout atheists once they are too grown to take marching orders?

At best, church attendance provides only a temporary reassurance for parents who want to raise "good" children. That the young so often and so enragingly turn out to be adults with little visible goodness and still less visible connection with the family faith suggests that the goals are wrong. Religion is trivialized unless it opens the child's mind to the beauties of service to others. All of the enduring religious teachers—Buddha, Moses, Jesus, Mohammed—insisted that worship of God is hollow unless based on a commitment to ease the suffering of human beings. Of what use is it to rear children who have the facts and stories of the Bible down cold but have learned little about using one's skills to aid the sick, imprisoned or the outcast?

This sense of service to others is not easily taught, at least not now in this country. The ethic of self-absorption and the glamorization of whoever at this passing moment is rich, slim or chic compete so intensely for the attention of the young that, even if a parent does know the value of getting his children to spend a Saturday afternoon doing errands for the old folks at the neighborhood nursing home or volunteering to care for the infants in the orphanage, a high-powered selling job is often needed. And that leads to problems of its own. If doing good in the world is so fine a pursuit, asks the young mind, why are they straining to sell it to me?

In the collision of questions between adults and children—we ask them to cite the facts of Easter, they ask us to prove that service matters—some crash survivors are around. These are the parents who boldly understand that the spiritual impulses of children don't need to be created, much less created by a stiff formula of instructions. The impulses are already present in the young heart. They need only be nurtured. But because this nurturing involves a careful mix of example, patience and wisdom, the days of failure outnumber the days of success. To the child, this isn't important. He perceives only that an adult is making the effort to pass along something valuable. Exactly how valuable will be known later. For now, it is enough in the child's mind that a sharing of faith is going on. No child yet has ever declined an invitation to share what is good.

# Confessions of a Halloween Wierdo          *1982*

In the what-they'll-think-of-next sweepstakes, some thinkers on the town council of Dudley, Mass., have thought up quite a next. They have banned Halloween.

No trick or treating this year for the kids of Dudley, the politicians ruled. Someone became sick from a cookie last Halloween, it seems. Worse, this year the Tylenol craziness is in the air. An evil spirit might put it into the head of a Dudleyite to lace a Halloween treat with cyanide.

The children of Dudley have yet to be polled on this banning, though a town spokesman said that violators would not be prosecuted. The cops have been instructed merely to tell the little ones to move on and go home.

Halloween alarmism about predator adults is an annual rite. It's usually been nuts who jam razors into apples or needles into candy bars who are on the minds of the Protectors of Children. I have some expertise in this issue because for the past 10 years I have gained, in some of the more fright-prone parts of my neighborhood, a reputation as one of those wierdos the kids had better avoid. My offense is that on Halloween night I open my front door and hand out vegetables.

Last year I gave okra. I had had a good year with it in my garden and had a few dozen pods left over. Okra is a late summer crop, so it was tough of skin by Halloween. I suggested to one kid wearing a gorilla mask that if he wasn't up to eating raw okra, despite his costume, he should boil it for 10 minutes.

The year before I was into kale. Don't be spooked I told a child dressed as a ghost, it's not spinach. In others years, I have treated the innocents at my door to carrots, potatoes, onions, broccoli and turnips.

Halloween is about the only time of year that I get near to proselytizing my vegetarianism. The kids are on my property, after all, and by the time many of them get to my house they are ready for a break from the nauseam pile of candy bars and other tooth-rots in their sacks. "You err what you eat," is the nutritional wisdom I quote on Halloween night.

A decade ago, other parents in my neighborhood warned that I was asking for retaliatory trouble by giving kids vegetables like kale and carrots. My windows would be broken, they warned, the porch railing bent and the doorbell ripped out.

None of these Druidic horrors has happened. Some years, I admit, the lawn on the morning after has been strewn with kale leaves and broken carrots. The sight causes me grief, and I wonder if I shouldn't go back to the civilized way of dispensing junk food. But I have never taken offense at the leftovers on the lawn. Instead I have taken the vegetables inside, rinsed them and cooked it all up for dinner—my annual post-Halloween stew, a high-nutrition and low-cost delight.

Harvesting my rejected crops has been a minor hurt compared with a larger joy: scaring the wits out of little kids by opening the door and standing there, as somber as Frankenstein, with a broccoli stalk jutting out of my mouth. The littler they are, the more frightened they get. It's not me, it's the broccoli. They've never seen it before. They've gone directly from processed baby food out of jars to plastic hamburgers and fries out of golden arches. The true fright comes when I hold out a trayful of broccoli and say, take one kid, you deserve a break today.

The children are brave. They look up at me and reach for the broccoli—quickly, as though either it or I might be catching. The veggie is dropped into the sugar-polluted sack and the friendly ghosts move on.

I have met few adults who believe me, but a growing number of my Halloween visitors actually eat what I give them. Not the onions that one year, nor much of the okra the other. But the carrots have been popular. Although it could be that the kids have been grateful not to have gotten a handful of bulgar or bean sprouts from me, I prefer a brush that paints a brighter picture: They certifiably and really do like the taste and texture of vegetables. Stranger things have happened on Halloween.

Each year gets easier for me. Kids began asking two weeks ago what I'd be passing out this Halloween. Gonna have to wait, I've answered. I had a decent bean crop but it's been eaten. I'm thinking now of tomatoes, which I've stewed and put into baggies. Except they would be unretrievable on the lawn the next morning. I don't think I should be depriving myself of a treat.

# A Father's Day                                              *1981*

Father's Day is wonderful, and I'm for it. But one Father's Day is not enough. Three are needed—for the three climates of fatherhood that must be passed through before, weather-beaten but not broken, we can rejoice that God gave fathers the privilege of being co-creators.

Of the three climates—sunny; cloudy with daily air turbulence and tornado warnings on the weekends; and post-storm balminess—I know the first best. I've been warming in it for 13 years, since the first of three young males came into our household.

The sunniness of fatherhood when children are young, charming, have short hair and do not yet want their own phones is in having no tougher question to face than "Where did I go right?" This is the period of no-fault fatherhood. Where did I go wrong? is what the strung-out father down the street is asking himself—he with a 17-year-old son who is Mario Andretti behind the wheel of the family heap and a 21-year-old daughter who has the tastes but not the lineage of an heiress and has been to five colleges in three years.

I am entering the clouds of this second climate now. With one lad at 13, and his brothers rushing from behind at 12 and 9, I know it's been easy till now. Even the experts on fatherhood have told me so. In "Family Constellations," a sparkling book on how sibling positions shape an individual's personality, Walter Toman, a Viennese-born professor of psychology, writes of my ilk, the youngest brother of brothers: he "is not a conventional father .... Sometimes it is clearly more important to him to be understood by his children than to understand them himself .... However, often he is also a good companion for his children, and as such he is probably at his best in his role as a father."

If it's been a picnic so far, I can feel the ants crawling onto the blanket when someone accurately assesses the parenthood scene: "The children now love luxury. They have bad manners, contempt for authority, they show disrespect to their elders .... They no longer rise when elders enter the room. They contradict their parents, chatter before company, gobble up dainties at the table, cross their legs, and are tyrants over their teachers."

Who is this wracked soul? Socrates, just in with a fresh report on Greek family life in the Golden Age of 2,400 years ago. I have hope that his will be a useful text as I try to keep upright in these next few years of clouds, high winds and tornadoes. It's cheering to know that whatever I will be seeing in this second climate, Socrates braved it too. Not only that, but nothing he saw was so over-powering as to keep him from being a philosopher, the noblest of all crafts. All I do is practice one of the lowest—putting a few words into the newspaper, which is to philosophy what a shanty is to the Parthenon.

When I ask fathers of the second climate how long it is before the third climate of post-storm balminess arrives, I get mixed answers. If young Mario has just squealed out of the driveway and has floored it to 90 before reaching the light at the corner, I am told "never." Or if the daughter of the house has just done her parents the favor of graduating from college, after trying six of them at $8,000 a year, then the answer might be brighter—"Oh, half a century or so."

Is it going to be that bad? Once more, a philosopher rides to what looks like an impossible rescue. Mark Twain said, "When I was a boy of fourteen, my father was so ignorant I could hardly stand to have the old man around. But when I got to be twenty-one, I was astonished at how much the old man had learned in seven years."

With seven years of learning ahead of me, one safe bet is that not much of it will be book learning. An estimated 300 how-to-parent books have been published in the past 20 years, excluding reprints of Piaget, Montessori, Gesell and Erikson. But most of these are books about how to change an infant's diaper, when the mystery for me is how to change—and shape and inspire—an adolescent's mind.

It's not books that can tell us that—only other fathers. Which is another reason a few more Father's Days would not hurt: we have a lot to talk about.

*Chapter 3*

# Our Brother's Keeper— Sometimes

T he poor have it hard, the saying goes. Well, the hardest thing they have is us.

—*Daniel Berrigan*

## On Chicago's Margin                                      *1982*

My spiritual counselor at the Pacific Garden Mission, fingering an opened Bible on his desk, told me he was going to ask the most important question a person will ever have to answer in his life. In a hushed voice, he said, "If you were to die tonight, where would you go?"

Suppressing the irreverent remarks that immediately came to mind, I made a politic reply: "I'm not sure." How many people die in this place, I wondered.

The Pacific Garden Mission is one of the largest facilities for the homeless in Chicago, and it provides lodging and food in sparse portions to an increasingly large number of people. Since it is run by a group of evangelical sects—in the waiting room there is a photograph of the Rev. Billy Sunday—those seeking a cot for the night, as I was, must first be "counseled in the Bible."

My counselor, an earnest and well-meaning man in a pin-striped suit, gold me he deals with all kinds of people, from bums to engineers and lawyers. After twenty minutes of religiosity, sugared with frequent Jesus-loves-us smiles, he homed in: Wasn't it time I turned away from sin? I'm ready, I answered.

I was also bushed, although it was only my first day of the three I would spend among the homeless in Chicago. Three days and nights among the loners and losers of this city—shallow slumming. And my poverty was strictly voluntary. I have a family, job and home.

But one's initiation into poverty comes quickly. Only minutes after checking my wallet, my press card and other trappings of middle-class life in a locker at the Greyhound terminal, I felt what it is like to bear the stigma of lost respectability. As I walked along Michigan Avenue and State Street, shoppers and office workers gave me two kinds of looks: the hard why-don't-you-bums-stay-on-skid-row stare or the furtive there-but-for-the-grace-of-God glance. How many times had I looked at a bum and thought the same things?

It hadn't taken much to disguise myself. I omitted my morning shave, I donned a worn canvas windbreaker over a knee-length black raincoat, old running shoes and a stevedore cap. I walked with a slower gait. Soon I met others of my kind. They—we—seemed to be everywhere.

That first night at the mission, listening to the Bible counselor, who seemed interested only in converting me, I was overpowered by weariness. All I wanted was a bed and a few hours' respite from that world outside. But from the time I joined the line in front of the mission at 5 P.M. until I was assigned a cot, five hours elapsed.

After being "saved" by my counselor, I was led to the prayer room. Seated on the hard chairs were about 200 of America's unofficial missing persons. There were winos, the insane, the unemployed, the depressed, Vietnam veterans, the new poor. The majority were black. They sat slumped in silence. Large maroon signs bearing Biblical verses were hung on the walls. Until 9 P.M., we were subjected to sermons from a team of well-dressed evangelists who quoted Matthew 14 this and Luke 21 that. They were from a suburban church, one of them told us. They knew full weel that "Satan is out there and wants to take us to the bottom of the barrel."

The men in the audience, who had already reached the bottom and found leaks, listened impassively. After the sermons it was "testimony time." We were exhorted to "rise up and tell what's in your heart." About a dozen hands were raised. One penitent after another stood up and either testified that Jesus loved him or renounced Satan on the spot. Then a guitar player walked onstage and asked everyone to join him in singing "When the Roll Is Called Up Yonder."

Up yonder, as far as I was concerned, was the secondfloor dormitory, where my cot awaited. After the hymn, and after being frisked at the bottom of the stairway, we were taken to the Promised Land. As a "first-timer," I qualified for a bed; most of the regulars had to take their chances on floor space being available.

"Seven-A, take your hanger," the guard at the desk ordered. It took me a moment to remember that I was 7-A—that I had been assigned to the seventh cot from the wall, row A. I had been staring at the ranks of cots and the men walking to them, at last able to lie down after five hours of Biblegab. I took the hanger. "Get your clothes off and leave them in the hot box," the guard said. "Then get in the shower. It's down there."

The hot box is the room where everyone's clothes are hung for the night. The heat is turned up, frying any lice, bedbugs and other vermin nesting in the rags.

I slept fitfully. Less than two feet separated the cots. Each of us had only a coarse sheet to lie on and a blanket for cover, but the dorm was well heated. On one side of me a recently laid-off factory worker sat on his bed talking aimlessly to anyone within earshot. A guard finally came over and silenced him. On the other side was a gray-haired derelict, a veteran of the street who was asleep within minutes. The din of snores, whisky coughs, moans and shouts was constant. It was like a bedroom in bedlam, filled with men whose torments gave them no peace, even in sleep.

The morning bell rang at 5, two hours before dawn. It was 20 degrees outside, warm for a January day in Chicago. We were given the choice of hitting the pavement or going to the prayer room to hear a sermon. Although listening to the sermon would have earned me a bowl of oatmeal, I chose the street. I walked around until 11, when a soup kitchen run by Franciscans opened. There I lunched on bread and cheese, the latter compliments of the Reagan Administration.

My thoughts had already turned to finding a place to sleep that night. I had asked at the soup kitchen if the Catholic Worker ran a shelter in town. It was on Kenmore Street, I was told, about five miles north. I decided to try it.

Before setting out, I entered the first shop I saw—a liquor store—to ask directions. As I approached the counter, the clerk reached down and, without a word, handed me a miniature bottle of Bacardi rum. I told him I didn't drink, eliciting a now-I've-heard-everything look from him. Pushing the bottle back, I asked for directions to Kenmore Street.

After I'd walked a few miles, I spied a storefront library and went in to rest and warm up. I still had a good feeling about the generosity of the clerk. Perhaps other shopkeepers are like that, I thought. Back outside, at the intersection of Rush and Oak Streets, I noticed a bakery called LET THEM EAT CAKE. I thought I was suffering an optical illusion, but the name of the place was actually that. Rather than congratulate the woman who waited on me for the cleverness of the bakeshop's name, I got to the point. I was hungry. Could I scrub the floor or clean the windows—anything—in return for a bite to eat? No, she said. Have you any leftovers? No. Cakeless, I went back into the street and resumed my journey.

At the Catholic Worker house of hospitality, I was welcomed and invited to have tea in the living room. No beds were available, however, the young man in charge told me, not even for emergency crashing. We talked for a while, and he described the increasing financial pressure on private groups like the Worker in the current recession.

I headed back to the Loop; I probably walked about twelve miles in all, round trip. I was beginning to feel desperate about finding a place to stay. It was snowing heavily. Then I remembered a police-man telling me the day before that if the shelters were filled, one could always go to jail.

I set off to look for a cop but was distracted by a television crew filming the evening rush hour in the snowstorm. I went up to the announcer, a tall, handsomely dressed man, and suggested that instead of wasting his time on a film clip of cars and snow he cover the story of Chicago's homeless. Startled and a bit angry at this criticism, he said, "Where are they?" All over, I answered, but you have to go to them. He and his crew continued their search for the perfect fender-bender.

On a bridge over the Chicago River, two patrolmen approached me. I told them that I was cold and hungry and asked where the city jail was. "You can't just walk in," one of them said. "We'll arrest you first and call the wagon."

They seemed to be genuinely concerned about me. They explained that the judge would release me in the morning; it was routine. "What should we charge him with?" one asked the other. "It doesn't matter. Put down begging." I was reminded of the line in Shaw's *Major Barbara*: "The worst of our crimes is poverty."

That was my last literary reflection of the day. The paddy wagon arrived and, after stopping to pick up another homeless man, it dropped us at the city jail on South State Street. There were a half-dozen cops around the desk inside. They showered obscenities on the prisoners impartially—the cocky street-toughs, the old beggars and the mentally disturbed.

After a frisking—I was allowed to keep nothing, not even my pen or the book of poetry I was carrying—I was led to a cell. Seven of us were crowded into a space meant for two. Half an hour later, a guard bellowed at me and another prisoner to come with him. He took us to a different cell, in which there were only two other prisoners. It was 10 feet by 7 feet. Two thick bare boards extended from the wall and served as beds. There were no sheets, pillows or blankets. A little more than a yard separated the boards and the toilet, its bowl stained with dried vomit and fecal matter. It had no seat and there was no tissue. Urine stains yellowed the wall behind the bowl.

My cellmates said little. One was a 250-pound Hispanic who had been arrested for drunkenness in the subway; another was a derelict—a lean and morose man of about 30, who had been involved in a barroom brawl. The third was a high-strung drifter who paced the floor—what there was of it—breathing heavily and babbling incoherently. His body tremors suggested he was going through withdrawal. When I caught his eye he lurched toward me and snorted in my face, letting me know he wasn't to be stared at.

I wondered about sleeping arrangements. How would we decide who would get the "beds" and who would have to sleep on the grimy floor? The question was half-solved when the Hispanic heavyweight hoisted himself up and lay down on one of the boards. Suddenly, the drifter dropped to the floor without a word. In five minutes he was asleep, and I gained the second board by default.

As I was about to lie down, I noticed that the derelict, who had stretched out on the floor, had no pillow. I offered him my windbreaker, which he accepted with a look of incredulity, mumbling his thanks.

I lay awake all night, fuming because the jailers hadn't set aside a few cells for people like me, the voluntary arrests who only wanted a bed. Instead they threw us in with the petty criminals who had been caught in the night's dragnet. There were six men in one of the adjoining cages and five in the other. For hours they screamed at one another, asserting their manhood. Sometimes a man would roar his hatred for another prisoner ten cells away. On the rare occasions when the guards intervened, they added their shouts of "Be quiet!" to the general uproar. Through the long night the voices—raging, threatening—never stopped. Once again, the poor were venting their anger at the only available target—one another.

We were awakened at 4 A.M. In the mission, I recalled, the homeless can loll around until 5. After a breakfast of baloney sandwiches, two per person, about 100 of us were led to a small holding pen, to await our appearance in court. While we were there, fights broke out as some of the men settled the past night's scores. After thirty minutes or so, a guard entered and read a list of names. When mine was called, I walked through a corridor to a grubby courtroom. After two hours, at 8 o'clock, the judge arrived, a nattily dressed man in his early 30s. The number of prisoners in the courtroom had swelled to nearly 200, including a half-dozen prostitutes, but in a remarkable display of efficiency—this being Chicago, the city that works—all of us were run past the judge and sent out to the street in a matter of minutes.

I spent the rest of the morning at two soup kitchens and the afternoon in the reading room of the main branch of the public library. Part of that night, I slept sitting up in the Greyhound terminal. Had I found a heat grate, I would have tried it. After two nights of receiving the best—i.e., the worst—that society has to offer, I understood why so many homeless people prefer to sleep on sidewalks, in alleys and in abandoned buildings. If Chicago is representative, the homeless have a choice between spending the night in a shelter where religion is crammed down their gullets and spending it in the city jail, which offers them more terror.

Of course, some of the people who refuse to go to shelters are mentally ill. When I talked with them, I wondered if they had lost their minds before they went on the streets or if, thrown on the street through no fault of their own, they went crazy. In a harsh world without love, laughter, children, friendship, work or dreams, the poor are soon reduced to a mass of raw emotions: tenacity, fear, boredom, anger.

Private charity is no solution to the problems of the homeless. At best it buys time. Some have argued that as more people and more politicians learn of the suffering, they will provide help. But the available evidence suggests that politicians will only take action after they have been prodded by lawsuits and public demonstrations.

In New York, Mayor Edward Koch, pushed by the Coalition for the Homeless, in turn began pushing private groups. He scolded the Jewish community for not opening "a single synagogue" for the homeless. Some rabbis protested that such plans were already underway. Back and forth it goes.

Awakenings elsewhere are slower. In Phoenix, the city council has been on an anti-litter campaign for two years, the litter being the human kind—"transients and inebriates." The eyesores, it seems, have been hindering redevelopment of the downtown area. In 1981, the council, like railroad cops in the 1930s routing tramps from boxcars, passed laws against sitting or lying in streets and sidewalks.

That, predictably, did nothing. Currently, more homeless than ever are in downtown Phoenix. Forced into action by the failure of its drive-em-out program, the council recently gave support for an emergency shelter for 300—in a warehouse.

One council member, fearing that fair Phoenix might be over-taken by masses of the great unwashed as word spread that a luxurious warehouse had opened, warned about letting the city "become a mecca for every transient in the United States."

The trouble is, we rarely go beyond the stereotypical to speak to the destitute, much less go among them. If we do, our eyes are opened, and maybe our hearts. In his 1933 book, *Down and Out in Paris and London*, George Orwell wrote: "Still I can point to one or two things I have definitely learned by being hard up. I shall never again think that all tramps are drunken scoundrels, nor expect a beggar to be grateful when I give him a penny, nor be surprised if men out of work lack energy.... That is a beginning."

At the least, a similar beginning—a jolt to awareness—is required now. Personal or institutional generosity is no more than a symbolic message to missing persons that help is on the way. Except in too many cases it isn't. What's on the way are more homeless: people doomed to be driven from their homes tomorrow by cuts in housing programs today. News stories tell of cuts in housing aid for rural poor and elderly citizens. The walking wounded are now having their crutches yanked away.

For many of the homeless, getting back up will be impossible. Emergency shelters—clean, civilized and humane places, not mini-chapels, nor jails—must be provided for this group as a matter of the poor's rights not civic charity. But even the public shelters, which fill as quickly as they are opened, won't mean much if citizens don't have the jobs, or welfare and mental health programs, to remain in the private shelters they have now—their own homes.

Among Chicago's destitute, I found people who, if they worked in my office or lived in my neighborhood would come off as sociable and decent citizens. That they happened to be on the streets didn't lessen their humanity. If anything, each time the rest of us look away, we lessen our own.

# Curing the Fear of Cancer          1982

They are cancer *patients*, they insist, not cancer victims. They meet weekly for between two and three hours of attitude therapy. For them, cancer is not a Death Row disease that you automatically die from but an illness you can live with: live fully, and perhaps live longer than originally thought.

Each in the group has undergone surgery in hope of stopping his cancer's spread. All have decided that whatever treatments they had placed faith in before—from daily drug therapy for one patient with ovarian cancer to three surgical operations for another—they now want to fight or control their cancer other ways than only medically. They are calling on the powers of the mind, on emotions and group support as helps in strengthening the body's immune system to defeat cancer cells. They nod approvingly when one member of the group says with passionate conviction about the weekly meetings, "This is the best medicine I've got."

Cancer attitude therapy has been an established part of American psychiatry for a number of years. It has been bolstered, on the

popular level at least, by the death-and-dying movement that
stresses the quality of life as the quantity of life itself ebbs away. Its
best practitioners are neither pain-control quacks preying on the
desperate nor are they debunkers of the traditional cancer treatments—surgery, radiation and chemotherapy—who offer the
psychological approach as a laetrile of the mind.

The leader of the group that meets at the Washington School of
Psychiatry is Dr. Robert Kvarnes, a 66-year-old psychoanalyst who
for 29 years has been director of the school, at 1910 New
Hampshire Ave. in northwest Washington. The other four
members include Dr. Morris Chalick, 45, a psychiatrist who underwent surgery for melanoma, a skin cancer, a year and a half ago;
Gail Polsby, 43, a clinical social worker who practices privately as a
psychotherapist and who had a rare cancer that required the
removal of her bladder in 1975; Monsignor Geno Baroni, 51, who
has peritoneal mesothelioma, a rare abdominal cancer; and Dorothy
Joyce, 57, administrator of the treatment clinic at the Washington
School of Psychiatry, who has ovarian cancer.

This group differs from conventional attitude therapy programs.
The guide for the group, Kvarnes, is a psychoanalyst who has
cancer himself. His approach to cancer attitude therapy is no
exercise in wellness chic. His own health—and life—is on the line, a
thin line, he is the first to admit.

From mid-April to early June 1982, I was an observer at six
therapy sessions, all on Thursday mornings between 9 and noon. In
addition, individual interviews were conducted with Kvarnes and
Baroni. Initially, it was undecided whether pseudonyms or actual
names would be used. But as time passed, "going public," as one
member put it, was a difficulty for no one. In fact, because all five of
the patients were in caring professions—four in medicine and one
in religion—the giving of permission to use names was seen by
them as an extension of the positive attitude they were trying to
affirm in themselves and spread to others who have or may get
cancer.

It is a group that has freed itself of the cancer pall. In none of the
sessions, not even for a moment, did anyone give in to gloom or
despair. Most Americans have been conditioned to equate cancer
with slow, agonizing, unstoppable death. Cancer is the handy
metaphor for inevitable destruction. In the Watergate hearings,
high drama was reached when John Dean told of going to Richard

Nixon to say that a cancer was eating away at the presidency. He was telling Nixon the rap wasn't to be beaten. But we operate on a double standard. A Henry Kissinger can suffer heart disease and he's off to the hospital and the public is regaled with the details, before and after. But a Hubert Humphrey or a Steve McQueen can contract cancer and a great effort is made to hide it.

The get-cancer-and-you're-a-goner syndrome came up in several of the sessions. Everyone had stories about what it felt like to be on the receiving end of people wondering why they were not yet dead and buried. In one session, a member, breaking in bittersweetly, said, "In the last few weeks, I've had several people confronting me. I don't know whether I—related or unrelated to my cancer—have provoked them. Or whether it's coincidental that it's happening now. Or whether people confronted me because they felt, 'Oh well, he has cancer, we don't know how much time we have to tell him this so we'll tell him now.' Or that they see me still okay a year and a half later and have a certain feeling of resentment—after they have felt sorry for someone, pitied them, done something for them—and everything's fine."

Baroni, a cheerful spirit who has a gift for extracting the wry, laughed and shook his head knowingly. He said that had happened to him, too: "'You look well,' they'll say, 'What's wrong with you? You're not supposed to be this well. You're supposed to be pretty sick.'" Baroni, a former assistant secretary of HUD during the Carter administration and currently an aide to Archbishop James Hickey, suffers from the same type of cancer Steve McQueen had.

Another, agreeing with Baroni, said that with cancer "you're supposed to have sunken eyes and really look terrible."

No one in the group had The Terrible Look. Nor did anyone look at his cancer-interrupted life with fear. Much of this seemed due to positive feelings generated by Kvarnes. He is reflective, fatherly, well-read, a man given to drollery and held in affection by many of the more than 100 mental health professionals who teach at the school. His third-floor office is roomy, green-carpeted, brightened by house plants and four abstract paintings but otherwise undisturbed by a decorator's touch. Kvarnes, whose mother died of cancer at 66, underwent radiation treatment in late 1979 for prostatic cancer. A year later it was learned that it had spread extensively to the bones. An orchiectomy—the removal of the male hormone glands—followed, on the medical theory that this type of cancer, when it spreads to the bone marrow, often depends on the male hormone. A recent bone scan revealed what Kvarnes calls, with guided delight, "a marked reduction" of the cancer.

Kvarnes organized the group in late 1980 at the urging of his colleague, Gail Polsby. Married with two adopted children, she saw the need for the therapy program because "I had had a hard and lonely time that year (1975) when I thought I was going to die, and where most people who had my kind of tumor died quickly. I couldn't find people to talk with me about my illness."

In the sessions, Morris Chalick sat between Polsby and Kvarnes. Chalick, a bicyclist, amateur actor and who came to Washington in 1968 to work for the Peace Corps as a staff psychiatrist, sees a surgeon and oncologist every six weeks. "I'm at a stage where there is nothing. But something can always pop up." Chalick, introspective, well-groomed and respectful of his elder, Kvarnes, was, as much as anyone, keenly sensitive to the group's mood.

Dorothy Joyce often arrived a few minutes late. But gladness would lighten the faces of those already present when she came in the door. They knew she had just driven into town from her daily drug treatments at NIH. It was as if her being physically able to come to the therapy session symbolized a victory celebration for life.

Baroni was the natural storyteller who ranged from jovial tales about his early days as a priest in the coal fields of western Pennsylvania to accounts of people being dumb-struck when they casually ask "how are you" and him replying, "not so hot, I have cancer."

As the leader of the group, Kvarnes is cautious against over-selling the benefits that might result from the weekly meetings. But neither does he see the process as an exercise in aimless faith healing. The middle ground, he explains, is that the group is organized "on an experimental basis."

"We're going on the hunch that what we're doing makes a lot of sense," said Kvarnes. "But it will be a while before we compile a record that would sway any skeptical physician. There's an absence of a caseload. Say you have 100 cases that you've worked on. You can report that 78 percent of the time you get this, in 21 percent you get this and one percent that. We don't have those kind of data at all. The hunch that we're going on is that the person's attitude affects the way that the body works against the cancer cells. The mediating agent seems to be the immune system. We're going on the pretty strong hunch that we can, by our efforts, influence the way the immune system works. I say hunch because it's not something that's verified by our or anyone else's statistics."

Between the poles of hunches and scientific verification is Dr. Nicholas Hall, an assistant research professor in psychoneuroimmunology in the department of biochemistry at George Washington University Medical Center. He is working with Kvarnes on this project and is enthusiastic about it.

"Physicians have known for a long time that emotions affect disease," Hall said. "But what is the mechanism? I'm optimistic that Dr. Kvarnes' group will provide for us a model for which there is no lab animal counterpart. The results of his investigation, coupled with the results of ongoing animal studies, will help us to better understand the complex interrelationship that appears to exist between the central nervous system and the immune system."

Although Kvarnes and Hall have arranged to conduct outside tests to determine if the ability of the patients' white cells to fight off the cancer cells is changed during the course of the therapy, the talk within the sessions is predominantly on the human, not the scientific, level.

On April 15th, the session began conversationally. Kvarnes, as he was to do every session, loosened his collar and tie and unwrapped a morning munchie, a thick slab of peanut butter between two wheat crackers. Baroni, on a green leather lounge chair with his legs slung over a footrest, recalled the earlier bouts he had with cancer, in 1973 and 1980. Both times he told almost no one of his illness. The group was curious about this, and questions came:

Chalick: "Wasn't it tough on you to have a secret?"

Baroni: "A secret? Yeah, I had a scar [on the neck from a lymph node operation] so I wore turtlenecks a lot. I really didn't want to talk about it. I even avoided doctors."

Joyce: "Why didn't you want to talk about it—because you were afraid you would have to identify it?"

Baroni: "I was afraid. I just didn't want to talk about it. I would keep my appointments. I went to get my regular checkups. Those times it was surgery. This time, though, I had all those treatments for eight weeks, every day. I went through various degrees of feeling good and feeling bad and wondering what's happening. No predictions. The prognosis was different, too. When you talk to a surgeon, he always says, 'We got it all!'"

Joyce: "That's the great line." [Group laughter]. "I heard that, too. That's the first thing I heard when I came out of anesthesia: 'I think I got it all.'"

Baroni: "Yeah, and you want to believe that, too."

Kvarnes, enjoying the dialogue as well as the last bite of his peanut butter, broke in: "Did I tell you about my mother's cancer? It was in 1959—I would have been 43 at the time and with no experience with cancer after medical school. She developed a carcinoma of the bile duct. It was about September when the diagnosis was made. We got the news that it was inoperable. We all broke down as a family. No one said anything to anyone else. She was in the hospital from September to December. No nurse, no doctor, no son, no daughter who is a nurse—nobody said to her that she had cancer. My mother knew it. She never brought it up. I waited for her to bring it up because I didn't think I could. I think I was afraid of some kind of emotional reaction that would be beyond my control. Which was absolutely nuts. My mother was fully capable of talking about it. She didn't think I was. She knew she was dying. And here we had this conspiracy that included the whole damn hospital. No one came to talk with this intelligent woman. And a very gutsy woman who, if she were in a group like this, would be working like crazy to conquer her cancer."

Joyce leaned forward in the chair: "Bob, the surgeon who did the hysterectomy on me came in and talked to me and said, 'I think I got it all.' He never used the word cancer. This is last year."

At this session, as at all of them, references to other people's attitudes about cancer were not an occasion to put down friends or the medical establishment for their inadequacies as much as they were a means for the group to try to make an intellectual advance. They were seeking to push away the inert blob of fear that represents the common attitude about cancer and replace it with the activism of the therapy sessions. Passivity was being singled out for defeat.

Included in each session are from 30 to 45 minutes of guided imagery therapy, with Kvarnes or Chalick as leaders. These are therapeutic techniques designed to evoke the patients' thoughts and feelings about their cancer. In guided imagery, the leader might direct the members (whose eyes are closed and bodies relaxed) to imagine that they are in a pastoral scene—garden, meadow, hillside—and that they meet a wizard (mentor). The "imaging" that follows—what the wizard says, how the individual reacts, what the individual finds as he moves through the scene—is meant to provide usable information to help shape the person's attitude toward his cancer.

On May 13, with every member present and the group in chairs arranged in a circle in front of the office couch, Kvarnes began by asking the patients to limber themselves into a relaxed position. Eyes closed, feet and legs spread forward and bodies sunk softly into chairs. Kvarnes spoke quietly and slowly, spacing his sentences:

"This is called 'The Thread.' And the thread is going to lead you to a sight where you either have some cancer activity or where you want to be sure you don't have any... You're going down some long, long stairs... A very long descent... When you reach the bottom—take your time to reach it—you find a thread line there... You pick up the thread and start to follow it through many corridors and rooms before you come to the room where you're going to do your work; that is, where there's some cancer presence or some monitoring that you want to do... Don't forget that you have a crystal, and the crystal not only can ward off something fearful but it can be pointed at something and shine some light on it so you can see it better. And if you need to, you can call on a guide, like a wizard, to help explain things to you... When you get to the place where there is cancer activity, then you plan some attack on the cancer. You figure out some way to do something about it, either using the crystal or imagining something that calls out to be done..."

Kvarnes stopped, and many minutes of silence passed. No one stirred. Eyes remained closed, bodies relaxed.

Then, in a low voice, Kvarnes asked the patients to open their eyes and come out of the imagery.

Baroni spoke. "First I thought I was going down the Dupont Circle Metro, that long stairway. There's one over at HUD, a steep one, too. Then I thought I was going down a coal mine. Eventually I got to this lab or clinic. I found the thread, a green thread, and I followed it. In the clinic, my oncologist was with me. He put the CAT scan X-ray on the wall, looking at it. He said, 'We're not sure if some [of the cells] look like they're dead. Some look as if they're dormant. We don't want to stir them up because they could become reactivated.' I thought about nuclear waste. What do you do with it? He said, 'If you stir up [the cells]; they might go somewhere else. Just try to contain them.' I said, 'What about flushing them out?' He said, 'No, just contain them. Some look like they're dead, some inactive. Just wait and see.'"

Baroni finished and Chalick told of his imaging. "I went down the stairs. I was in the basement of the house where I was raised. I kept going into another room that was darker and then finally crawled through some carbony black hole in the wall to a small cave-like room, I was looking around with the crystal. Something's got to be written on the wall. There were hieroglyphics that I couldn't understand. I went to a fourth wall and focused on [the words] 'stay where you are.' And I kept peeling away layers... There was something stuck in the wall, a little piece of marble or ivory, and I had to look under a microscope. There was the image of a tulip leaf on it. I didn't know what to make of that. A little worm came. And I said, 'That may be what's left of my cancer.' I burned it. I don't know how I lit a fire. I just burned it."

Kvarnes took his turn. "I went into a long curved tunnel. It was fairly dark in there, so I was using the crystal to guide myself. Suddenly I came across a great big hulking mass of poorly defined something or other. So I turned the crystal on it. I could see it was just a kind of an amorphous mass. I used the crystal to outline it very clearly. And the whole point of that was to aid the immune system and recognize it's cancer and that one spot on my rib still shows up on the last bone scan. I wasn't burning it with a crystal but was lighting it up so it could no longer be missed."

Gail Polsby confessed that she had trouble getting started. "I couldn't get into it. I got down there but it was all empty. Nothing was there—no cancer, not anything...Just an empty cavernous mass. I've got to get out of here... My mind just spun around and went nowhere. The problem is more what to do with the mutilation of the surgery rather than the cancer."

Kvarnes broke in. "Maybe that's what we should use as the equation for you in these things. Most of the guided imagery doesn't exactly fit you. You're pointing out what the problem is— somehow accepting yourself as you are now, with all the mutilation that's gone on. Maybe that's what you could be working on. The thread could lead you to something that makes things better."

The idea of using the sessions—the sharing of information, experiences and feelings, exercises in guided imagery—as a strengthening of the mind, which in turn could strengthen the body in its fight against cancer cells, was important to Kvarnes. But as the sessions progressed, it became clear that the importance was greater for him than for the others.

On May 20, a philosophical clash erupted between Kvarnes and Chalick. The two psychiatrists differed on how the immune system could be affected by information gathered by the brain. The discussion had moments of both clarity and cloudiness.

Kvarnes: "It's not enough to go from the idea that believing—or religious faith or faith-healing—makes an illness go away. There's a gap there. I've got to know how that happens."

Chalick: "There's still a gap anyway. There's no connection that anybody has between this thing that we call thinking and whatever this stuff [an illness of the body] is."

Kvarnes: "That's a very important part of it. [But] there is the left brain, right brain organization."

Chalick: "That's a thought."

Kvarnes: "No, it's not a thought. Goddam it, it's definite.

Chalick: "But that still doesn't reach how it goes about . . . You do have thoughts, and whether they may be left brain or right brain, but how they then affect some other part [of the body], no matter what you say about chemicals or electrical currents, there is still a gap."

Kvarnes: "The right brian is a pattern forming . . ."

Chalick: "Look, I know that stuff. You're going over old stuff . . ."

Kvarnes: "That's pattern recognition. I think what we're doing here is pattern *formation*. We talk to the right brain and the right brain makes a pattern that can somehow be conveyed to the endocrine and the neural system, and that it isn't just wild or that terrible gaps are there. We have all kinds of evidence of that in other areas. You take a basketball player. You go through the steps with him until he gets a sequence for a very tricky shot. At the point where his right brain has taken over and organized that activity, he no longer thinks about it. He goes through the motions step by step.

And that's organized by something. That pattern is created by the player, with the left brain coaching. And then it gets converted into a right-brain directed activity."

Chalick: "I think you're on dangerous ground when you just leave it in terms of left brain, right brain . . . All of that's a guess about how it's working."

Kvarnes: "Well, sure."

Kvarnes: "You have to have a hypothesis."

Chalick: "*You* have to. That's what I'm getting at. I think there's something Western and culture-bound about the idea that we have to do something about it, and that we have to understand what we're doing."

Kvarnes: "I'm not a Buddhist."

The exchange between the two psychiatrists—gentlemanly but pointed—reflected not only a philosophical disagreement but a tension of expectations. More than the four others, Kvarnes is watchful: first of the fluctuations in the cancer's progress, or lack of progress, in the most vulnerable members of the group—Baroni, Joyce and himself—and second of what beneficial role the therapy sessions might be having in those fluctuations.

Kvarnes obviously believes the exercises in guided imagery are beneficial. But as the sessions progressed, he began to wonder whether he was being unduly cautious about the positive news coming from his and Baroni's doctors. Both men had been improving and the improvements were unexpected. "Geno and I," Kvarnes said with warm feeling at the sixth session, "have had rather spectacular reports and I'm a little bit worried about how we handle them."

Kvarnes had learned from blood tests and bone scans that his cancer was no longer the threat to his life that he thought it was two years ago. "We're trying to adjust to this information, individually and as a group," he said. "I don't think any of us would want to stand up and say, 'This is an enormously successful program. Kvarnes has gotten rid of his bone metastasis and Geno has cured his mesothelioma.' But something's going on. And we're at such an early stage in this that I'm both excited and terribly cautious about it. There's no question in my mind that if the change in me is genuine—and there seems to be no question about that—the imagery process has had a big part in it. And the fact that I've taken an active role in my illness has been a big part. I'm no longer victim, no longer helpless. I don't have any uneasiness about calling the doctors with my questions..."

This bouyancy was a feeling shared by Baroni, though he is less concerned than Kvarnes about the provability aspect. He told of talking to his doctor about the latest good news. "I called him this week [late May] and said, 'Let's start all over.'... He told me that the other doctors [on the tumor board] he showed [the new results] to are pleased, delighted and, quote, surprised. Because there's no known cure [for mesothelioma], nothing works and it goes fast— six months, nine months. He said, 'We're delighted, happy and surprised.' That's the first time he's used these words. I asked him, 'What do I do now? Am I in remission?' 'No,' he said, 'there are still tumors there. But they're not going anywhere. They haven't gone to your kidneys. They haven't gone to your liver, they haven't gone to your lungs, they haven't run through your system like they're supposed to. So you're on hold.'"

Baroni is the only one in the group who speaks in religious metaphors about his cancer. The others have an appreciation of his spiritual life, and they listened raptly when he told of going before his old congregation at St. Paul and Augustine. It was during mass, and, instead of a sermon, he led "a healing service" based on guided imagery.

"I asked them to follow me or just listen," Baroni said, "I asked them to relax and close their eyes. Most were older people. There's a great tension between the will to live and the will to die. You've got to have both. You can't say 'to hell with it, I'm going to die,' or 'the hell with it, I'm going to live.' You have to work them both. A lot of these people said, '27 years ago, the doctor said I wasn't supposed to live, and here I am.' Here's a spunky little lady—blind, 94 years old— and she says, 'I'm ready to go any time. Every day I say, 'Lord I'm ready.' So she's dealing with both sides. And other anecdotes: 'The doctor's dead who took care of me...'

"I told the people that this was the first time in nine months that I've stood in a pulpit. What's interesting is that I came to this church in 1960. And I said you took me in. It's a black church. I was a stranger. You welcomed me. You healed me. Nine months ago I was in the hospital and didn't expect ever to get out. But nine months later, here I am. I believe in healing, I believe in believing. I want to share something with you. Close your eyes and relax. Concentrate on your head. Try to feel the blood. Let the blood come down through your hands. Let your hands get warm. Put your hands to your face. Then I took the garden. I went to the house. I went inside. That's the body. And inside the house was the master—the guide, the teacher—and the teacher had a light and said, 'You are the light. This aching body is still a light. We are created by Divine light and are becoming part of a Divine light. God is within us. And this little light of mine is struggling to survive. We don't have to go anywhere. We have to look into ourselves.'"

In the group, Baroni was the most expressive about the uplift he received every week, and never mind if his immune system was or wasn't being manipulated into a new toughness. For him, it was plenty merely to have this intimate gathering of friends who had looked cancer in the eye and not blinked.

At the sixth meeting, Gail Polsby, moved by Baroni's accounts of his improvement and his guided imagery sermon at mass the Sunday before, smiled and said to him, "You seem to be a little more full of your self today." Baroni agreed: "I've been annointed five times. But that's passive. They used to call it last rites. They've changed it to annointing of the sick... That's not enough. I need more. What I've learned here is to do these meditations—guided imagery meditations—and to do a combination of the physical and the spiritual. I add the spiritual part to the technique I've learned here. In religious terms, it's a new way of praying, a new way of meditating—of dealing with your health, your healing and your believing. It's something I never learned in the seminary. I've learned from all of you a legitimacy and credibility in terms of guided imagery and the mind and the emotions.

"And if stress and distress and my father's death and a lot of other things may have set me up for my cancer, then you can choose how you deal with yourself when you're sick: You can panic, be fearful, wary, distressed or you go on. You can say, 'I have to learn how to live,' and not let something die within you while you're supposed to be waiting for the end. So you fight against that. I've learned a lesson: The legitimization of the secular knowledge of guided imagery and the religious. My attitude is healthy and [perhaps] that's helped my body to be healthy. I don't say I know that yet. Later on I might know. They keep telling me that with mesothelmia there are no winners, no survivors."

The "they" was never long out of any therapy session. Oncologists, radiologists and surgeons were the experts whose soundings couldn't be muffled. If the attitude therapy sessions were exercises in self-help, they were not, therefore, rejections of the help that standard medicine might offer. The group knew that often enough nothing could be done with cancer patients.

A colleague who had come to the group before I joined—he had been to four sessions—died of lung cancer in early May. His death was discussed. The Thursday newspaper carried his obituary, which Baroni read aloud to the group. Reactions to the death varied. Kvarnes felt frustrated because he wished the man had had more time with the group. Baroni confessed that he often had looked at his dying friend—losing weight, slowing visibly—and saw himself as he might be as his end approached: "Is that how I will look?"

But the death did not alter the agreement that held the group together: that managing one's own cancer ought not to be handed over to the experts when a vast amount of expertise—in one's own mind, emotions and spirit—was available. It mattered to some more than others exactly how that interior expertise was acting on the body. But attitudinal changes were separate from medical changes. No one in the group remotely believes that he has moved closer to the magical "cure of cancer." But they are saying, tentatively, that they are moving closer to discovering a cure for the *fear* of cancer.

# The Homeless Belt of Washington   1982

They are homeless street women, but on this afternoon in early autumn, Sara Malone, 67, and Helen Pick, 58, are receiving rare comforts for their tired, exiled bodies and beaten spirits. They are in the hospital. Someone cares about them.

In room 4E21 of Howard University Hospital, Malone sits in a chair at the foot of her bed and looks up expressionlessly when two visitors appear. She is thin-waisted, nearly toothless, has a pale weathered face and speaks in halting, monotone sentences.

Malone recognizes one of the visitors: Connie Ridge, a generous-hearted volunteer social worker who has served several years at one or another of the city's shelters for homeless women. As an update on her progress, Malone lifts her partly bandaged left arm. On it, as well as the right arm, are scabs and scars—from human bites.

At 10 p.m. Sept. 3, Malone, about 100 feet from the entrance of Mt. Carmel House, a 40-bed overnight shelter for women at 471 G Place NW, was attacked by a vagrant man who pummeled her face into bloodiness. He sunk his teeth into her arms. Malone managed to get away and stagger back to Mt. Carmel House. Sr. Maureen Fultz, the Carmelite sister of charity who opened the door, saw only the blood and wounds and did not at first recognize Malone, a regular at the home. Sr. Maureen cleaned the wounds and took Malone to the Howard University Hospital emergency room where she was treated and released.

Several days later, after Malone believed she had recovered, she returned to the streets. Her left arm became infected. It ballooned grotesquely. Sr. Maureen took her back to the hospital where she was to remain through the early part of October.

Across town at George Washington University hospital, Helen Pick, in a wheelchair with two pillows, was resting in a corridor at a 5th floor nursing station. Her face was lightly rouged and her greying hair well-coifed. She was amiable and enjoyed talking with her visitors.

Pick was in a wheel chair because both her legs were amputated in early June, the left one at the upper thigh and the right one above the knee. She doesn't recall the details of what happened, nor does anyone close to her. It is believed that after cashing her Social Security disability check in the first week of June, Pick fell asleep in an abandoned building. A beam loosened from the ceiling and dropped across her legs. Or robbers may have heaved the beam over her after stealing her money. Somehow, she did not come to and call out for help until the blood circulation in her legs had been cut off. Gangrene had set in. When brought to the hospital, no choice was left but to amputate.

Pick, who said her husband had worked for Pepco for more than 30 years and where she worked for 15, began sleeping in such shelters as the House of Ruth and Sarah's House in 1977 shortly after she was widowed. She was ill and could not keep her apartment going. No options remained but the streets by day and the shelters by night.

Last winter, Pick often spent mornings and afternoons at the Mt. Vernon Place Methodist Church day shelter at Massachusetts Avenue NW, now closed. As a teenager in a middle-class Washington family in 1940, she sang in the choir at the church.

These two women might appear to be worst-case examples of homelessness. But after two weeks of interviewing unhoused women, visiting the staffs at five of the core-city shelters and attending two emergency meetings of the D.C. Coalition for the Homeless, I learned that worst-case stories are the rule more than the exception. No woman who falls to this life of raw deprivation has had a soft descent. If the crash to the bottom was less harsh for some, it is because the support system that kept the person within the bounds of security—a job, a family, government programs, a place to get medical help—was pulled away slowly, not abruptly.

"I don't want to talk to you," said Ada Moore, at first, in a grainy voice, throwing a hard look in case I missed her mood. I had said I was from a newspaper. "Every year," she continued, "it's the same thing. They go around and take pictures of us."

Moore, 68, on the streets and in the shelters of 20 years after coming to Washington from New York, rested on a plaza bench near the shopping mall kiosks at 10th and G Streets NW. It is not hard to see why cameramen find her photogenic. Her poverty is classic: a hunched back, shriveled face, irregular teeth, eyes abjectly vacant and a presence, as Henry James described a female character, "without bloom."

Moore was one of a dozen women on the benches waiting in the early evening for the dining hall in the basement of the First Congregational Church at 10th and G to open at 6:30. Between 50 and 60 women are fed a full meal there daily.

The conversation was brief but it revealed the art of her survival. "Mt. Carmel's is all filled up. Maybe I'll get in someplace else: The Lutheran church at 14th Street. They were filled up,too, last winter. There aren't enough shelters. A lot of women are on the streets. The year before I was at Carmel, with the sisters. Another year, a lady took us in. I've been robbed 10 or 12 times. I don't carry money anymore." She expressed no doubts that she could take another winter.

On both hands, Moore wore rings. "This ring? Oh, I found it. I was looking for some paper one day and it fell out with the paper." Moore laughed. "So I got it. This other ring, my girl friend gave it to me. She went back to Sweden." Moore nodded to the bundle next to her. "It's just a few clothes, that's all. A change, so I can keep clean."

A companion came over to Moore and said it was time to go in to eat. Dinner in the basement was fresh zucchini with melted American cheese, lettuce and tomato salad, toasted rye bread, an apple and tea. Seven tables, with room for eight women at each, were spread near the buffet line. From the dress of the women, it would have been impossible to guess the weather outside. A few wore heavy woolen pullover hats and thick overcoats buttoned to the knees. Another wore a sportshirt and jogging shorts.

During dinner, the conversations, like the clothing, ranged from hot to severely cold. One woman in her mid-40s, high-strung and bugle-voiced, ranted for 25 minutes. She addressed no one in particular and no one in particular, for sure, listened. Many ate in stone silence.

Next to Ada Moore was a rotund woman who said she had been to St. Elizabeth's that afternoon "to deliver a paper." She had copies of the text and passed them around. It was three single-space well-typed pages titled "These Are Some of My Thoughts and Experiences Which Took Place Two Years Ago." It began: "I was very angry that my sisters and brothers committed me to St. Elizabeth's ... I was diagnosed as schizophrenic for 15 years and after 25 hospitalizations. However, after I came to St. Elizabeth's for the third time, they diagnosed me as a manic depressive."

The paper ended: "It has been over a year since I have been in a hospital and I don't plan to go back anytime soon ... I feel like I am sane in an insane society...."

No one at the table read the paper. A woman told everyone that Jesus Christ would be returning in three months. That was also ignored.

A small flame of interest was sparked by the story of a pretty young black-haired woman, barely out of her girlhood, who said she was a Harvard-trained "efficiency consultant." She told the women she was from "Trans-Jordan, which is overseas." One dinner companion asked about her visa and her Social Security status. The answers were unfocused: "You've got to have verified diplomatic status if you're doing any kind of consulting within the federal government. You know, you've got to have that."

A woman in a woolen hat and thick overcoat, Ruth Schreiber, ate alone and took tiny bites of her zucchini. Pleasant spoken, with wisps of gray hair falling from her hat into blue clear eyes, Schreiber said she sleeps outdoors on the back stairs of the Labor Department building. "My doctor told me to sleep outdoors for four years. I did that. And I'm all well. I used to have chest problems."

Schreiber likes the Labor Department stairs, but she is suspicious of the police. "I was robbed so many times that the police didn't even write up the reports anymore. Some of the worst thieves I've ever encountered were the city police. The last two chiefs have taken my raincoats. When it rains I just walk in the water."

The meal went as pleasantly as the six volunteer staff workers could make it. On one level, the scene was a large damp bag of misery. On another, some of the women in the dining hall had come together to form an outpatient mental health clinic. Except there were no doctors, nurses or professional help.

At Sarah House, a 15-bed overnight shelter at 1329 N St. NW, Kathy St. Clair, the director, spoke of herself and her small staff of volunteers: "The longer I work here, the more I'm struck at how lucky any of us are not to be on the street. It doesn't take much to get there—just a little twist of fate, really. We shouldn't be quick to look at a homeless person and think to ourselves, 'That will never be me.'"

Estimates on the population of homeless women in Washington range from a few hundred to a possible few thousand. Among the urban exiles, the streets are meaner for homeless females than the males. Women are more vulnerable to personal attacks. The beating of Sara Malone was one of several known assaults, including three rapes, in early September.

The women have such a fear of male drifters or winos suddenly going berserk and venting their fury on them that they tend to avoid the city's soup kitchens for meals. Mostly men are served at places like the Zacchaeus Community Kitchen. Unlike the men, the women are loners, not pack members. Women prefer not to join "barrel gangs," the clusters of people who huddle around barrel fires in open lots to heat themselves during the winter.

The male homeless are depicted as bums and derelicts, a stereotype that is as false as the one imposed on the female homeless: bag ladies. Few women who sleep in shelters at night and pass the day wandering the streets are either especially ladylike or carriers of bags. Most are destitute, lonely women who are often mentally or physically ill and have either given up hope of recovery or have decided to settle for the scraps of human warmth at from the all-encompassing kindness of people like Sr. Maureen.

Only a few are so defeated as to have gone permanently beyond concern about keeping up some form of human contact. The bundles that some women haul around with them often represent the last ties to a happier past, when the material possessions inside were worn in good health or were gifts of love from a family member. Or perhaps the bundle is an accumulation of "finds" picked out of rubbish cans or discovered on park benches. In the madhouse of the streets, the bundle is a thin link to sanity.

The closest neighbor to the president of the United States is a homeless woman named Mary. She sleeps on the sidewalk next to the police guard stations at the Pennsylvania Avenue entrance fronting the White House.

She is small and stooped-over, and wears a gray all-weather poncho with a hood that flops over her face. Next to her, like a faithful pet, is a pullcart of belongings. Mary, who appears to be in her early 60s, speaks in a flattened-out voice about such great issues of the day as national security, the communist threat and her neighbor, Ronald Reagan, who she says is not really the president. Jimmy Carter was never president either.

The executive police have developed a protective attitude toward Mary over the years. They estimate she has lived on the White House sidewalk for better than a decade. The cops talk with her and share food and coffee. During sub-freezing nights with heavy snowfalls, the woman's tiny body is all but immobilized by drifts that pile up between Pennsylvania Avenue and the White House fence.

The security guards' kindness toward this modern Lazarus at Caesar's gate is as close as we come to a federal policy for homelessness.

The city has a Homeless Belt. It stretches from near-Northeast's House of Ruth (65 beds and under contract from the city) to the edge of Georgetown where "bridge people"—considered more resilient than barrel people and friendlier than grate people—live under the Whitehurst Freeway.

In between are the stationhouses of survival. Some are serene, inviting places. Hannah House at 612 M St. NW is a sparklingly clean three-story house run by a Sister of Mercy and a laywoman who recently left her religious order after 40 years.

It is a "house of gifts," one of the women explains. A motel gave 20 bedspreads, a kitchen-supply company donated a sink and metal cutting tables, some Jesuits in Georgetown passed on their richly designed wool broadloom carpet. The priests, the sisters said, were redecorating.

A block south, at 612 L St., NW, is the Zacchaeus kitchen. As many as 400 men, and a handful of women, appear every morning for a bowl of vegetable soup and whatever breads, crackers or fruit may have been gathered from the Foodbank or donated by friends. Judges send convicted criminals to work at Zacchaeus as alternative sentences. A religion teacher at Carroll High School brings his students to expose them firsthand to lessons not found in the textbooks.

In the past five years, according to a report from the Community for Creative Nonviolence, 29 citizens have died from exposure in the city. This winter, with everyone involved saying that the homeless population is burgeoning, the death toll again is expected to be high. The population grows because, in addition to the waves of deinstitutionalized former mental patients, the lack of low-cost housing is pushing people to the margins. Some 9,000 families are on the waiting list.

Beginning in mid-September, women have been sleeping on the sidewalk outside Mt. Carmel House. First one woman, then two, soon five. They knocked at the door of the four-story building, which was once an orphanage owned by St. Mary's Catholic Church next door, but were told by one of the four sisters inside that every bed and every available inch was taken.

Mt. Carmel House, a clean, well-run and brightly decorated home that is known as the Hilton of the city's half-dozen women's shelters, has filled to capacity since its opening two years ago under auspices of Archbishop James Hickey.

The youngest woman spending the nights is 19, the oldest in her late 70s. The persistent reality is the phone. Everyday calls come with dead-end pleas from the city Department of Human Services, the Department of Protective Services, St. Elizabeth's, the courts, the police, hospitals, churches and families. Every call has one statement and one question: "We have a woman with no place to go. Can you take her?"

"In the last three or four months," said Sr. Maureen, who is in her late 20s and who had risen at 5 a.m. to keep watch over the women, "the demographics have been changing. Younger women are coming. Many had kids, were living on AFDC and were probably marginally employed. They gave their kids up to Protective Services and then took to the streets and came to the shelters. That's a drastic difference I've seen in just the past few months. Once they give their kids up . . . . They give up hope. This is a new population."

One of Sr. Maureen's closest friends is a staff member at Mt. Carmel's, Diane Dougherty, a lay social worker paid by the archdiocese. She has a fairly large reservoir of grit mixed with hope, but it is rubbed raw by the friction of dealing with officials of government programs. "These are the programs that are supposedly in business to prevent women from being put out on the streets. That's the frustration we meet everywhere we go, whether we're talking about the public-welfare system, the mental-health system or the health-care system."

Both Sr. Maureen and Dougherty confess to feeling "guilty" because the women they care for, though at the bottom, are not rock-bottom. "There are some out there," said Dougherty, "who might be called sub-hopeless. They won't ever come to a shelter or if they do come they are violent and we have to ask them to leave. We're not really getting the worst of the worst."

A few days after Sara Malone was beaten and bitten, another woman came to the door with a wide gash on the back of her head. A man had tried to undress her on the street. She resisted, but, before fleeing, the man pounded her head on the curb.

"Our initial response to the men who do violence to the women here," Sr. Maureen said, "is anger. It should be, because the men should be responsible. But it's the infighting of the lowest classes of society. It's almost beneficial to the system to keep that kind of anger and hostility down at the bottom all the time: victims attacking other victims. Calling the police—and we don't feel comfortable doing that—does nothing to relieve the problem. It never will. It takes care of the temporary situation, but the reason there is so much violence against the women on the street is because the men are feeling the same type of oppression the women are. And even some of our women get violent with each other. It's almost a normal response to the type of pressure they have in their lives. Until the overall structure that's causing the oppression on the one on the bottom changes, the violence isn't going to stop."

One morning, after leaving an overnight shelter where I had been talking with the director about an 85-year-old woman who had appeared a few days earlier, my stomach knotted. On the sidewalk, in a cluster of the homeless, was a woman with a familiar face. She had been a coworker at The Post for a time. I went over to her. After an awkward few moments—I didn't remember her name, she didn't remember what floor I worked on—her story came out. She left work about a year ago. "Pressure," she said. She talked of several things she had been learning lately about life, including the fact that the shelter I had just come out of was one of the best in the city. She had stayed there for a time and knew.

Back at the office, I asked about the woman. She had worked in the newsroom. Someone said that she began talking aimlessly to herself. It became disruptive. Another said she had trouble concentrating and had become unpredictable. It wasn't a case of going off the deep end, everyone agreed, only the shallow end. But it was enough to sink her.

# The Bullying of Joann Newak                           1982

In a U.S. Air Force court of appeals in Washington on Oct. 15, a bizarre and nearly unbelievable story of heavy-handed military justice unfolded.

At the center of the case is Joann Newak, who joined the Air Force in August 1979. She was a recent graduate of Marywood College, a small Catholic liberal arts school in Scranton, Pa. For the past four months, Lt. Newak, now 25, has been imprisoned on a six-year sentence at hard labor in a military jail at Ft. Leavenworth, Kansas.

Newak finds herself locked away, and with her life possibly in ruins, for being found guilty by an Air Force court of first offenses that were not only nonviolent but would probably not be prosecuted in civilian courts.

During off-duty hours at Hancock Field near Syracuse, N.Y., where she was stationed and where she assumed that her private life in her off-base apartment was not subject to the military code, Newak occasionally smoked marijuanna, had an affair with a woman and believed some pills in her possession were amphetamines when, by the Air Force's own tests, they were actually diet pills.

In civilian America, recreational pot users are rarely if ever imprisoned. People aren't jailed for their sexual orientation. And someone who mistakes diet pills for speed has yet to be seen as a dangerous criminal.

But under the military code, these are major crimes. What is hapening now to Newak was described by Robert Sherrill in his 1969 book, "Military Justice Is To Justice What Military Music Is To Music": "It is one of the ironies of patriotism that a [person] who is called to the military service of his country may anticipate not only the possibility of giving his life but also the certainty of giving up his liberties ... The Bill of Rights has had little or no relevance to the code of justice governing the military."

Over the phone last week from her prison, Newak, an intelligent woman who is able to retain a sense of hope despite her ordeal, told of having liked the Air Force. She was proud of her excellent performance record that was leading, at the time of her court-martial in March, to a sure promotion to first lieutenant.

Newak is from a small town in Pennsylvania, the daughter of a registered nurse and sister of a schoolteacher. Her father is deceased. At Marywood, she earned a degree in health and physical education.

Newak recalled that even during her trial—when Air Force prosecutors flew in low to strafe her case with the full firepower of the letter of the law—she did not believe she would be sentenced to prison for these minor first offenses. At worst, she expected a reprimand. Possibly, if the book were to be thrown and knowing that her interpretation of the military code about one's personal life differed from the Air Force's, she might be dismissed from the Air Force.

During the appeal of this case, evidence presented by Newak's civilian lawyer, Faith Seidenberg of Syracuse, suggested that Newak was badly served by the Air Force attorney first assigned to defend her. He had a conflict of interest, because he was also defending an airwoman he had persuaded to testify, under immunity, against Newak. He admitted to telling the airwoman that Newak "was going down the tubes." That was an out-of-place comment for a defense lawyer to make about his client.

This lawyer was removed from the case once the conflict of interest and his biases became apparent. But Seidenberg argued persuasively that by then, in the tight Air Force circles in which Newak was being accused, tried, judged and sentenced, the damage had been done. It was a fair assessment because, in fact, Newak did eventually go down the Air Force tubes.

The height of military wackiness in this case is that Newak was found guilty of having amphetamines because she "believed," as the Air Force charged, they were amphetamines. Thought control may be a major juridical priority of the military, but in civilian courts it is a legal impossibility to think you are commiting a crime when nothing in your possession or actions actually is criminal.

Newak's appeal is expected to be decided in three weeks by three Air Force judges. Of Seidenberg's argument that her client has been unfairly treated and excessively punished, the chief Air Force lawyer in the case attempted to put it down as mere "interesting social commentary [that] is not persuasive here. [Newak] was not tried in a New York court; she was tried in a military court. And in a military court, appellant's offenses are criminal acts."

That states it with chilling preciseness. Newak, who in the Air Force was neither a hardened drug abuser nor anywhere near being a troublemaker, thought she could serve her country and still keep her personal life to herself. She now knows she had a delusion.

*This column, and the two following, were credited by Joann Newak with helping her get out of prison much earlier than otherwise. She was released in August 1983, 14 months into a six year term. A source in the Pentagon told me that the Air Force released Newak because the besmirching it had earned was no longer worth it.*

Two months ago, I wrote about the imprisonment by the Air Force of 2nd Lt. Joann Newak. The young woman—25, intelligent, a graduate of Marywood College in Scranton, Pa.—was given six years at hard labor in Fort Leavenworth, Kan. She began her sentence in June.

Newak had been found guilty by an Air Force judge of marijuana, sodomy, amphetamine and conduct-unbecoming-an-officer charges. A few days ago, three Air Force appellate judges upheld the decision.

Something is ludicrously odd about this case, and I recall first sensing it during the appeals hearings in October. Newak was having her day in court by having another day in prison. Instead of being free while her case was under appeal, which is routine in civilian courts for offenses of far greater severity than Newak's, the lieutenant was locked away in Leavenworth. Should a reversal eventually come through, the Air Force presumably will give Newak a cheery "sorry about that."

The oddity expanded to bizarreness when the disparity between the harshness of the sentence and the mildness of the so-called crimes was examined. I say so-called not to be arch, but because New York—the state in which Newak was stationed—does not prosecute, much less imprison, its citizens for minor marijuana involvement or for their sexual preferences.

Newak was a recreational user of pot who occasionally shared the substance among friends at her off-base apartment at Hancock Field, near Syracuse, during off-hours. Her crime of "sodomy" demands another so-called. Newak was involved in a personal relationship with an Air Force woman. Lesbianism is not a crime under the military code, so the Air Force, with a stab at unisex justice, nabbed her for sodomy.

The amphetamines, equally alarming to the Air Force, were discovered to be diet pills when tested in a lab. Newak's offense was to think the pills on her dresser were illegal.

As the Air Force carried Newak off into the wild blue yonder of military justice, it appeared at first that this was another example of martial excess. What cost overruns in Air Force bombers are to national defense, sentences to six years at hard labor for nonviolent first offenses are to sensible justice. In the past four years, an Air Force dragnet has been spread wide to catch more people.

On the last day of 1978, there were 176 Air Force people in prison. By June 1982, with only a perceptible increase in the ranks, the prisoner roll reached 692.

An Air Force spokesman explained this surging increase of nearly 400 percent as "a change in administration and stricter approaches to discipline." He didn't mention that with more young people seeing the unemployment lines and turning in last resort to the armed services for jobs, the new harshness is a way of announcing to recruits that the military is toughening its standards.

Jailing decent and up-front young women like Joann Newak is a dubious way of toughening anything. The standard it leads to is a double standard, one that lays bare the extreme that the separation of military and civilian justice systems can lead to.

The argument of many in the military—at least those who think Newak got what was coming—is that the Uniform Code of Military Justice applies to everyone in the armed services—24 hours a day in all places—and that the Supreme Court recognizes the need for this separate legal system. In theory, fine. But where is the line between a separate law and law-unto-itself? Are constitutional rights meaningless upon putting on the uniform? If anything, with the military priding itself on being the first line of defense in defending the constitution, those rights ought to be more honored, not less. Instead, the extremes are being honored.

Those extremes didn't bother the three Air Force appellate judges who ruled that Newak's sledgehammer sentence was appropriate. In one opinion, Lt. Col. Edward Miller concludes by suggesting that not only are the civilian and military judicial standards justifiably different but also that the military's is, by far, superior: "Had the accused (Newak) been tried on these identical charges in a civilian court, which would probably have been unfamiliar with the laws and traditions developed by the military during its long history, it is likely the court would not have had full capacity to recognize the complete impact of damage to the national security resulting from such conduct on the part of a commissioned officer."

So that's it. A few puffs of pot in your living room, some no-no friendship with another woman, and before you can say Air Force Dense Pack, "national security" is dealt a first-strike hit.

Faith Seidenberg, the Syracuse lawyer who is defending Newak for no fee, is bringing the case to a higher military appeals court that has three civilian judges. The National Lawyers Guild, and other groups, have joined the appeal. A new test case, involving basic constitutional questions, is developing.

Meanwhile, when Joann Newak writes to me, and when I answer, the letters both ways are opened, read and stamped by her jailers. In the mind of the military, some correspondence between citizens is also a threat to national security.

When she was locked away in a military prison in June 1982, Joann Newak had no illusions about either military justice or military vindictiveness. Both were harsh. The 25-year-old Air Force lieutenant—once praised in evaluation reports for her integrity, ethics and morals—had been sentenced to six years at hard labor for offenses that would not have been prosecuted in a civilian court.

Off duty and off base, she used pot recreationally, had a brief relationship with a woman and believed that some diet pills in her possession were illegal amphetamines.

When I reported the case in columns last October and January, Newak wrote letters to me from the Fort Leavenworth, Kan., military prison, saying she believed the worst was behind her. She understood the trap she happened to be caught in.

The military, swamped with applications, had entered a new era of choosiness. By making an example of her, it was sending the message to gays, and others whose private behavior was suspect, to keep away. To those already in, a warning—love the wrong sex or smoke a joint, and you'll be jailed.

At worst, Newak's punishment should have been a dishonorable discharge. A minor reprimand would have been suitable. She wanted to serve her country.

A few days ago, the Air Force showed that it was determined to keep on flying high in the bullying of this young woman. It denied her parole. The Air Force Clemency and Parole Board required, as one condition for release, that Newak attend a community-based drug rehabilitation program. The board said the rehabilitation was "essential" for her "return to civilian life."

Newak declined. I'm not a drug addict, she said, I don't need to be treated as one. Had she less integrity and a fuzzier sense of justice, Newak would have gone along with her jailer's game. This was a moment to agree to anything that could get her out of prison. She said no.

Just as she had refused to accept an Air Force's Court of Military Review opinion against her—that her sentence was justified on national security grounds—she now rejected the lie that she was an addict in need of treatment. A drugless year in prison was ample proof that Newak was not an addict, which, as a mere occasional marijuana user, she never was in the first place.

Newak's determination to protect her integrity is no surprise. She is currently in federal court in Kansas to protect the privacy of her correspondence with her lawyer and the media. When Newak writes to me, the letters are stamped "reviewed." My replies are opened and read.

Sometimes my letters, apparently seen as dangerous to the stability of Fort Leavenworth prison, are returned. One rejection was made when I sent a running magazine to Newak. The censors didn't think this notorious drug addict should be reading about the latest on LSD (long slow distance). The magazine came back.

In federal court in Topeka last February, the Fort Leavenworth commandant defended this snooping by referring to a letter I had written last year. To the military, it must seem that I was conspiring with Newak to foment prison unrest. She told me that among other deprivations at Fort Leavenworth there were inadequate exercise facilities for the women inmates. I wrote back: "Start a little protest group there to get the women access to the running track, or at least some open spaces where you can put in a few miles each day. I have some friends who started a running program for prisoners and it does wonders for everybody."

The argument of the military is that Newak's mail must be opened and, if necessary, blocked because she is both a national security threat and a danger to the institutional security of the prison. All this borders on the comical, except that a young woman's life is being devastated by the Air Force's cruelty.

The military can't even get its story straight. An Air Force official recently wrote to Newak's congressman, Rep. Joseph McDade (R-Pa.), that the opening of her mail had "no relation to the possibility of compromise of national security."

It's only raw harassment, which is the spike the Air Force first drove into Newak and now, through denial of parole and continued mail snooping, is driving deeper. Civilian lawyers involved with military courts say the treatment given Joann Newak is not unusual.

One concession has been made. Because of the national attention given to this case—from "CBS Evening News" to The Village Voice— Newak's sentence has been reduced from six years to three years. That is only partial justice. Until Newak is freed, and her record cleared, the Air Force's disgrace will continue.

# Hunger in the Neighborhood                    *1983*

Ronald Reagan, nervous in the stomach that he is perceived as stone-hearted to the poor, suddenly wants to know about hunger. Media stories about soup kitchens and cheese lines look real on television, a Reagan aide said, but you never know. A presidential Task Force on Food Assistance has been formed, sent forth by Reagan with the customary words of true leadership that he wanted to "solve the problem of hunger in America once and for all."

If learning about hunger is Reagan's goal, he could have skipped the commission gambit and taken instead a quicker, cheaper and more mind-shattering approach: a tour of his neighborhood in central Washington.

Within walking distance of the White House are four soup kitchens, each serving serveral hundred of the poor in their daily search for food. Less than two miles away are several emergency food centers that dispense free groceries to families. And everywhere are the dumpsters behind restaurants and supermarkets in which rotting but still edible morsels—the snack foods of the poor—are found.

The soup kitchen I know best is a few blocks north of the White House, at 14th and Church Streets in the city's prostitution and drug corridor. The Zacchaeus Community Kitchen was opened in 1972 by Edward Guinan, then and now one of the country's unstopable friends of the poor. The day the kitchen opened, Mother Teresa, then an unknown nun from Calcutta, happened to be in Washington. Guinan asked her to join him at Zacchaeus. She ladled the first bowl of soup.

I have been volunteering there one morning a week for several years. I don't do much—soap some bowls in the sink, ladle soup, wipe tables. Subconsciously I am probably there for selfish reasons that have more to do with the practice of my profession than my religion: to see close up the effects of an economic system that for many is inhumane. For these citizens, the Reagan policies are only the latest brutality.

Odd turns and surprises keep occurring at this particular kitchen. The other morning, a new group of the hungry appeared: Salvadoran refugees. The three men were working as farmers a year ago in rural El Salvador. They were forced to flee. Now they are part of the kitchen's expanding clientele. It wasn't so long ago that this haven was visited by only street alcoholics with grizzled faces. Now it is common to see well-shaven young men who, out of work for a few months but still resisting the fall to the bottom, commute between the unemployment line and the soup line. Of late, women have been appearing in larger numbers also, as have children.

The hard work of running this operation is less in cooking and serving food than in gathering it from the markets and warehouses. Food companies and farmers, with a better sense of the poor's misery than the Reagan administration, are generous in donating their surpluses. The problem is in the costs of distribution.

Last month, word came to the group that runs the kitchen that some farmers in North Carolina had an extra 40,000 pounds of sweet potatoes. They would be plowed under if no one came for them.

Money to rent a truck was raised by a coalition of church groups. When the vehicle returned from the North Carolina farms, it was parked in a poor neighborhood. Local families were invited to help themselves. Fifteen hundred people came. In less than three hours, the potatoes were gone.

Several blocks to the east of his residence, Reagan would come upon a soup kitchen at 6th and G Streets NW. It operates from 5 p.m. to 6:15 p.m. When I went by the other afternoon, a line had already formed at 4 o'clock. I recognized a few faces from the 14th Street soup kitchen. The men have soup for breakfast at one and soup for dinner at the other.

In the alley that is the entrance to the dining room, the heat was in the 90s. What hung heavy in the air was the recently announced news that the building temporarily housing the kitchen at $300-a-month rent would soon be demolished. Several blocks were being cleared for high-rise apartments and businesses. Once again, the poor were in the way of progress.

One block over is a shelter for homeless women. Food is also provided. One of the Catholic sisters who run the 42-bed facility says that volunteers are needed for more than merely serving the meals. People are needed to talk with the women. A kind word, or a warm conversation, is often the last solace anyone thinks of giving to the hungry, though it is food for the soul.

On large letters on a cloth wall-banner in the dining room, the courageous sisters proclaim the ideal they try to live by: "Be of love a little more careful than of everything."

If Ronald Reagan is too busy to visit the hungry who surround him, he should send his commission to the kitchens and shelters of his neighborhood. The hungry, who suffer "the problem" that Reagan says he is out to solve "once and for all," have time to talk. It's the shortage of listeners that is their deepest destitution.

# Chapter 4

# Kindly Mentors

In time of war, as in time of peace, admiration is lavished upon physical bravery, and the prevailing hero is one who has risked his life for a presumably holy cause. Such men, I confess, leave me cold, for it must be obvious that their merit, such as it is, is very far from uncommon, and I have a considerable doubt that it is really admirable. I can see nothing superior in a man willing to trade his life for public applause, and I can see no more superiority in him when he is a soldier than when he is a prizefighter, a lion tamer, or a parachute-jumper at a county fair... The kinds of courage I really admire are not whooped up in war, but cried down, and indeed become infamous. No one, in such times of irrational and animal-like emotion, ever praises the man who stands out against the official balderdash, and seeks to restore the national thinking, so called, to a reasonable sanity. On the contrary, he is regarded as a shabby and evil fellow, and there is not much protest when he is punished in a summary and barbaric manner, without any consideration whatever of the evidence against him. It is sufficient that he refuses to sing the hymn currently laid out.

—*H. L. Mencken*
*Minority Report*

# Sargent Shriver                                        *1976*

When he declared his candidacy dead, and wafted to the after-life of
Washington, where losers can, without fear, be put on hold by
nobodies and ignored by waiters, Sargent Shriver was characteris-
tically buoyant. At the wake for his presidential campaign, he called
it a "remarkable success." That was vintage Shriver: ever the mole,
boring his way through piles of defeat and fatigue, and coming up to
sun himself on whatever ray was left. It is one of the traits by which
Shriver has endeared himself to so many of us who once worked for
him. It is also the kind of behavior that has caused him to be
dismissed as a lightweight by many reporters.

There were, at the outset, a few exceptions. Theo Lippman, Jr. of
the *Baltimore Sun* saw something more in Shriver. Michael Novak,
who has worked in both of Shriver's campaigns, praised him.

As one who cared about the Shriver candidacy—because I had
cared about Shriver himself since about ten years ago when he
invited me to Washington to work for him at the Office of Economic
Opportunity—I was elated by these signs of regard as Shriver's
1976 campaign got underway. Someone else had perceived something that I had seen over the years and had been telling friends
about all along. "Wait until he's President," I had said more than
once to those who, unable to benefit large doubts, saw Shriver as
little more than a well-plumed careerist looking to nest in any roost
of Washington power.

The waiting goes on. Shriver fell after the Illinois primary in
March, after he had stumbled into and staggered out of Iowa, New
Hampshire, and Massachusetts. To reflect on the failure of Shriver
is, first, to examine how elective campaigning can be a death rite to
an inexperienced candidate who makes an early mistake or two in
tactics and, second, to suggest that the Democrats are not so talent-
rich a party that someone like Shriver can now be dismissed as
obsolescent. He has lost out but that is no proof at all that he is worn
out.

A candidate's basic strategy in political campaigning is to make it
hard for the baying press to discover his weakness. The pack gets its
thrills by sniffing for scents of naivete (Romney's "I was brain-
washed"), or simplism (McGovern's $1,000 to every American), or
stupidity (Reagan's $90-billion scheme). Romney, McGovern, and
Reagan had all survived earlier hunts, so when running presidential

campaigns they were nimble enough to force the press to work a little to sink in their teeth.

With Shriver—a 60-year-old innocent who had never run for office on his own—it was as though he couldn't wait to expose his vulnerability. His announcement speech at the Mayflower Hotel on September 20 was hardly into its first syllables when he was claiming the legacy of John F. Kennedy. The packed and high-mood celebrators in the ballroom cheered and stomped at their Sarge's taking up the fallen banner of JFK, but for the detached observers the message was different: Shriver felt insecure about running on his own record and ideas, so he was hooking jumper cables to John Kennedy to be energized by a winner.

Candidates traditionally ride coattails, but this was too much to ignore for even those in the press who had affection for Shriver: a candidate using the coattails of a man dead 13 years. For those who felt no affection, the urge to move in and chew up Shriver was irresistible. The opportunity came the next day on "Meet the Press." The interviewers forced Shriver into an immediate defensiveness about the Kennedy legacy: forcing the new candidate to explain that Ted Kennedy "is the logical claimant, but he decided, you know, not to be a candidate"; to say that "my success in business did not start when I married the boss's daughter"; to dodge a question about why he stressed the Kennedy legacy but not the McGovern legacy, although he had run with McGovern in 1972. Each of the four questioners—Bill Monroe, Jack Germond, Martin Nolan, and Robert Novak—pawed Shriver with legacy questions.

The program was dispiriting because Shriver not only had a weakness revealed so soon but he had openly cooperated in exposing it. And this was before Ms. Judith Exner stepped forward with tales that gave new meaning to *Johnny, We Hardly Knew Ye.* But the real irony of Shriver's making himself dependent on John Kennedy was that, of all the Democratic candidates—the announced ones then and those running now—only he had a record of service and innovation that was unique and substantial on its own. Shriver was the only candidate who could go back and say that something he began 15 years ago—the Peace Corps—is still alive today and retains much of the philosophical purity that he originally gave it. He was the only candidate who could point to ten-year-old programs and ideas—Head Start, Job Corps, Legal Services,

Upward Bound, among others—and claim that they were still productive and working today. Nixon tried to kill many of them, but failed.

By stressing this kind of association, Shriver could have forced the debate about him to revolve on his skills as a social innovator. In Washington, it is acceptable to dismiss such programs as Head Start and Job Corps, but in trips I have made around the country in the past few years, whether to the migrant worker camps in southern Florida or the coal towns in east Tennessee, I have come upon people still being served by the administrative structures that Shriver set up a decade ago in OEO programs. If there was a legacy crying out to be claimed, it was Shriver's own: one to take immense political pride in and one that separated him in obvious ways from the Jacksons, Carters, and Udalls. None of them could point to something initiated 15 or 10 years ago and say, honestly, that it was functioning today.

The best-selling position in politics today—anti-bureaucratic, pro-lean government—was Shriver's over a decade ago. Government employees traveled first class in 1961; Shriver's Peace Corps went tourist. There were no carpets on the floor at OEO. There was no tenure at the Peace Corps to guarantee lifetime employment to time-serving bureaucrats. The evaluation and inspection system at Peace Corps and OEO encouraged whistle-blowing, and communication between the top and bottom of those agencies that was unprecedented. Legal Services at OEO represented the first break in the liberal tradition of throwing money at problems. Instead of a giant new agency to deal with social problems, a handful of lawyers was turned loose with minimum cost and maximum results.

That Shriver, with such a record, didn't offer himself as an unattached candidate—avoiding any self-announced association with John F. Kennedy—was a mistake, and instantly perceived as a crippling flaw by reporters happy to kick the crutches out from under a candidate.

But Shriver was insecure at the prospect of running on his own—despite his record at Peace Corps and OEO, and in Paris as ambassador, and as a corporate lawyer who negotiated contracts with the Soviet Union. It was a form of personal uneasiness common to Washington. Few of those who have attachments to one form of power or another don't rely on them. Journalists use the phone and announce themselves not as John Smith but as John Smith of CBS

News or John Smith of *The Los Angeles Times.* Some of the power-reliers are such habitual self-linkers that even as dinner guests they introduce themselves by saying not merely who they are but whom they are with. When you ask someone "Who are you with?" it is code talk for "are you important?"

Shriver's psychological inability to detach himself from a source of power was standard Washington behavior. To imagine his agony is not hard. He was suddenly a free lancer. For 15 years, he had been safely associated with a force larger than himself. He could dash around the country, hold forth on the issues and win victories that had to be noticed, because it wasn't really himself that he was putting forward. It was someone else—JFK, LBJ, McGovern—or another cause: poverty, diplomacy. He had no difficulty battling the Albert Quies and Charles Goodells who led the congressional fights against OEO. He wasn't asking Congress or anyone else to do anything for Shriver; he was only the agent serving another, whether it was the Mississippi Head Start director who needed funds or Lyndon Johnson wanting to be seen as great. Writers who have been on the payroll of a newspaper or magazine for years but suddenly try to stand on their own as free lancers can sympathize with Shriver's situation. Now it's just me, not me and CBS or me and *The Los Angeles Times.*

That Shriver felt distinctly uncomfortable with his free-lance status is suggested not only by his sticking with a dead brother-in-law but by associating himself with a group of the glitteringly alive. Much time was devoted to organizing the "Shriver for President Committee," a list of names that included Lauren Bacall, Paul Newman, Arthur Rooney, Roosevelt Grier, Carol Channing, Morton Downey, Ara Parseghian, Mrs. Aristotle Onassis, G. Mennen Williams, Jr., Scottie Fitzgerald Smith, L. Sam Shoen (chairman of the board of U-Haul-It), among others.

The committee list wasn't all like that, but reading the names it was clear that here was a candidate who may have had a lot of friends but he must be the last of the sophomores to believe that many voters would be impressed by his knowing so many of the beautifuls. The committee list made it easier to dismiss Shriver as a lightweight, which Johnny Carson regularly took vacuous glee in doing. At Shriver headquarters, the list became an embarrassment. One volunteer told of phoning field workers in Massachusetts to ask how much more campaign literature they needed from Washington. "They'd always tell me, send up speeches, press releases, but for

God's sake burn those committee-list booklets. Nobody in the neighborhoods is impressed by Sarge's celebs."

This was another irony. On the list—among the Morton
Downeys, Carol Channings, has-beens and never-was-beens—
were citizens whose judgment, values, and ideals were politically
and morally sound. That Shriver was friends with someone like
Prof. John Raines of Temple University's department of religion, or
Charles Frankel, a philosophy professor at Columbia, suggested a
side to him that set him apart from the other candidates even more
distinctly than his record at Peace Corps, OEO, and Paris. Shriver
was a passionate reader of philosophy, theology and literature, one
who sought to make the connection real between daily politics and
the resources of the inner life. It was not a pose of piety, but an
effort to go out of himself to seek communion with minds and
spirits larger and deeper than his own. It is standard American
politics for public men to display their reverent side, but as Nixon
exemplified with his White House prayer services, what we get is
not religion but religiosity. It is useless for a candidate's supporters
to claim that their man is holier-than-thou's, which is why Shriver,
both in 1972 and in the six months of running just past, kept his
interior life where it should be: hidden and within.

My own glimpse of it came when I began working for Shriver as
his speechwriter in 1966. I had been roving the country and sending
in articles to some of the smaller magazines. One of them appeared
in the *National Catholic Reporter*, then and now a lively weekly.
Shriver, a NCR subscriber, had read a piece of mine on Harlem. A
week later when I was in Kansas City, he called. He enjoyed the
article and needed a speechwriter. Could I come to Washington to
talk about the idea. It was a heady moment for me, discovering that
something I'd written in a small circulation journal was read by one
of the few national figures that I respected. This was also the first
job offer I'd ever had. But on coming to Washington, I had no reason
to be overjoyed. I would blow it when I met Shriver, I thought,
because he would ask me—having been well out of circulation for
five years—what I knew about Head Start, VISTA, Foster Grand-
parents, and I would know no more about them than about
molecular physics. We went to dinner. For the next four hours, not
a word passed between us about OEO, Peace Corps, or anything
else of political Washington. Instead, the discussion involved the life
and thought of such philosophers as Leon Bloy, Ronald Knox, Henri

DeLubac, and Romano Guardini. At one point, Shriver went off on a long conversational discourse on the differences between the early Jacques Maritain, the middle and the late Martain. I had spent enough time reading this French philosopher to know that Shriver wasn't bloviating and that he did indeed have a sensitivity to ethics and moral theology. I was amazed, because Shriver was then much the worldly success that Washington embraces. His enthusiasm for ideas and moral issues had to be respected because he was no recent convert—a Chuck Colson—whose candlestick talk dripped with the wax of piety. Shriver told me that while a student at Yale, 30 years earlier, he had invited Dorothy Day to come speak to a group of students there, and that he had kept up with the Catholic Worker people since. One of those he most admired was Daniel Berrigan. In 1965, when Berrigan was known only as a promising poet, Shriver had asked him to baptize one of his children.

Because I knew a little about Maritain and Leon Bloy (author of *The Woman Who Was Poor*), Shriver hired me. In three years of helping him with speeches, it was always striking that rather than my sprinkling in quotes from the heavies—as most politicians, wanting the wise sound, demand of speech writers—the quotes would come from Shriver. He would pass along the latest book he had read—Unamuno's *Tragic Sense of Life* or something of Bergson, Teilhard, or Ralph Ellison—and suggest that some of the underlined material be used for the next speech. A few months ago, when I went to his headquarters to talk about his campaign, he rattled on about the progress he was making in New Hampshire and Massachusetts. Others were in the room then. But when they left, he asked the secretary not to be interrupted. He reached into a drawer and took out a book. He began reading aloud. "Let's see if you recognize this," he said. He read a page and a half. It was from Maritain's *Social and Political Philosophy*. Shriver would read a sentence, and exclaim, "and just listen to this!" He would go on, get excited, stop, read on. About half an hour passed and, recharged, he was ready for the outside world again.

It is maddening that Shriver's early campaign botches made it so easy for him to be dismissed. Nothing worthwhile he said or did seemed able to free him from the self-inflicted damage of the Kennedy connection or the sheen of his beautiful people image. Yet, going back, much of what he actually was saying not only has sharpness and insight now but was able to command serious attention when he said it. In January, he issued a 22-page economic position paper with the kind of persuasive arguments and careful analysis that no other candidate—before or since—has presented.

Shriver was also the only candidate to try to arouse a campaign discussion about family life and the effect—usually disastrous—of government policy on parents and children. *The New York Times* and other papers devoted editorials to Shriver's ideas, but how much did anyone want to hear those ideas? In April, a month after Shriver retired, Jane O'Reilly ended a column in *The Washington Star:* "The problems of families and children in the United States are extraordinarily complex and important. Why aren't all those men running for President talking about it?" One was.

For all the commotion about the supposedly religious natures of Jimmy Carter and Jerry Brown, a Shriver paper on "Religion and the Presidency" represented the only specific statement of a candidate's uses of religion should he get to the White House. "I can assure you of only a few things," he wrote. "If I am elected President . . . I shall establish a Council of Ethics Advisors, similar to the Council of Economic Advisors . . . for most presidential problems have ethical, not just financial, scientific, military or political dimensions. Frequently the more important question is, 'Should we do it?,' not 'Can we do it?'"

Shriver is as thoughtful, candid, and creative a person as we have in public life. He just should be kept from running for office. He botches it, whatever the causes, in or out of his control. But should the Democrats win in November, the need will be present for someone in the cabinet who has survived countless struggles with Congress (as he did at the Peace Corps and OEO), brought government to the citizens—through Community Action programs, neighborhood Legal Services offices—well before "down with Washington" became a slogan, and came forward as a presidential candidate with careful thoughts about economics, family life, and ethics. Besides that, he has read Jacques Maritain, early, middle, and late.

# Paul Engle                                                       *1983*

IOWA CITY—Paul Engle, an oral anthology of stories about storytellers, remembers after class one day in 1946 when a graduate student stopped him. Flannery O'Connor brought Engle a manuscript, one of the early chapters in "Wise Blood." Engle told O'Connor, then 22 and away from her Milledgeville, Ga., home for the first time, that "this scene of the attempted seduction just is not correct. I want to explain. She said, 'Oh no, don't, not here!" So we went outside, across the street to the parking lot and into my car. There, I explained to her that a sexual seduction didn't take place quite the way she had written it—I suspect from a lovely lack of knowledge."

With or without sex ed courses, O'Connor would claim Engle as her mentor until her death 18 years later. It was one of dozens of literary relationships that has marked the 50-year-career of Engle as poet, essayist, teacher, spotter of talent, developer of genius, guardian of English, prairie philosopher and fundraiser.

Wealthy angels as diverse as W. Averell Harriman and the Exxon Corp. have given Paul Engle money for his University of Iowa writing programs. Kurt Vonnegut and Philip Roth, who came here to teach under him in the 1960s, shower praise on him for his nurturing of writers. John Irving and Gail Godwin were among his students. And a Nigerian chief, Okogbule Wonodi, wrote to say, "I am personally convinced that you have done more in creating an atmosphere of peace and mutual respect between citizens of different parts of the world than most loud-talking politicians."

As the receiver of all this, Paul Engle says of himself: "I grew up in the world of the family farm, of the horse. You won't believe how much stuff I've shoveled in my life, and I go on doing so but on a different level."

The level is the high one of literature, which Engle has been serving most of his life. It isn't in New York or San Francisco where two one-of-a-kind writing programs flourish, but here in a slumberous heartland town where corn and books, two of life's necessities, are equally valued. In 1941, Engle took over the University of Iowa's creative writing workshop. He directed it for 25 years. In 1967 Engle and his future wife Nieh Hualing, a Chinese-born novelist and translator, cofounded the International Writing Program. Nieh directs the program now, with her husband as consultant, while he writes his next book, "Engle Country: Memoirs."

As Iowa's leading importer of talent—and a fair exporter of his own through a dozen books—Engle raises up to $400,000 annually for the international program. "Watch it when you're with Engle," warned a Des Moines editor. "If he thinks you have money, he'll talk it out of you for his programs."

Though he hasn't done as well as some of Iowa's farmers, whose bins overflow with surplus grains, Engle has reaped well over $3 million from foundations, corporations, the U.S. Information Agency and individuals for the International Writers Program. In 15 years, more than 400 foreign writers—novelists, poets, playwrights, essayists—have settled in for annual three-month stretches of unhassled writing time and classwork. The idea, Engle wrote in the mid-'60s, was "to run the future of American literature, and a great deal of European and Asian, through Iowa City."

The running has been nonstop. Other "Iowa authors" brought here by Engle include Robert Penn Warren, Robert Lowell, William Stafford, James Dickey, Herbert Gold, Vance Bourjaily, W. D. Snodgrass, Donald Justice, Philip Levine, Paul Horgan, Karl Shapiro, Josephine Johnson, Mark Strand and Richard Kim. Every major American literary prize, and scores of minor ones, has been won by Iowa products.

In the early 1950s, Engle had poets Snodgrass, Stafford, Levine and Justice under his care. "I had them all in one class," he recalls. "It was exactly like being a lion in a den of Daniels. It scared the hell out of me. It's a frightening thing to be a teacher and walk into a class-room of absolute brilliance."

Once, while teaching briefly in the late 1930s in Chicago, Engle had Gwendolyn Brooks in his class. Brooks was to win the Pulitzer Prize in poetry in 1960. "The class," Engle remembers, "was mostly rather over-weight upper-middle-class Evanston women. Every time they'd pick up a piece of paper, you could hear their expensive girdles going snaaap. We had a poetry contest in the last class. I was the judge. All poems were anonymous. I read them and said the winner of the first prize is: And it was a pseudonym. So I said, would so-and-so please stand up. This extremely black girl rose, really rather scared. This was up in Evanston, the upper-middle-class [area] of Chicago, and she came from 63rd Street by the hill. Every-body gasped. And I said the second prize winner is—another black girl from 63rd Street stood up. At that time, it was obvious that it was a good idea [for me] to get the hell out of Evanston before nightfall! All these pudgy Dior types hated my guts."

That began a friendship with Brooks. The class, Engle believes, helped to "start her career. I don't take credit for her talent. Nobody does that, I just say I recognized it—quickly. That's why so many got here [to Iowa City]."

A porchlight flicks on, breaking the evening shadows. The front door opens and, in a flurry of courteous words of greeting to a visitor, Paul Engle moves through the iced air to the end of the walkway. In front of his two-level home, on the upsweep of a headland that overlooks the Iowa River, Engle is not fully visible in the darkness. Even without a physical image, his voicefulness— undulate baritone vowels, heavy consonants—suggests size.

Bad news, he calls out. "Hualing isn't here. She's on the way to Singapore. Landing right this minute, as a matter of fact. Exactly now. She's there for a conference with writers."

It's a husband talking of his absent wife, putting her in the lead paragraph of his thoughts, which is her place in his emotions. Instead of some gab about the whip of the Iowa winter wind, about to become unignorable, Engle announces right off that tonight he is a cup with no spoon. Conversation will be a hard stir.

It doesn't turn out that way. Nieh Hualing, who succeeded her husband as director of the International Writing Program in 1976, is at Earth's end, spreading and bringing back the word. But Engle, inside now and coat hung, keeps her present the way he will keep fresh ties tonight to every love in his life: By descent into earthy stories as rich as Iowa loam and by soarings to high feelings of justified pride that have made him a literary figure like no other in America.

The Engle living room is a full browse of a place. On one wall 30 hand-carved tribal face masks are hung, a peering-out of craftsmanship that matches the writing talent Engle drew from his former African students, who gave the masks as gifts to their teacher. Bookshelves, house plants and knickknacks soften the other walls. Near the fireplace is a Chinese coffee table, its top set in mother-of-pearl and with oriental women in a garden.

With a poker, Engle upends two logs already kindling but which could be doing better, and then teases the upper licks of the fire to flame higher. In a minute, they do, and Engle, happy with his manual labor, draws back to the comfort of his chair.

Like his voice, he is large. Approaching 75, he retains the straight-up hulk of a 6-2 frame, built both for farming and towering over the classroom lectern. Blue and alert eyes are set in a long face with ample room at the top for high eyebrows that lift up like exclamation points when his sentences need one. His hair, not the mane it once was, still has body enough to be mussed when he runs his fingers through it while talking.

Engle exudes localness. "My job," he began, "is to be an old Iowa boy. I was born in Cedar Rapids, 25 miles north of here. When I became 50 years old, my first wife, who's now deceased, said to me one morning, 'Look, what in the hell have you done? In 50 years, you've gone 25 miles.'

"How could I deny it—I'd gone a half mile a year!"

Not really. Engle has made several around-the-world journeys in only the last two decades. He has bed and board guaranteed in scores of nations where his former students live. His first venture from Cedar Rapids was in 1932. He had graduated from the local Coe College that year before and did postgraduate work at Columbia University in New York. He won a Rhodes scholarship and enrolled in 1934 at Merton College in Oxford. "I had horse manure on my shoes. From my father's barn. That was my life. That was my father's career—farmer and horse-trainer. The horses ate pure oats. We ate oats ground. I arrived over there and a servant was assigned to shine my shoes. Can you believe it?"

He turns over the rough-hewn back of his hands to show that anyone can get a callus or two on the palms but only the seasoned farmer has weathery skin on the other side. As a farm boy, of German stock, he cared for the horses that helped give the family its living. When he was to earn his own living at writing and teaching, he remembered: "It was invaluable in dealing with colleagues and deans to have learned how to handle horses. A blacksmith shop is better training than a university—it is fundamental and primitive. You learn that a horse usually twitches a little just before he is going to kick. Our blacksmith was Czech and could swear in both languages. He chewed Horseshoe Plug—what else?—and when he took a shoe out of the forge for the last time he would spit on it to 'cure it,' shouting, 'By God, she's a beauty.'"

In his childhood in the 1920s, Engle earned money for the books he was devouring by being a *shabbas goy* for local Jews who observed the Hebraic law of the Sabbath. "I was a Gentile who lit their fires on Saturday morning and put them out Saturday evening. This was in Cedar Rapids for the Jewish community. I got 15 cents a Saturday. Their religious regulations forbade them to light a fire from dawn Saturday to sunset Saturday. I would go down in the winter and shake their stoves, and put in corncobs, wood, coal, set the grate and then go back in the evening."

A school librarian in Cedar Rapids nudged young Engle into the world of literature by skipping the McGuffey Reader routine and giving him instead an anthology of English and American poetry. "It changed my life. It's amazing the power that a sympathetic, alert librarian or teacher can have over the young. They can speed up your life by 20 years."

The speeding-up came into public view on July 29, 1934, when the entire front page of the New York Times Book Review was given over to a review by J. Donald Adams of Engle's "American Song: a Book of Poems." The banner headline read, "A New Voice in American Poetry," with a subhead, "Paul Engle's 'American Song' May Prove a Literary Landmark." Engle was 26.

The review was effusive. Noting that first books of poetry were rarely placed "on the front page of this section, or for that matter any book of contemporary poetry," it celebrated in New York what Engle writing in Oxford was celebrating about heartland America. "He drinks deep," Adams wrote, "from that well from which every creative artist must—love of place, the sense of being somewhere rooted." Lines from a poem were quoted:

O wood thrush crying in Kentucky hills,
O gray gull poising over Puget Sound,
Sing down our hands from cursing at the sky,
Give them again the feel of friendly ground.
Under the Chippewayan woods, the wide
Iowa prairie, Illinois loam sheet—
O meadow lark in blue stem—we will watch
The birds of Francis gather at our feet.

Launched by the front-page review, Engle had every reason to forsake the boondocks to become the new literary darling of the New York or Parisian salons. He had been traveling throughout Europe during this period and could read Descartes in French and Kant in German. The manure was off his shoes. Instead, the cosmopolitan came back to the Corn Belt. In 1937, newly married to a local woman, he joined the university's English department as a teacher of writing and lecturer in poetry. The bonding was to be permanent. "I decided that the United States was the place where I wanted to live, but that I really wanted to settle here—in this small, agreeable and very adventurous university town . . . Unlike a great city, Iowa City is not dispersed. Here we have a real community. All the people know each other well. It's a reasonably safe town. You can walk around. Kids have a good life. Our people do go to New York, Washington and San Francisco. They visit. But basically they live here in the heart of the country. They meet businessmen. This is very important in the United States. We're a business country. They meet farmers. They go to John Deere in Moline, where tractors are being made. They go to art museums. So they have the kind of varied life they couldn't have if they lived in a big city. This is not putting down New York. It's a great city. But it doesn't have any farmers. And it doesn't make many tractors."

The number of writers forged by the big cities is also open to question, if compared with the products of Iowa City. Philip Roth believes that "Paul Engle's Iowa Writing Workshop is one of those places, like Elizabeth Ames' Yaddo, that made life easier and pleasanter for hundreds and hundreds of writers. Iowa City is what a whole generation had, instead of Paris. And it wasn't so bad, either."

One of the earliest signs that Engle was onto something special at the workshop was Flannery O'Connor. Like Engle, she was rural. Both had their doubts about the cities: Engle that they don't make tractors and O'Connor's nervousness at New York cocktail parties. She said of one Upper East Side event: The trouble with everyone there was that they didn't come from anyplace.

When O'Connor arrived in Iowa City, Engle knew definitely she was a child with origins. "She came out of the red dirt country of Georgia. She walked into my office one day and spoke to me. I understood nothing, not one syllable. As far as I knew, she was saying 'Aaaaraaaraaarah.' My God, I thought to myself, this is a retarded young girl. Then I looked at her eyes. They were crossed! Finally, I said, excuse me, my name is Paul Engle. I gave her a pad— believe me, this is true—and said would you please write down what you're telling me. And she wrote, 'My name is Flannery O'Connor.

I'm from Milledgeville, Georgia. I'm a writer.' She didn't say 'I want to be a writer.' She said 'I am a writer.' I said do you have any writing with you. She had one of the most beat-up handbags I've ever seen. It must have been put in an old-fashioned water-powered washing machine and churned for a day. She handed me this paper. I read four lines. You don't need to eat all of an egg to know if it's good or bad. I looked at her and said to myself, 'Christ, this is it. This is pure talent. What can I do? I can't teach her anything!' I taught her a little. She had a few isolated problems—with her society, her illness."

O'Connor's first book, "The Geranium: A Collection of Short Stories," was submitted in June 1947 as a thesis for a master's degree in fine arts at the university. It was dedicated to Engle. In a letter in 1971 to Robert Giroux, the publisher, seven years after O'Connor died of lupus, Engle remembered that her "will to be a writer was adamant; nothing could resist it, not even her own sensibility about her own work. Cut, alter, try it again ... Sitting at the back of the room, silent, Flannery was more of a presence than the exuberant talkers who serenade every writing-class with their loudness. The only communicating gesture she would make was an occasional amused and shy smile at something absurd. The dreary chair she sat in glowed."

In 1965, Engle invited Kurt Vonnegut to the workshop to teach. Vonnegut, living in semistruggle on Cape Cod at the time, arrived in Iowa City in an old Volkswagen, his enthusiasm for writing in about as poor shape as his car. He had written six novels, but the several passes at the book he wanted to write most—about the American firebombing of Dresden in World War II—went nowhere. He was in a creative airlock. His two years with Engle loosened him. He wrote "Slaughterhouse-Five" in Iowa City.

Vonnegut has been an Engle fan since. He recalled recently that he has twice proposed his former colleague for membership to the National Institute of Arts and Letters for his enduring service in assisting writers. "He's an extremely important man culturally. I can't think of any institution, except maybe the Guggenheim Foundation, that has encouraged as many writers as the Iowa workshops. In my time, a Chilean novelist was there. So was Nelson Algren. We all needed to get pumped up about the importance of writing. Of course, that was the magic of Iowa—getting a whole bunch of writers in one place and talking about nothing but writing.

You decide pretty fast that writing is important after all. Paul was a raffish soldier-saint leading us into battle against the Philistines. I don't know why he's chosen this role, but it's been tremendously useful to all of us."

Vonnegut didn't offer specifics on the names and locations of the Phillistines. But if he had in mind the businessmen who populate corporate America, then he may have placed Engle on the wrong battlefield. ITT, U.S. Steel, Rockwell International, Amana Refrigeration, Atlantic Richfield, Mobil, Reader's Digest, Time Inc., Northern Natural Gas and Bankers Life Insurance are among the companies that have been persuaded by Engle to give money to the International Writers Program. "Fund-raising is a major activity for me every year," Engle said, "going back to the times when I did the same for the Writers Workshop. Money-raising is a dog's life and sometimes I tire of barking at the golden moon." He tires more of academic intellectuals who look down their educated noses on the business world. "Ultimately," Engle said in an interview a few years ago, "all salaries come down to the productive enterprises of the country—people working, often harder and longer hours than professors work."

If Engle's closeness to businessmen is a twist, perhaps a twist with double English is his friendship with Averell Harriman. "Ave's an old friend. I lived in his house for two years [in the early 1950s]. At Harriman, N.Y., up the Hudson River. The Harriman estate is called Arden."

Engle met Harriman in 1954 in Hobe Sound, Fla. He had won a Guggenheim Foundation fellowship and through good fortune found an affordable house to rent for a few months. Engle was unprepared for the swank of Hobe Sound: "Beautiful houses with large lawns. Each blade of grass cost a dollar!" A neighbor was Philip Barry, the playwright. One evening at dinner at the Barrys, Harriman and his then-wife Marie were at the table. A close and enduring friendship began. "I admire Averell Harriman as really almost the greatest man this country has produced in this century—in world terms. Ave can take an objective view of people he hates: This is marvelous! Few of us can. Ave can, for the good of the country."

Engle told of the time his daughter Mary was staying in the New York apartment of the Harriman's. On the day she left, a car was called to driver her to the airport: "You know who went and got her bags and carried them out to the street? Seventy-nine-year-old Averell Harriman. He carried my daughter's bags. There is a thing called character, and Averell Harriman has it. It's going out of fashion. But he has it. And he treats a young girl from Iowa elitely."

It's no less for her father and stepmother. "Over many years," Harriman wrote in a 1976 letter supporting the Engles' nomination for the Nobel Peace Prize, "I have known the Engles and watched their dedicated efforts to bring peace and understanding to the world by bringing writers of every country, language and culture to their program in Iowa City ... It is important to note the they were not asked to undertake this difficult program by a government. They invented the idea and gave their years to raising the funds to finance it from many sources, most of them private individuals and corporations. This is unprecedented in the history of international relations, which are almost always governments talking to governments."

Toward evening's end, Engle walks through a hallway off the living room to his office. In neatness, it's the opposite of the straight-lined Iowa cornfield, being instead a scatter seed of books, envelopes, papers, letters. Crops are rotated here. On a table, like a tractor ready to plow, is an Olympia manual typewriter. It is in this workroom that Engle spends much of his time writing "Engle Country: Memoirs." The dissoluteness of the room tells the un-written story that this is a place where work is sweated out, where Engle takes the advice he has been giving to students since he took over his first writing class in 1936: "A work of art is work."

When he is reminded of the line, he talks of what is currently passing for education in the classrooms. "Did you read about this basketball player—6-foot-8 who's taking third and fourth grade after graduating from college. This is a travesty and a tragedy. He couldn't do that in the Soviet Union. Nor China. *We're* the country that's destroying itself. [Our children] aren't being taught simple facts, simple grammar and clear mathematics. What's going to happen in 20 years? We'll be an ignorant country. I think we're in desperate condition, and for survival it has to change. We must no longer indulge ignorant teachers and ignorant students... It absolutely scares me when I see how badly many students write.

"I think education has given itself far too much to abstract concepts, abstract testing. What's the point of having an extremely good test which proves that your students haven't learned anything? What's the point of *that*? Teach them, teach them, teach them in a way which motivates them. There's no day that goes by without stories in the newspaper about students who go and vandalize the school at night that they attend by day. This is not only vicious but is dangerous to the country. It's destructive of any respect to intelligence . . . If you get the young involved in what they are learning, they won't be destructive."

In the book he edited, "On Creative Writing," which is as much a classic on the art of language as Strunk and White's "Elements of Style," Engle wrote that "the simple, often grunt-like puffs of air which we call words must be used by the writer with such skill that they can bring to a reader, who cannot even hear whatever tone of voice the writer would give them, a form and sense which will move him. This is by no means as easy as lifting bricks all day or breaking stone."

It is a vintage Engle thought: joining the work of the mind with the labor of the body. For more than 40 years, he has been bringing people who write to a place where people farm, rejoicing in the talent of the Czech blacksmith and celebrating the kindness of the Hobe Sound millionaire—and pulling it off in a circle 25 miles wide, if necessary. In "Who's Who," Engle provided a few biographical details of his life and ended with a summing-up line: "A grindstone does its job by a perpetual turning in one place, wearing itself down slower than the steel."

*A few months after this article ran, Paul Engle was visiting Washington. I invited him to The Post to give a lecture about writing. He accepted joyfully. For an hour one afternoon, he shared his ideas and stories with a roomful of editors and reporters. It was one of my best days at The Post, and for many others, too, I suspect.*

# Daniel Berrigan                                        *1980*

I last saw Dan Berrigan at one of his favorite haunts, the river entrance to the Pentagon. I thought to myself that here is the lithest and youngest 60-year-old in America. His hair is graying, it's true; but I thought he ought to be inside giving the fitness-conscious generals seminars in keeping youthful.

Berrigan is the son of parents who lived into their 90s, and he has already given himself over to longevity: he has been faithful to his Jesuit commitment for 42 years. Small wonder he called his last book, *Ten Commandments for the Long Haul.*

He was even more youthful in 1966, when I first met him in Washington. Back then, he was known mostly as a poet with something of a moral edge to his words. He was a teacher in an Upward Bound program in Colorado. This was funded by OEO under Sargent Shriver. Since Berrigan was technically a government worker, Shriver regularly had Berrigan come to the agency to give talks to the staff. I saw him there mostly as a poet.

Today he is known for his emphatically unpoetic defiance of the nation's drive toward militarization. His critics see him as an unrepentant rebel with both a taste for grandstanding and a passion for simplistic interpretations of national security issues. His admirers look to him as a prophet of peace in a culture of violence, as an Amos denouncing the gaucheries of power and a Francis crying out for a new era of love.

Whatever other judgments are being made these days about Daniel Berrigan, the predictions of a few years ago—that he was a dated figure of the 1960s who would have no relevance to the 1980s—were dead wrong. In 1982 American bishops are publicly thanking him for his early witness against the madness of nuclear weapons. He has an overflow of invitations to speak on the nation's campuses, from Notre Dame to Onondaga Community College in New York to Millsaps College in Mississippi. He maintains his ties with his readers by turning up in newer magazines like *Sojourners* and *Notre Dame Magazine* as well as old reliables like *The Catholic Worker.* His 30th book was published last summer and another is due this spring. A Berrigan biography by John Deedy recently was published by Fides Claretian Press. For someone who was pronounced "washed up" by the trend keepers, Berrigan endures as a public figure of remarkable durability.

In 1968, as a burner of draft records, Berrigan was among the Catonsville Nine. Now, as the hammerer of a General Electric missile, he is among the Plowshares Eight. His protests remain as relevant to the immediate danger as is his belief that he will never stop "making noise and being congenitally unhappy with false peace and wrongheaded power."

Berrigan believed the United States was a morally under-developed nation in the 1960s, and he believes it now. He asked citizens then not to cooperate with America's military machine, and he asks it now. He engaged in civil disobedience then and was willing to go to prison for it, and he does the same today. He is today where he has always been: in a state of smoldering resistance to a culture comfortable with the terror of nuclear weapons.

The last long conversation I had with Berrigan was a while back in the small apartment he shares with four other Jesuits at 220 West 98th Street in New York City. At the time, he was teaching black prison literature at New Resources College, a low- and no-tuition school in the neighborhood. He also was volunteering one day a week to care for the dying at Saint Rose's Home for Incurable Cancer on the Lower East Side.

The apartment's furniture was Jesuit spare. On the bedroom wall hung the "Trident Crucifix," a stark bodyless cross shaped out of barbed wire cut from a fence guarding the submarine base near Seattle that the local archbishop, Raymond Hunthausen, has called "the Auschwitz of America." The bookshelves were heavy with the work of pacifists such as Gandhi and Thoreau. Berrigan's own books were not on display, though one piece of literature about him could be found: his arrest record, complete with fingerprints, compliments of the New York Police Department.

Among Berrigan's family pictures is one of Monsignor Joseph Buh, a Croatian priest who married the future Jesuit's parents in 1911. In his apartment that day nearly seven decades later, Berrigan talked about his parents and his childhood.

He was born in Virginia, Minn., on May 9, 1921, the fifth of Frida and Thomas Berrigan's six sons. His mother was a German immigrant; his father was a son of Irish immigrants. A few years after Daniel's birth the family, hovering just above poverty, moved to New York State, near Syracuse.

In a verse published in his book, *Prison Poems*, Berrigan wrote movingly of his father:

*Whatever you denied us, you*
*gave us this which enemies name*
*distemper, madness; our friends,*
*half in despair, arrogance.*

*Which I name, denying both—the*
  *best of*
*your juice and brawn—unified*
*tension to good purpose.*

Berrigan's mother was quieter than the stormy Hibernian socialist she married. She opened her sons' eyes to the world and to the merciful response that should be made to it.

In spare prose, snapping like the sounds from a hard-wire snare drum, Berrigan wrote of his mother in *Ten Commandments for the Long Haul.* The passage is as necessary to a full understanding of the priest as anything else he ever wrote.

"We were farm people in upstate New York," Berrigan began. "We had 10 acres of clay, a few livestock, and a deep reserve of stubbornness. So we made it through some of the leanest seasons on record since the Egyptians hoarded wheat.

"One day, there arrived at our kitchen door a portent the likes of whom a child's eye is seldom granted to behold. [He was a] poor, wild-eyed, ragged creature, a figure out of *Les Miserables.* He had undoubtedly passed nights and days in the swamp nearby; in face and crouch and growl, he was like a ravenous wolf.

"In the house were my mother and two small children, Philip and myself. She opened the door, while the two of us sprats peered out from her skirts. And without missing a beat, she waved this inarticulate bag of bones into her house.

"She laid a cloth and began to prepare a meal: a dozen eggs and trimmings, fresh bread and butter, coffee snarling from the pot. The wolf at the door was wolfish at table. Without a word, he polished off everything within reach. He was silent as stone, and my mother silently came and went, serving him. Then, in the pantry, she worked away preparing sandwiches and fruit for him to take along. Which he did, departing, mumbling something incomprehensible into his beard, maybe a word of thanks.

"Within 10 minutes, a carload of state troopers swarmed in the yard, yelling word of an escaped convict in the area. My mother, calm and usual in manner, stood between the listening children and answered: Yes, someone of that description had been in her home, and yes she had fed him, and yes he had gone off in that direction. They raced off like the hounds of hell on the spoor of our poor guest.

"And I, age five, knew something instinctively: that she had pointed the pursuers in exactly the wrong direction. I knew too, as children will, that ... everything of her life, her aura, her courage, born of poverty and crushing labor and the bearing and raising of six children, everything was predictable, like a healing shadow cast ahead of her at evening. The shadow of one who invariably shelters the victim. And who, having fed a fugitive at her table exactly the way she would feed her family... after this spontaneous, congruous conduct, by no means would she cap her good act by surrendering so sorry a creature into the hands of police.

"Brave, dear, dead lady! Ineradicable example! You showed two little children a way, without ever pausing to recollect that they would remember such an hour, such a woman, the event stamped on them like a birthmark, to their dying day."

Berrigan would be on the lam himself in due time, leading the FBI on a four-month chase that would end in August 1970 with his capture on Block Island. A photographer of beady eye caught the scene: the handcuffed Berrigan, smiling and striding with purpose, being hauled away by scowling G-men. The prisoner was the free man, the posse the captured.

Berrigan joined the Society of Jesus in 1939, when he was 18. He liked the Jesuits' revolutionary spirit, though he found that at the novitiate at St. Andrew-on-the-Hudson the daily regimen was along the lines of the military training found nearby at West Point.

By 1945, Berrigan was studying at Woodstock in Maryland, the ivory tower for East Coast Jesuits. He told John Deedy about the time Philip Berrigan, home from the war as a dashing young infantry officer, came to Woodstock to see his brother.

"V-J Day had just occurred," Daniel recalled, "and the whole seminary organized a spontaneous victory demonstration," including a parade, patriotic songs and a uniformed Phil Berrigan up front carrying the Stars and Stripes. "It was really a weird combination of emotions," Berrigan remembered. "All of us had relatives in the war; some had relatives who had been killed. It was a great relief to have the war over. But there was no moral understanding of what this war, or any war, was all about."

Berrigan followed the traditional regimen of the Jesuit seminarian: he taught and studied and did a bit of fieldwork. He might have ended up as one of the order's respectable middle-roaders had he not come into contact with Dorothy Day and her Catholic Worker movement.

This great woman—a ladler of soup, a defier of warmakers, an opener of doors for the homeless, a passionate Christian—opened Berrigan's mind to an authentic kind of religious witness. She moved him in what he later called "a direction of modest possibilities."

Following his ordination in 1953, Berrigan taught and served as Sodality moderator at Brooklyn Prep. In 1957, he returned to Syracuse to teach the New Testament at LeMoyne College.

Under Day's inspiration, he was becoming an activist, though still within academia. It would take several years at LeMoyne for him to learn that a tight institutional structure was not for him. He was searching for other ways than the classroom lecture to teach the New Testament.

As the 1960s began, he made contact with members of the Catholic Worker network, including Thomas Merton, the Trappist monk with whom Berrigan shared numberless discussions—in visits to Merton's monastery and in correspondence—about non-violence and opposition to America's war culture and the meaning of the priestly vocation.

Berrigan and Merton were more than fellow pacifists. Each had religious superiors who tried to silence him, in one shifty way or another; each was tempted to bolt his order, and each was a writer of powerful prose. A year after Merton's death, Berrigan dedicated one of his most trenchant books, *No Bars to Manhood*, to "my father, Thomas Berrigan" and "my brother, Thomas Merton."

He grew closest, though, to his blood brother Philip, who is larger physically than Daniel and more the outgoing spirit, more at ease with buoyant joviality. In the early 1960s Philip, while still a priest, found himself exiled from the seminary staff of the Josephite Fathers in Newburgh, N.Y. His views on social justice put him out of sorts with the rightwing Hudson Valley locals. He was dispatched to a parish in the Baltimore ghetto. "He started over," Daniel recalls of his brother. "He was incapable of meanness of spirit, even in dark hours, and wasted no time licking his wounds. He set about organizing in the inner city. Housing was a main issue locally, as was the war, for the poor were the first victims of the roundup. In all the troubled days that followed, I remember how the poor people stood with him."

Philip, now married and gone for some time from the Josephite order, today is a leader of Jonah House, a Baltimore community that lives and works among the city's poor. It is a national resource center for the peace movement.

Daniel Berrigan speaks with admiration of his brother's work at Jonah House, which he says "requires a very large measure of maturity to enter and become a member in a way that will contribute to the future. The pace there is very hard," he continues, "but I've seen people turn into healers there. Like myself. When I go there, I come back with my heart doubled."

With the emotional support of the Jonah House community behind him, Daniel Berrigan for the past two decades has had a free-roaming apostolate of peace. No other priest in the church has a ministry like his.

Of himself and his brother he writes: "What I am proud of is the consistency that binds the last 20 years in a coherent and even exciting unity. We have never reneged in difficult times on what we promised is rosier times. We have spoken the truth in public, in years when such activity had a bloody price tag attached. When the country was engaged in a mad international hunting party, we refused to ride to the hounds after human pelts and parts. More, we objected to the game, and raised a cry."

The cry has been upsetting, not only to the posses, prosecutors and judges who believe that one more jailing will "rehabilitate" Berrigan, but also to the intellectual critics of American radicalism. One of those is the Rev. Andrew Greeley, who in 1971 wrote in *The New York Times:* "The truth is that Catholic 'radicals' don't make any difference at all .... On the contrary, all the available data suggest that Berrigan-style protests are counterproductive to the causes they support." Time has proven that Greeley was merely displaying in the *Times* his uncanny knack for being wrong.

For a time, Berrigan's most threatening critics were members of his own order. In 1965, Jesuit superiors in the New York province bounced the priest to Latin America, in hopes that his heated peace protests would cool off. Berrigan never learned the specific details of the reasons behind that exile.

Today things are different. The Rev. Joseph C. Towle, S.J., Berrigan's current superior in the order's New York province, wrote recently to his fellow Jesuits: "If there is some truth to the comment that Dan has been on the fringe of the Society of Jesus, it can be said that we his brothers have not been where he was either. To me, the sense in which he has been on the fringe is like that of a weight being whirled at the end of a string, the escalating force of events shifting the center more and more away from the axis.

"The creeping threat of nuclear war, considered by many as potentially the second greatest evil in world history—second only to the crucifixion of Christ—has changed all of Dan's priorities .... The New York province itself, in its own searching way, has come to establish two major social priorities: world hunger and the arms race. Would we be at the latter point without Dan Berrigan? I wonder.

"As his superior and brother I think much about his life, his words, his writing, his friends and the world I share with him .... I have offered these remarks not to debate anyone else's views of Dan or law or violence but simply to sketch a reasonable basis for the province's support of him.

"Dan Berrigan is missioned by the New York province to the ministry of peace and to advocacy against nuclear war and weapons proliferation. I do not specify the details of that mission any more than I do for anyone else. I do trust—and have never found that trust betrayed—that Dan's decisions in the area of civil disobedience are based on prayer, discernment, counsel and proportionality, and that they are guided meticulously by the principle of nonviolence. I can only hope that his unique way both of seeing and dramatizing issues has some effect upon myself and other Jesuits."

At times, Berrigan has been harsh on his order. He accuses it of harboring "masters of invention. They come out of the culture, they know how to take its pulse, try its winds and trim their sails.

"We're not running the Little Brothers of Jesus," he continues. "We're not running the Catholic Worker. We're running Georgetown University, the school of foreign service. We're a nursery for the State Department; only the brightest and best get born here. So connections are everything, and dollars are nearly everything."

Unarguably, plenty of Jesuits are toadies to the rich and powerful, and more than a few are pliant in giving their blessings to worldly schemes. But that is not the whole story. The order also runs deep with men fervent for peace and ornery in their dedication to the poor. Throughout the world—from Central Appalachia to Central America to innercity Washington—Jesuits, like Daniel Berrigan, are paying heavily for siding with outcasts.

At the moment, a three- to 10-year prison sentence, plus 10 years' probation, hangs over Berrigan. The state means to keep him controlled until he is 82.*

At the trial of the Plowshares Eight, the presiding judge, Samuel Salus II, called Berrigan and his colleagues "malcontents." The group had entered a General Electric munitions plant to confront a Mark 12A nuclear missile nosecone. With hammers in their hands and Isaiah on their minds, they began beating the weapon into a plowshare.

Initial charges against the eight included violence and terroristic threats, but these were dropped after some GE employees called the group "nonviolent and peaceful." The eventual conviction came on burglary charges.

That was fitting. Berrigan and the others, who included his brother Philip, were burglarizing a storehouse of false security. "Everything in our history points to one dolorous conclusion: the eventual or prompt discharge of nuclear weapons," Berrigan maintains. "Indeed, history is appallingly consistent with this outcome. No weapon, once conceived, ever rotted or rusted unused."

From the bench, Judge Salus stated that his court was not a proper place to debate the likelihood of nuclear holocaust. In a letter to a journalist he went further: "Don't be fooled by the broad sweep of inner conscience, justification and peace as asserted by these people," he wrote. "History has yet to prove them correct or their assertions sound in logic and experience. What it has proved is that they have tried this kind of thing eight times before with the same political arguments. It is part of their policy and tactics to delude people about their good intentions when their sole purpose is to have no master, no government and, really, no God."

The judge's palaver about godlessness aside, using the courts as a forum for questions of life and death is not a decision Berrigan makes lightly, as though a few moments of speechifying are worth up to a decade in prison. Instead, he argues that if allegations of criminality are the domain of the judicial, then why should such questions be off-limits in the courts?

Five years ago, when Berrigan was before an Alexandria, Va., court on civil disobedience charges following a peaceful dustup at the Pentagon, he asked the judge: "Is it [not] true by Nuremberg statute, as well as domestic law, that it is a criminal act to conspire to commit a crime? Then we say the conspiracy is under way. The weapons are concocted. The plan is well-advanced .... We claim that the most horrid crime in the history of humanity is being planned [at the Pentagon]: a conspiracy to Hiroshimize every city of the world, to pulverize and vaporize all flesh and bones."

That is grisly talk, but not grislier than the pictures of what American atomic bombs did to citizens in two Japanese cities.

If Berrigan's frankness is out of place in a judicial setting, where will be the courts of last resort? Is the debate on disarmament to be confined to congressional committees, seminars of experts and windbags, and the offices of military analysts?

That these have become the normal outlets for protesting history's most massive weapons buildup may be why this militarization strikes so few as heinously abnormal. It may also be why, in these times of backward values, Daniel Berrigan may soon be back in prison.

*In early 1984 an appeals court overturned the conviction.*

# Tom Hamilton                                             1983

SOUTHBURY, Conn.—Elemental honesty and mettle mark the character of Thomas J. Hamilton. I knew this 35 years ago when I was a 10-year-old fourth grader in the village grammar school in Glen Head, N.Y., and he was a reporter for The New York Times. Tom Hamilton, who lived in Greenvale, the next town over, came to my class during Career Week to talk about one of the lasting loves of his life and what would become, in the private list of bedrock joys, one of the loves of mine: journalism.

The houselights of memory have dimmed on that distant day. But a long-lingering debt has remained. The other afternoon I took a sentimental journey to look up Tom Hamilton to pay off the accrual of thanks that I owed him. He took the time, half of a life ago, to scatter seeds among a few schoolchildren, a planting that at least for me caused a new growing. That year—1948—I started my own class newspaper. It was my first experience of writing and I have been at it since.

Tom Hamilton is now 74. He retired from The Times in 1972, after 35 years of reporting. Before that he had reported six years for the Atlanta Journal and the Associated Press. He lives in this quiet western Connecticut community with his wife of 49 years. What the numbers unmistakably add up to is a life of beautiful consecutiveness, of a writer finding at a young age a profession and a mate to devote his heart to and never being lured to think that he was missing out on better deals elsewhere.

Physically, Hamilton had the carriage that I remembered: tall, firm shoulders, no extra weight. His voice retained the southern ease of his Georgia childhood when he was the son of an Augusta newspaper editor.

If what he said at my school 35 years ago left an impression—that a career in journalism could lead to a life of purpose, excitement and service—so also did his reminiscences the other day over lunch in a Southbury restaurant. The former U.N. bureau chief for The Times, the former chief of the Bonn and Geneva bureaus, the onetime correspondent in London, Madrid and Washington didn't waste a breath recalling the big shots he met or the big stories he wrote. He was a refreshing contrast to those journalists who bloviate about the presidents, senators and other grandees whose elbows they have rubbed, as though first-name acquaintanceship with the mighty helps the reader understand how the mighty, in no one's name, keep messing up the world.

Tom Hamilton's ego didn't need that kind of self-massaging. Instead he went back over the workaday world of reporting, of the obligation of journalists to push beyond the conventional and get at news that the rest of the pack ignores.

The stories he told were mostly of other journalists he admired, from Ralph McGill, who was a fellow Georgian, to James Reston, a fellow Timesman. Reston worked with Hamilton in the London bureau in 1939. He came from AP and started work the night before World War II began.

When I asked Reston of his recollections of those days, he remembered Hamilton's "kindness to me, his gentility, intelligence and his lovely quiet voice." It is possible, it appears, to be both a tough reporter and a warm human being.

I knew none of this during Career Week 35 years ago, though perhaps I sensed it. Following Hamilton's visit—only the appearance of Eddie Stanky of the Boston Braves would have been a greater thrill to me—I looked for his byline in The Times. My father subscribed to the paper, though his emotional allegiance was to the runt of the New York media, the Brooklyn Eagle. The international politics that Hamilton wrote of wasn't what Glen Head's fourth graders talked about, but the way he wrote it—in polished, fair-minded prose—was like growing up with a trusted companion.

With my visit to Southbury, a cycle has been completed. I am older now than when Hamilton first shined a light in my life. As visitor to classrooms myself, to speak of writing, I am joining the chain of lives that passes on the treasures others once held out to me. In a happy coincidence, Bill Hamilton, Tom's youngest son, is an editor in The Post's newsroom. He makes it a pleasant place to work.

In Southbury, Tom Hamilton and I had the warmest of times. Much of the enjoyment is that I have begun to know the delights that Hamilton surely felt: helping along young journalists, getting them fired up and seeing their writing get into print. When the bylines fade, what we pass on could be all that endures.

# Dorothy Day                                         1980

NEW YORK—The funeral procession of Dorothy Day, her body in a pinewood coffin, moved out of Maryhouse on Third Street on the way to a requiem mass at Nativity Catholic Church, a half-block away. Someone wondered aloud why more of the poor were not present. The street, as mean as any in this cloister of harshness on the edge of the Bowery, was certainly not overflowing with homeless souls come to mourn the woman who had served them in a personal ministry for half a century. A few men and even fewer women—blank-eyed, dressed in tatters—stood in clusters, while others wandered down the street from the city shelter for derelicts, one of Manhattan's unseen hellholes. But that was all. Most of the 800 people following the coffin were either old friends of Miss Day who live outside the neighborhood or members of the Catholic Worker community who run St. Joseph's and Maryhouse, the two local shelters for the homeless.

Large numbers of the poor did not come, for a reason as obvious as the open sores on the face of a wino opposite Maryhouse: they are too busy trying to fight death themselves. To mark the passing of someone who loved them—accepted them totally by living here, raising money for them through her newspaper, *The Catholic Worker*—would, of course, make sense in the rational world of the comfortable, where public tribute to the deceased great and the seemingly great is the proper way of dealing with grief. But here on this street that is full of the homeless and jobless, death was not needed for grief. Hope gets buried every day.

If the turnout of the poor was not strong, there was also an almost total absence of Catholic officialdom. This was the genuine affront. Few of the faithful in this century were more committed than Dorothy Day to the church's teachings, both in its social encyclicals—on the distribution of wealth, the evils of the arms race—and its calls to private spirituality. She was a daily communicant at mass, rising early to read the Bible and pray the rosary.

Dorothy Day used her faith as a buffer against burnout and despair. Fittingly, it will have to be taken on faith that her life of service made a difference. She issued no progress reports on neighborhood improvement, summoned no task forces on how to achieve greater efficiency on the daily soup line.

Nor did she ever run "follow-up studies" on whether the derelicts of the Bowery renounced their drunken and quarrelsome ways. As her favorite saint, Theresa of Lisieux, taught, results don't matter to the prayerful.

On the subject of results, Dorothy Day had a philosophy of divine patience: "We continue feeding our neighbors and clothing and sheltering them, and the more we do it the more we realize that the most important thing is to love. There are several families with us, destitute to an unbelievable extent, and there, too, is nothing to do but love. What I mean is that there is no chance of rehabilitation— no chance, so far as we see, of changing them, certainly no chance of adjusting them to this abominable world about them, and who wants them adjusted, anyway?"

That was from the June, 1946, issue of the Catholic Worker newspaper, a monthly that has been a voice of pacifism and justice since 1933. The jobless and homeless are so thick in the streets that "Holy Mother City," as Miss Day called it, makes no pretense of even counting them.

It may be just as well. Counters get in the way when there is soup to be made. Even worse, getting too close to the government means a trade-off that Miss Day resisted in words and action. "The state believes in war," she said, "and, as pacifists and philosophical anarchists, we don't."

Because she served the poor for so long and with such tireless intensity, Dorothy Day had a national constituency of remarkable breadth. She was more than merely the conscience of the Left. Whether it was a young millionaire named John F. Kennedy who came to see her (in 1943) or one of the starving, she exuded authenticity.

It was so well-known that she lived among the poor—shared their table, stood in their lines, endured the daily insecurity—that the Catholic Worker became known as the one charity in which contributions truly did reach the poor. It is at St. Joseph's House, 36 E. 1st, New York 10003.

"It is a strange vocation to love the destitute and dissolute," Miss Day wrote a few years ago. But it is one that keeps attracting the young who come to the Catholic Worker as a place to brew the soup and clean the toilets, which is also the work of peacemakers. They are against military wars for sure, but their pacifism resists the violence of the economic wars. "We refuse to fight for a materialistic system that cripples so many of its citizens," the Catholic Worker has been saying for half a century.

The only Catholic bishop of the church on hand was Terence Cardinal Cooke of New York. As the procession rounded the corner from Maryhouse and went on to the sidewalk leading to the church, the scarlet vestments of the Cardinal came into view. The contrast was powerful. In a neighborhood of drab colors, where even the faces of the poor seem to be grayed with depression, the scarlet robes of the Cardinal, his scarlet skullcap, had a touch of mock comedy to them; the vestments seemed almost the costume of a clown—a clown who was lost in the saddest of landscapes.

A Catholic Worker priest, a young Dominican who works at Maryhouse and was to celebrate the mass, made the best of the situation. At the head of the procession, he shook hands with Cardinal Cooke. The Cardinal took over and prayed aloud, commending the sould of "dear Dorothy" to the mercy of the Lord. While cameramen from the Associated Press, *The Daily News* and the Religious News Service clicked away—getting the coffin in the foreground—the Cardinal finished praying in two minutes.

It was just enough time for many in the processing to think beyond the Cardinal's brilliantly hued presence at the church door. Some recalled the pacifists from the Catholic Worker who have been standing for the past few months outside Cardinal Cooke's offices uptown and in front of the splendid St. Patrick's Cathedral. They have been leafleting the churchgoers on the immorality of the arms race and pleading with the unseen Cardinal to issue a statement in favor of nuclear disarmament. In the most recent issue of *The Catholic Worker*, one of Dorothy Day's writers said sharply about the vigil at St. Patrick's last August: "We want to remember the victims of the [Hiroshima and Nagasaki] bombings, and to mourn the fact that the hierarchy of our archdiocese is so silent about nuclear disarmament, when statements from the Vatican Council, recent Popes and the U.S. Catholic Bishops Conference have been so clear in their condemnation of the arms race."

Six grandchildren of Miss Day, carrying her coffin, nodded their thanks to the Cardinal and proceeded into the church. A moment later, John Shiel went up to Cardinal Cooke. Shiel, a short, half-toothless man who has been repeatedly jailed in peace protests, is something of a lay theologian who can quote every Pope back to Boniface I on the subject of war and peace. A friend of Miss Day, he left Washington at 4 A.M. to be here for the mass.

"Hello, John," said His Eminence, who knew Shiel from his persistent lobbying for peace at the annual meetings of the hierarchy.

"Hello there, Cardinal," said Shiel. "When are you going to come out against nuclear weapons?"

His Eminence gave no answer, and shortly he was driven off in his limousine to "a previous commitment." The day before, according to a Catholic Worker staff member, Cardinal Cooke's secretary had phoned to request that the mass be held at 10 A.M., because it would then fit into the Cardinal's schedule and he could preside. But Miss Day's daughter had already decided on 11 A.M. because that was when the soup kitchen was closed for the morning break between cleaning up after breakfast and getting ready for lunch. The Cardinal's presence would be missed, the secretary was told, but with all due respect, feeding the poor came first.

Inside the church, with its unpainted cement-block walls and water-marked ceiling, the breadth of Dorothy Day's friendships was on view. In the pews were Cesar Chavez, Frank Sheed, Michael Harrington, Ed and Kathleen Guinan, Paul Moore and Father Horace McKenna, the Jesuit who for decades has been serving the poor at his own soup kitchen in Washington.

In the back of the church, after the sermon, the undertaker, a friendly man, tall and properly somber-looking, was asked about the arragements. "She was a lovely lady," he said. "We're doing this way below cost. The Worker gives us a lot of business, and besides, Miss Day is part of the community."

The undertaker said that the archdiocese was picking up the tab of $380 for opening the grave at the cemetery. If the patron saint of irony were listening in, he or she would call out to the heavenly choir: "Stop the music." During the archdiocese cemetery workers' strike in the mid-1950s, Dorothy Day was personally denounced by Cardinal Spellman for siding with the underpaid gravediggers.

After mass, a young Catholic Worker staff member, who was the candle-bearer at the head of the funeral procession, told the story of the candle—a thick white one, almost three feet tall. "We went around to neighborhood churches. We asked the sacristans for their old candle stubs that would be thrown out anyway. Then we melted them into this one large candle." Another form of brightness was present—a thought from one of Dorothy Day's books, printed on the bottom of the mass card: "We have all known the long loneliness and we have learned that the only solution is love and that love comes with community."

At about 12:30, some of the crowd drifted back to Maryhouse where lunch was being served. Pea soup was ladled from a ten-gallon kettle. Brown bread was on the table with milk, tea and oranges: enough food for all.

# Eddie Stanky                                           *1978*

SPRING HILL, Ala.—A doubleheader against Ohio State was two hours off, so Coach Eddie Stanky of the South Alabama Jaguars was receiving visitors in his tiny office beyond the right-field fence. I came as a sightseer, squinting backward to the ancient scenes of the

1940s when Stanky and his Dodgers were giving artificial respiration to a dying Brooklyn.

At Ebbets Field, he played second base like a tantrum, using bad behavior for a mitt. The athletic despotism by which he ruled his part of the infield caused him to be called "Eddie the Brat." Freud said that childhood is anything but an age of innocence, but the brattiness of Stanky was the youthful id that drove him, spikes and fists, into guileless combat against the Musials, Kiners and other archetypes of the National League. They had poise and power; Stanky had the talent of the intangibles. Branch Rickey of the Dodgers said, "He can't throw, he can't run, he can't hit—but he's the most valuable player on the team."

Today, at 60, weighing a playing-days 156 pounds and wearing his old No. 12, Stanky is regarded as one of the best coaches in college baseball. This week he is completing his ninth winning season at South Alabama, a state university outside of Mobile flowering as brightly as the spring azaleas. A believer in graduate work for his boys, he has produced an average of three players a season for the major leagues. On some days, more fans come to Jaguar Field than do Bostonians to Fenway Park or New Yorkers to Yankee Stadium.

For all of these brags, what Stanky boasts of with the most feeling has nothing to do with winning or losing. "I'm a believer in participation," he said. "The one record I care about came in a game against Vanderbilt in 1972. I played 38 men in one 9-inning game. Everyone got in. Some seasons, I've carried as many as 45 players on the team. I've never cut anyone from the squad."

I first met Stanky in 1958 when I played a round of golf with him at the Spring Hill College golf course. I was on the golf team. An off-season resident of Mobile, Stanky played regularly at the college course. He was teeing off by himself and, seeing I had no game, suggested I join him. I liked him instantly. He was manly and warm, qualities he radiated 20 years later.

As a manager in the majors for seven years—his last team was the White Sox in 1968—Stanky was known as a brooding terror who would fine his players for such offenses against cosmic probity as missing a bunt or not advancing a runner from third with fewer than two outs. As a 5-foot, 8-inch runt who force-fed himself on desire, Stanky had no peer in devising ways to get to first base. As a Chicago Cub, he began his major-league career by going to the plate and stopping a pitch with his head. He went on to discover less fracturing ways of advancing himself: He holds the National League record for most bases on balls in one season (148 in 1945). A mutt among the Rin Tin Tins of baseball, Stanky preached that "what counts is not the size of the dog in the fight but the size of the fight in the dog."

What happened to change all this, to convert a brat into a father figure? Stanky believes the mothers of his players have gotten to him: "The greatest thrill I have these days is when my players graduate and their mothers come up and embrace me for helping along their sons. There is something about a mother's tears at graduation. I can't weigh it. I'm a second parent to boys who are away from home for the first time. There's a key to every lock in a youngster. If we can find the problem, we can solve it."

For all of us almost-athletes (I almost made it in pro golf, one of my older brothers almost signed with the Yankees) few comforts in our fretful middle age should mean as much as the maturing of Eddie Stanky. As a Polish-German boy who might have gone no further than the stickball finals in the poor neighborhood of his native Philadelphia, here he is at age 60 saying that what counts is not the score. When he went to South Alabama in 1969, he told a reporter, "I considered whether a year is successful not on the won-lost record but on how many boys I have helped physically and mentally." On recruiting: "I always talk to the parents first, rather than the ballplayers. My idea is that baseball is not as important as the education that the boys can get to prepare them for a career. So I sell the parents on the education opportunity first, then the baseball."

The days of innocent aggression are well behind him, and an emotional continuity now flows between Eddie-the-Brat and Eddie-Among-the-Crying-Mothers: He is still extolling the intangibles. As a ballplayer, he told the fans that getting to first by a base on balls was the same as a long single to the outfield. Now he says that sports mean something only if the social context means more. By this he believes that games are not only a way of enjoying youth but of getting beyond it as well, so that when the other delights come along—education, raising children, tears at graduation—we will be wise enough to value them.

*Chapter 5*

# What Better Time to be a Catholic?

**I**f the Catholic Church is not today the dominant social dynamic force, it is because Catholic scholars have failed to blow the dynamite of the Church. Catholic scholars have taken the dynamite of the Church, have wrapped it up in nice phraseology, placed it in an hermetic container and sat on the lid. It is about time to blow the lid off so the Catholic Church may again become dominant social dynamic force.
                                            *—Peter Maurin*
                                            *Easy Essays*

## Among the Trappists, True Seekers                    *1980*

After shocking everyone with my plans about entering a Trappist monastery, that summer of 1960, I went about the important things—like taking bets at the country club that I would last more than a month. If I had been raised in a Jewish family, I imagine that at 22 and wanting to get some traction before lurching into the rat race, I would have gone off to an Israeli kibbutz for a few years. Or if I had had a childhood of no religion at all, I would have gone to sea on a freighter to learn a bit about life that way. Some of my classmates were joining the Peace Corps, which was taking its first recruits in the early '60s, and would spend their first post-college years in Africa or Latin America. It was a moment for choosing a route, even if, as in my case, it was to be a circular one that, in five years, would lead me out the gate that I was then entering.

I had recently finished college. I ducked the fact until I had back strain, but I knew that all I had gotten out of college was myself. Worse, I was terrified by the prospect of adulthood. I wasn't ready for it, not yet to be jailed in one of life's cells nor ready to disbelieve that T. S. Eliot was right when he said that he never wanted to grow up. In the lead-time of the subconscious, I think it takes about a decade or two for a person to look back and give a definition to his earlier acts.

Friends have told me that my going into the Trappists was a try at finding a womb, with Holy Mother Church's being warmer than any that secular society could offer. I don't discount this fully, though in debates with myself the winning argument is that of my terror of adulthood. What a frightening absurdity, I thought, to throw away my youth on making a living when, at this time of freedom for good from the academic clamor of college, living itself should begin.

I don't recall what I told the guestmaster about my reasons for wanting to try out the Trappists. Stay around for a few days, he suggested. Room was available in the guesthouse. Some help was needed on the farm, if I wanted to work. Come to Mass, if I wanted to pray.

The ifs fell into place. I stayed for about a week. Some work clothes were found for me and I shoveled manure in the cow barn half the day and climbed a manure-spreading tractor that lumbered over an alfalfa field the other half. Being assigned to the manure pile was, I suppose, "the harsh treatment" that St. Benedict spoke of, though to me, the pungent earthy smells of the farm, the freshness of the land, and the feel of my own muscles actually being used for a purpose pleasing to heaven and not mere recreation, it was a budding of joy that I can feel to this day.

For those with a taste for history and religion, 1980 promises a special kind of richness. It marks the beginning of the year-long observance of the 1,500th anniversary of the birth of St. Benedict, the Italian who set out to save his soul and ended up saving Europe. He was the right man at decidedly the wrong time.

Between 480 and his death in 547, a time when the Roman Empire was enduring the aftershocks of the sieges of Attila, Genseric and other plundering statesmen from the north, Benedict was becoming the father of western monasticism. He established a number of Christian settlements that were similar to the earlier monastic communities in the deserts of Egypt, Syria and Palestine.

He would have preferred to have been a hermit rather than a revered abbot, except he discovered that when a hermit gets good at it he attracts followers. He and his disciples settled for the slightly wider path of spirituality, being alone together. Benedictine monasteries, coming as they did when the sun was setting on the West, are credited by historians, first, with keeping European learning, culture, art and the Word alive, and then centuries later, helping it to flourish.

Inside the monasteries, the problem to be solved, aside from each person's figuring out in his own subterranean how best to cooperate with God's grace, was the eternal one of Christian living: how to be a saint if you have to live with other saints. In the 40 years that he guided his monastic communities, the best that Benedict could do was put together a few jottings that, after his death, became codified into the 73 chapters of the Holy Rule. It was to become one of the world's major historical documents, even though it was intended "for beginners."

Benedict waits to his final line in Chapter 73 to explain that. It was really a sly move because by then a disciple might have thought he had advanced a bit in the way of perfection. No, said Benedict, when you think you are getting ahead, that's a sign you've fallen back. Be content to be a beginner, just as the Holy Rule contains only "the rudiments of the religious life."

I have two copies of the Rule, one at home and the other in my office, though it's been several uncontemplative and severely secular years that I have opened either. 1980 will be a good time for another reading. It will be a moment, also, for reflecting about a few years in my life—from 1960 to 1965—when I lived under the Rule in a Trappist monastery in a rural remoteness of central Georgia.

*Chapter 58. When anyone is newly come for the reformation of his life, let him not be granted an easy entrance; but as the Apostle says, 'Test the spirits to see whether they are from God.' If the newcomer, therefore, perseveres in his knocking, and if it is seen after four or five days that he bears patiently the harsh treatment offered him and the difficulty of admission, and that he persists in his petition, then let entrance be granted him, and let him stay in the guest house for a few days.*

The guestmaster at the monastery of the Holy Spirit, one of about 90 priests and laybrothers in the community, had seen more than a few young men, devout and earnest, show up in full convincement that the Trappist life was for them. The Trappists, known officially as the Order of Cistercians of the Strict Observance, lived in the irony of being both practitioners of the hidden contemplative life and the objects of steady public attention. The writings of Thomas Merton, a New York intellectual and worldling whose account of his conversion to the monastic life, "The Seven Storey Mountain," was a best seller in the late 1940s, had created a boom in Trappist applications. For decades, America had only three Cistercian monasteries, but between 1944 and 1960 nine more would be founded to absorb the crush.

For me, the appeal of the Trappist life was in the intensity of its vision. If I was going to trouble myself to believe in God, then why not really make trouble and get into it fully by scrapping, cold turkey, as much of the nonsense that might interfere.

The prayer life was intense: daily Mass, the recitation of the Psalms in seven daily offices of Gregorian chant, constant spiritual reading and regular theological guidance from seasoned people who, despite their modest protests, were well along in the love of God and His creation.

The manual labor was strenuous. The Georgia community, settling in 1944 on a former cotton plantation amid hardshell Baptists, had spent more than a decade building a large, architecturally flawless and wondrously beautiful church. Nearly all the work—scaffolding, pouring the concrete, stonecutting, tiling—was done by one group of priests and brothers, while the other worked the fields or cared for the large herds of cows and pigs.

Crowning it all was the jewel of simplicity: a diet of mostly vegetables and fruit, rising in the country quiet well before dawn for Matins and Lauds and going to bed at dusk after Compline, and a routine that Benedict himself of the 5th century could walk into.

*Chapter 27. For the Abbot must have the utmost solicitude and exercise all prudence and diligence lest he lose any of the sheep entrusted to him. Let him know that what he has undertaken is the care of weak souls and not a tyranny over strong ones.*

No doubt about it, laughed the abbot, Father Augustine Moore, your back will be sore for a week after all that shoveling. I was speaking to him about the possibility of coming into the community. It was a moment for an on-high Holy Joe sermon, but the abbot, a man untouched by pretensions, spoke simply about the life of grace and the spiritual rewards (to be found in cooperating with God's will). He had been through this many times before—counseling the young innocent Alyoshas who want to abandon the world and capture the truth of Father Zossima—but nothing he said to me was outworn. His words gave life to the oldest of truths: We are on earth for a purpose, the Church provides the sacraments and we serve each other in the mystery of our vocations.

Fr. Augustine wasn't scornful of the world beyond the cloister. I was surprised. The Trappists had a right, if anyone did, to put their noses high into the air, so reeking I thought, had American society become with its malodorous hedons and materialists. But if Fr. Augustine, I was to learn then and numberless times after, had had a temperature rise, it was over the grumblers and fault-finders who let themselves be contaminated by hard judgments about others.

I was only a newcomer, with no more than squatter's rights in this spiritual territory, but he welcomed me with deep priestly kindness. In the five years I was to spend under his guidance—his expansive Irish manner, his appetite for humor and a quietude of having access to God's mercy—I came to depend on him as a practical lookout in much of what I was searching for.

Go home for awhile, he suggested. Think about things and come back in about a month. I had no desire to be a priest, I told him. Which meant that I would go into the novitiate as a laybrother. Fine, he said. In many ways, the brothers had the freer life; more time in the fields and fewer obligations to structured prayer. Manual labor can be the purest form of prayer, he said, although it depends, as in everything, what kind of disposition the individual brings to it.

*Prologue to the Rule. "And so we are going to establish a school for the service of the Lord. In founding it we hope to introduce nothing harsh or burdensome. But if a certain strictness results from the dictates of equity for the amendment of vices or the preservation of charity, do not be at once dismayed and fly from the way of salvation, whose entrance cannot but be narrow."*

By reputation, the Trappists were known as the church's strictest order. It welcomed God's fools but not if they fooled around with the distractions that others of the church's orders allowed themselves. Join the Jesuits or Dominicans for that, where, like the priest in "Morte D'Urban" by J. F. Powers, the good life could be had by those whose wallets carried both holy cards and credit cards.

As braced as I was for the penitential severities of the Trappist regimen—the lean diet, the absence of newspapers, the silence (maintained by a sign language that a French abbot devised centuries ago to keep the brothers from carping about him behind his back), the unchanging schedule—I spent the first two years realizing what a subtle practical joke, at least in the matter of externals, Benedict had enjoyed. What was hard about any of this?

Life without the New York Times or Newsweek wasn't a penance. The hard beds were healthy. The vegetarian diet was the essence of physical fitness. The silence was a relief. The manual labor—milking cows twice a day and pitching silage in between—was invigorating.

And best of all, the company was good. The fathers and brothers in the monastery were a robust mix of intellectuals and workers. I could hardly not delight in being among them. A few were eccentric—as perhaps I was to them—but benignly so. Many were second-career people who came here after wrestling for years with the classic "there's-something-missing" feeling. This included a former Latin teacher from Philadelphia, a social worker who helped run a flophouse for homeless men, a construction worker who had been to Saudi Arabia with an oil company, a New York financier who was a pal of Toots Shor and Sherman Billingsly, a priest who had been a missionary in Bolivia. They were men, surely, who were investing a lot of their time into reflecting on "utlimate realities," and on that holy account they had rights to be what Flannery O'Connor, a frequent visitor to the monastery, called "Christ-ridden."

But they weren't, at least not in my line of vision. The love of God had become so sensible and reasonable a passion with them that it wasn't necessary to lock away their emotions in some vault of the supernatural. Human warmth and friendliness were compatible with the self-abandonment that a lifelong commitment necessarily demanded.

Everyone has incommunicable parts in himself—spaces for privacy—but it was a major surprise for me to learn that large amounts of other personalities in the monastery became vividly obvious (and in that way lovable) in the close and constant contact of community life. An old priest told me how his sensitivity to others could grow. He could tell, he said, merely by noticing how the man in the choir stall next to him moved his hand and arm to turn the page of the large chant psalter whether he was depressed that particular day or whether his heart was light.

Enjoying the company of these good men was a major easement of any strictness that Benedict speaks of. If I was supposed to be undergoing a piercing to my depths of all earthly pleasures, I should have also felt guilty about enjoying other parts of life; the exquisitely beautiful Gregorian chant, which was sung at the daily High Mass, or the quality of the library by which I was able to form a personal reading program of more than 200 books a year, or of being close to the land and the animals that pastured on it. One of the writers I was discovering then was Rabbi Abraham Heschel, who wrote that "wonder is a form of thinking. It is not the beginning of knowledge but an act that goes beyond knowledge; it does not come to end when knowledge is acquired; it is an attitude that never ceases. There is no answer in the world to man's radical amazement."

*Chapter 53. Let all guests who arrive be received like Christ, for He is going to say, 'I came as a guest, and you received me.' And to all let due honor be shown, especially to the domestics of the faith and to pilgrims.*

I thought at first that if indeed the fathers and brothers were cut off from the world they were like the blind Milton, who learned to see more than most men of healthy sight. But they weren't cut off. 1960 and 1965 were the years of Pope John XXIII's renewal, when the old protectedness of Catholicism was forced to give way to new risks. It was to create considerable bitterness among many of those who gave their lives to the church but who suddenly saw the church leaders changing some of the rules. Supposedly the renewalists were bringing together irreconcilables that could only destroy the faith.

That wasn't true, but the feelings behind the falsehood were still authentic. Fr. Augustine relished the developments of the second Vatican Council. The New Yorker articles about the council were read at the table. Protestant and Jewish theologians would come to the monastery to share their views, among them Thomas Altizer of Emory University in Atlanta. He was the "death of God" professor in the early 1960s, a thinker whose reputation has since suffered death pains of its own. Writers came: Flannery O'Connor, who lived a few hours south in Milledgeville, and Ignazio Silone, the Italian novelist. Journalists like Ralph McGill and Eugene Patterson of The Atlanta Constitution were regular visitors. Patterson, now the editor of The St. Petersburg Times, would come out in work clothes and throw himself into a weekend of manual labor. Black pastors of rural Baptist churches were invited to speak of their ministry. When some of these churches were firebombed and burned by racists, Fr. Augustine asked a team of brothers to design stained-glass windows for the rebuilt structures. The same brothers left the monastery to install the windows.

All of this was new. To some it was the dangerous persiflage that threatened to turn the place into a fun house or a monsignor's rectory. To my taste, it was a bright opportunity for the order to move away from the days of French Jansenism and begin reviving the tradition of a monastery being a center of learning. For centuries, it had been that way, when the sacramental life was ambient to the arts and culture of the larger society.

In looking back, perhaps my appetites were too wild for this renewal. I know that I was surely being revived, at least intellectually. I couldn't get over the beauty of the Old Testament, nor of the force in the social encyclical of the modern papacy. As an additional exercise, every year, I would take a different writer and read every one of their works: Dostoevski, Tolstoy, Saul Bellow, Flannery O'Connor and Shaw. I had language books sent to me, with a new language studied every year: German, Hebrew, Mandarin, Spanish and Norwegian. I have long forgotten most of these tongues, though I did stick with the most foreign language of all, English. I studied the dictionary and tried to learn a new word every day. I wrote in a journal for an hour a day. The prime opportunity for reading came while I worked in the dairy. I was one of four who milked a hundred Jerseys every day. I discovered that when the milking machines were on the cows, I had about eight to 10 minutes of idle time. I could read four or five pages of "The Idiot" or "Wise Blood" in those moments. After a couple of years of this, I knew which cows were the slowest to drain. I would herd them into my section of the barn, which meant that while the machines milked the cows I had a longer time to milk the books.

I asked my confessor once whether he thought my taking the slow-drainers for myself was a sinful deed, since it left someone else more work to do with the quick-finishers. He was a priest of expansive theology, and he said no. In fact, it was a little Biblical. You're just being a good shepherd with a peaceful flock: you know them and they know you.

The guests I looked forward to were my mother, aunts and cousins. Families were allowed one five-day visit a year. One aunt, for whom only hermits were lower than Trappists in God's plan for the world, wrote counseling letters to me during my first year to be sure I didn't lose the use of my vocal cords. Go to the woods everyday and talk to the birds, she said.

When she came down from New York for the first visit, I thought I'd give her a scare. I walked into the guest house and started talking to her—except I made no sounds. Only my lips moved. My aunt turned ashen, as if all her fears had come true. "It's happened," she called out. "He can't talk!"

Some of the visitors to Holy Spirit would have strained the charity of even St. Benedict. These included a couple of generals and colonels from Ft. Benning. They had come to the monastery, through the abbot's benevolence, to tell the community about the Vietnam war, which was just then beginning. How pompous and cocksure they were in their plans for keeping the peace in Southeast Asia. I would have been happy if they preserved the peace merely in the monastery barnyard. They would fly up from Ft. Benning in helicopters, coming in low every time over the cows in the south pasture. I was bringing the herd in one afternoon when the choppers appeared over the horizon. As they came near, the cows, as terrified as I had ever seen them, stampeded across the pasture heeding nothing but the impulse to escape this noisy monster in the sky. A few of the beasts, their eyes looking up in blank frenzy, careened full gallop into the barb wire fence, gashing their legs and udders in one bloody tangle. That gave the generals a good laugh. One of them joked about it later.

Standing near the fence, I watched the helicopter come down. I caught sight of a general looking at me. I raised my arm, bulged my muscle, and gave him a vehement finger. I wanted to call out. Like my Trappist piety? I prayed to the Virgin Mary that his eyes were strong enough to see me.

Inside, the army men took over the chapter room. After listening to them explain how they would be doing God's work in Vietnam— and asking the brothers to pray for their patriotic exercise, no less— I tried to rally some anti-war feelings among a few of those who were close to me. I made little headway. There was no sense of it. Catholicism isn't one of the peace churches, like the Quakers or Mennonites. Its theologians argue the just war theory. It ignores its pacifists like Daniel Berrigan and Dorothy Day. It even honors warriors, like St. Bernard the Cistercian abbot who helped preach one of the Crusades. It shouldn't have surprised me that, with all this at work, I was about the only one in the community who was sickened by the talk of the generals. The country was in for a fine war, I remember thinking, in 1962 with the first casualties a couple of meek Jersey cows in rural Georgia.

*Chapter 51. A brother who is sent out on some business and is expected to return to the monastery that same day shall not presume to eat while he is out, even if he is urgently requested to do so by any person whomsoever, unless he has permission from his Abbot.*

I had done so well shoveling manure and milking cows that after four years of it, Fr. Augustine elevated me to the position of cook. I relished the chance. The brother before me was on the somber side. It came out in his cooking. Boiled potatoes and collard greens one day, collard greens and boiled potatoes the next. The third day the soup was Leftover Special. Skilled hands could ladle up only the broth, missing the potatoes and greens.

"Liven things up a little," the abbot said. "Some imaginative cooking would be good for morale."

Cooking for 90 meant multiplying my recipes by about 12 if the servings were for eight or by 22 if for four. I learned that exactitude often didn't matter that much, because the ovens themselves were relaxed about it all. One was at 350° when the thermometer said 425° and the other was at 450° when the reading was 300°.

I began serving up what I thought were zestful meals. Potatoes could be German fried, French fried, mashed, scalloped or pancaked. I would heave some diced onions or peppers over them, and sometimes sprinkle cheese or parsley over that, if it were a liturgical feast day.

Morale did indeed pick up, I was told. It may have peaked the Sunday I served strawberry pizza. It was in late May, when the strawberry crop was being harvested. I had about 20 large pizzas coming out of the ovens when the garden brother piled in with a dozen bushels of strawberries. I could make only so much jam out of them all, I thought. Why not do some more heaving and put strawberries on top of the pizzas? At first, it looked odd—bright strawberries amid the tomato sauce, mozzarella and parmesan, peppers, onions, the sliced carrots and the eggplant chips. But I put the pizzas back into the oven for five minutes to take the color out of the strawberries. I doused them with sauce and they mingled well.

The older members of the community, particularly a few Europeans who had joined the order in the 1930s and were unfamiliar with American cuisine, ate at the strawberry pizzas none the wiser. The younger members, Pizza Hut veterans, congratulated me, one of them suggesting that I could make millions for the monastery if I wrote a cookbook. Forget Trappist bread, he said. Let's market our strawberry pizza.

As electrified as the dining room was that night, it was nothing to a scene some time later when one of the old European fathers was in Atlanta for a visit to his doctor. It was late afternoon and he stopped into an Italian restaurant for supper. He ordered pizza. At the end of the meal, the owner of the place, honored to have this man of God eating his food, asked the priest how the meal was going. The pizza is excellent, the father said, but where were the strawberries?

*Chapter 58. He who is to be received shall make a promise before all in the oratory of his stability and of the reformation of his life and of obedience. This promise he shall make before God and His Saints, so that if he should ever act otherwise, he may not know that he will be condemned by Him whom he mocks. Of this promise let him draw up a petition in the name of the Saints whose relics are there and of the Abbot who is present.*

Near the end of five years, the time for permanent vows approached. I had decided not to take them. I had the kindly counsel of Fr. Augustine, as well as a psychiatrist from Atlanta who had been coming to the monastery to hold discussions about mental health and the spiritual life. The psychiatrist, who has since died, believed that the most difficult aspect of the comtemplative life was not the supposed austerity, or the solitude or the manual labor. It was the absence of seeing results. Faith in God, he told me, was easy compared with keeping alive a faith that your daily actions—so much of them linked with worship and prayers—actually made a difference. Only a few special souls can throw bread on the water and not think of its return.

The psychiatrist was talking of classic detachment, a state of spiritual mind located at the core of the religious instinct. He believed not only that I didn't have it then but never would. It was like that for most people, he thought. Even for the rare few who do spend all of their days uncorrupted atop one spiritual mountain or another, the taste for results is never stilled. One of the seemingly sainted can be detached from almost everything and yet still have gone nowhere. He is detached but he can't resist enjoying the pleasures of *knowing* that he is detached.

The psychiatrist, a well-read man who didn't share the prevailing analytic idea that someone who takes time for serious religion needs some therapy lest his life really get out of balance, thought that too many people had taken vows to the Trappist life out of a spirit of toughing it out. That could be destructive to the personality. He believed in temporary vocations. A person comes in, stays a while and leaves before taking on a lifetime commitment. That is one of the modern functions of a monastery, to be a type of graduate school where instead of working on a thesis, you can work on yourself. Few havens like this are available. If you have a permanent calling to the life, good. If not, that's all right, too. You were generous, to yourself and others, to spend a few years trying it out. The idea of "answering the call" was too narrow. A person doesn't have a vocation, he is a vocation.

Much of this confirmed my own leanings. Serenity, in rock-depth, was assuredly here, but the surface of life still had its pull. Even in the beginning, I came to look forward to trips with some of the brothers to the local town of Conyers every three months to give blood to the Red Cross. A small newsstand sat across the street from the blood bank. After giving my pint, and before the others finished giving theirs, I sprinted to the store to read through the newspapers and magazines. I was such a dry well for news that I asked the Red Cross nurse if I could give blood every month. She said I was already setting a Georgia state record with four pints a year.

A second pull also involved leaving the property. Often at dusk during my last year, with everyone else going off to bed, I would get a pickup truck and drive it around to the kitchen. I loaded it with food—10-gallon cans of milk, dozens of loaves of bread, bushels of vegetables and fruit, eggs and jam. I slipped out through a side entrance and found my way to the back hills where poor families were living in shacks. I brought them food. Some would invite me to eat with them. During the meals, usually livened by some old-timer's tales of how he and other black folks once picked cotton for 10 cents a day, I caught myself thinking that this was backwards. Here I was, living what the church proclaimed as a life of austerity and poverty, and yet having as many securities as anyone could want—access to good health care, a library, all the necessary food, clothing and shelter. And looking me in the face in those shacks were God's forgotten who truly were austere and poor.

I was troubled by the contrast, though I tried to keep clear of any hard judgments about those in the community who didn't feel as I did. In fact, food was always available at the gatehouse for any of the poor who could come for it. I knew also that the differences between direct and indirect service to society were as old, and as mysterious, as the story of Mary and Martha. For all any of us know, contemplatives like the Trappists—the ones who appear to be "unproductive"—may be the only reason that God bothers with this planet at all. Surely the rule of St. Benedict enjoys special favor, lasting these 1,500 years and as fresh today as at its first reading in the mid-500s at Monte Cassino.

In the 20 years since I went to Holy Spirit, and the 15 since I left, I have kept up with many of those who also came and went. Some had taken vows, others, like me, didn't. Whatever, all of them look on it as a resource period on which they still draw. When I run into college friends who went off to Peru in the '60s with the Peace Corps, or when I talk with people who did the kibbutz number or shipped out on freighters, I listen closely to hear if they also recall those experiences as resource ventures. Some do, but not in the tones of wonder and appreciation that mark the memories of the Trappist alumni.

# Why Aren't We a Peace Church?          *1982*

If I weren't a Catholic, and if I didn't believe that the chances for nuclear war have never been greater, I would likely be saying, as are many others, that the Catholic bishops are in over their heads when they introduce morality into the politics of nuclear arms.

To me, the bishops are not yet ankle deep in these waters of controversy.

In the essentials, their proposed pastoral letter is a needed statement of defiance to temporal powers—the Reagan administration, Congress and the Pentagon—that they cannot expect to keep making political decisions in a moral-free context.

But the letter, reasoned and cautious, lacks fire. It has none of the anger of men outraged that national security has become the new idolatry. They do not say that the Golden Calf of nuclear weaponry is in need of quick smashing. It is as though, in fear of being dismissed as incendiaries, the bishops step one pace forward and then one backward. Who needs blessed inaction?

They say, for example, that "we have judged immoral even the threat to use [nuclear] weapons. At the same time, we have held that the possession of nuclear weapons may be tolerated as deterrents while meaningful efforts are under way to achieve multilateral disarmament." This is a contradiction. To possess is to threaten. Are the bishops unaware of the history of weaponry? Every crossbow, saber, cannon or bomb devised by one nation has eventually been used against another.

This contradiction arises naturally from ambivalences built into the text. One of the stated intents is "to contribute to the public-policy debate about the morality of war." The bishops call for "public scrutiny" of nuclear politics, and ask for "limits" in the goverment's nuclear leanings.

This mildness would not stand out if in other questions of life and death the bishops also shied from moral firmness. To their credit, they don't. When the issue is abortion, they do not sprinkle their texts with "at the same times" nor do they modestly announce their wish to "contribute to the public-policy debate." Instead, and rightly in my view, they say that abortion is killing, no matter how many seemingly humane justifications an individual can make for having or performing one.

If there is no equivocation when the killing of the pre-born is involved, why not when the potential killing of tens of millions of people is at stake? When the bishops opposed the Reagan administration's sending of military aid to El Salvador, where the government kills its own people, they did not call for mere "limits."

One reason that the church's leaders move falteringly in their advocacy of peace is that they are uncomfortable in this new role. Until now, bishops have been builders of schools, hospitals, churches and seminaries. They have been able ministers of God's pork barrel. That work has been skilled and beneficial. But now a number of younger bishops are asking the obvious: Why put up buildings of peace in one generation, if they are to be leveled by nuclear war in the next?

American Catholicism, with a membership of 51 million, is still far away from being a peace church. The tentative moves toward nuclear pacifism do little to alter the church's other massive connections to the military. ROTC flourishes on Catholic campuses, Catholic colleges accept money for military research, seminaries train future military chaplains.

None of this is found among such peace churches as the Mennonites and Quakers. The challenge for the bishops is to accelerate, not slow, their efforts to begin a disengagement from military values. Nuclear war is only the extreme extension of those values. What risk, or sacrifice of status, is involved in saying no to a future holocaust?

But there is risk in saying no to the decisions that lead to conventional war, or no to the paying of taxes that buy weapons, or trying to educate the faithful and the whole country that Christianity in its origins was a religion of absolute pacifism.

A few bishops have been pushing hard to align the church to its original and enduring ideals. An immense educational program will be needed merely to get across the point that organized non-violent resistance is not weakness but a rational and effective way of settling disputes by other means than killing people. For this, the bishops should expect scorn and dismissal. They are getting a bit of this now, and it is a sure sign they are on to something prophetic.

# Bless Maryknoll                                           1981

MARYKNOLL, N.Y.—She is her sisters' keeper, the president of the Maryknoll missioners, an order that for 60 years has gone to exotic cultures and mysterious lands. But little in Sister Melinda Roper's training for the mission fields prepared her for the exotic and mysterious ways of the Senate Foreign Relations Committee.

She went there the other day at the invitation of one of the natives, Sen. Claiborne Pell (D-R.I.). In the name of God, and in the interest of getting a few profane facts on the record, Sister Melinda described how Maryknoll came to be in El Salvador—a local bishop asked four sisters to come work in the rural areas of the diocese in 1967—and how the last days of Sister Maura Clark, one of two Maryknoll sisters and one of four churchwomen slain in December in El Salvador, were spent. She read part of a letter from Sister Maura, written in November: "Being here ... and working for the refugees, getting them to refugee centers, obtaining and transporting food for the hungry *campesios*, displaced, hiding or in the organized groups, has its sweetness, consolation, special Grace and it is certainly a gift. Things grow tense and scarier. The way innocent people, families, children are machetied and ... thrown and left for the buzzards to feed on them, seems unbelievable, but it happens every day."

Sister Melinda then told the committee about her dealings with the State Department since the death of the sisters. An edge came into her voice when she said that "we have noted lack of communication, defensiveness, evasion and even contradictions. Furthermore, there have been innuendos as to the circumstances of the women's death. Why have two high officials in the present administration found it necessary—directly or by implication—to plant seeds of distrust and suspicion regarding the personal integrity of the women and their mission?"

A State Department spokesman said, "concerning the charge that we have smeared the nuns, we have already pointed out that this is not true." Sister Melinda's testimony was forceful, but after the hearings she was unsettled. The proceedings began at 10 a.m., but the first witness—Robert White, the former ambassador to El Salvador—went on until nearly 1 p.m. Eight senators came to hear White. After a five-minute break, only two senators returned to hear her testify.

After the hearings, Sister Melinda said she felt frustrated and disappointed. She had come to tell the committee about the Maryknolls who had in recent months become a name in the news. She wanted to tell her side of who they are and what they believe in. In the end, though, she confessed to having little sense that the committee shared her outrage about the State Department's treatment of Maryknoll following the killings.

The next day at the Maryknoll motherhouse—a pastoral enclave on a greening hill outside of Ossining, N.Y., overlooking the Hudson River in northern Westchester County where Washington Irving wrote his Sleepy Hollow stories—Sister Melinda confessed to being a bit bewildered by the recent attacks on her order. Aside from the speculation of Alexander Haig—that the sisters may have been running a roadblock and gunned down in the crossfire—and the suggestion of U.S. Ambassador to the United Nations Jeane Kirkpatrick that "the nuns were not just nuns, they were political activists" the order had been criticized in a National Review editorial that cited two earlier columns by Michael Novak.

On March 20, Ronald Reagan's favorite magazine stated the Maryknoll's leadership "espouses Christian Marxism in its grossest forms, inoculates its rank and file with these delusions, then sets them up like ducks in Central American shooting galleries. It does not lessen our abhorrence of murderous thugs to describe the order's conduct as despicable."

The editorial extensively quoted Novak's attacks on Maryknoll priests and the books they publish. The columns appeared, said the magazine, "three months before the slayings" of the sisters. That was an error. They ran in September and October 1979, 15 months before. Novak, a contributing editor to National Review who served recently as the Reagan administration's chief delegate to the U.N. Human Rights Commission in Geneva, said in his first column that, "The Marxists are plainly riding high" at Maryknoll. In a second piece, he said that "Maryknoll has been promoting Christian Marxism." With pride, he wrote about "a marvelous woman in Unionville, Ind., who stopped sending money to Maryknoll since reading my [first] column."

Novak said, "I was upset that National Review raised these questions at this time, and that it misstated the dates by a year."

Aside from issuing a slightly irreverent sigh that three out of four of these critics are Catholics—Haig, Buckley and Novak—Sister Melinda said that she didn't have much taste for point-by-point rebuttals.

"We're not going to be defensive," she said, taking a seat in a small conference room down the hall from the entrance to the convent. She was wearing denim slacks and jacket over a red blouse. She entered Maryknoll in 1957 at 19, after attending public and parochial schools in Chicago, and then two years at Michigan State. Most of her mission experience has been in Central America, including teaching school in Guatemala and parish work in the Yucatan. She was elected president of her order in 1978, becoming only its fifth superior since the Maryknoll sisters were founded in 1912. It's official name is the Catholic Foreign Mission Society of America.

"It's all right for our critics to get after us," she began, in what was to be a long and relaxed conversation in the company of two sisters and a visitor. "But then they will also have to get after the official Church in the United States. People keep trying to put us in a politically radical position. But the Gospel necessarily has political implications. Certain people will view the stance of the Church in this country on El Salvador as getting mixed up on politics. But I don't think that's the case at all... Take Jesus. They had to make him a political enemy in order to kill him. To eliminate him, the Romans had to be convinced that he was an enemy of the state. You have that dynamic working throughout history. Look at any of the martyrs of the early church. They were killed not because of their belief in Jesus Christ. They were killed because that was turned around and interpreted as a political act against the state. From the perspective of the state, they were political enemies. From their own conviction, from their own motivation, they were not. I would say it's the same with us. We will get accused by the state and other people of meddling. We're not meddling. Feeding the hungry is a basic, rock-bottom Gospel value. But it is also a very crucial economic, political and international issue.

"When you get to the issue of feeding the hungry, unless it's an emergency crisis, usually handouts are not the way to go. When you get to know the poor, understand and love them, you know—not just theoretically— that they have their own dignity and their own desire to live as responsible people. They don't want handouts. Then you begin to touch on why can't the poor produce enough food for their families, to have their own houses and land. And as soon as you touch that, you touch the structures of society and you touch political situations, the economic order. The whole thing. In that sense, yes, that's very much our realm of activity. And that will get interpreted in a thousand different ways."

One of the other women in the room as Sister Judy Noone. She is from Alexandria, Va., the daughter of a Washington tax lawyer and recently returned from 10 years of working with the poor in Bolivia. She said that although the deaths of the Maryknollers in El Salvador and the ideological attacks before and after from the

American right were a shock, they were not altogether unexpected. In 1978, the general assembly of the order said that "as participants in the mission of Jesus Christ, we choose to be in solidarity with the poor and enter into the universal struggle for justice." This statement was followed by a "list of implications" based on what could happen if the sisters lived according to that philosophy. "I'm afraid that much of what we thought might happen, has happened," said Sister Melinda. "Being labeled Marxist, (the) persecution, torture, death."

During lunch, Sister Melinda was joined by six other sisters. The dining room—low-ceilinged, large, with about 40 bare wooden tables—was adorned with a five-foot crucifix on the front wall and religious pictures on the side walls. About 100 sisters were taking their midday Lenten meal. A few of the elderly ones wore the traditional Maryknoll habit, a black headpiece that comes to a peak over the forehead, and gray and black robes that reach to the floor. These siters were exceptions, with most wearing conventional lay clothing. A few were in jeans and sport shirts.

Many in the room, like Sister Judy Noone, were home for a two- or three-year period of service or reflection at the motherhouse. Most will return eventually to the missions. Although the order is now linked in the public's consciousness with El Salvador, it has never had more than six sisters there at any one time. It remains heavily concentrated in the Far East and the Pacific as it was when the original group of sisters went into China in 1921. Many in the order—Maryknoll bishops, priests and sisters—were to be imprisoned or persecuted by Communist regimes.

According to the latest tally, 49 sisters are in Hong Kong, 44 in the Philippines, 28 in Japan, 30 in South Korea, 28 in Taiwan, 10 in Indonesia and 83 in the Central Pacific. In Africa, Tanzania has 38, Kenya 18 and the Sudan 4. Bolivia, Chile, Guatemala each have 35.

The order was founded in 1912 by Molly Rogers, an Irish-American woman who organized six other brave spirits—most of them Irish-American also—who had to wait eight years for Vatican approval. It was the first Catholic missionary group in America. Even today, an Irish flavor graces the order. A current booklet of photographs and essays on mankind runs keep with such names as Fogarty, McNally, Downey, McCormack, Kelly, Keegan, Murphy.

At table, the talk turned to the current demographics of the order. In 1960, the entering group of novices totaled 174. In 1980, only seven entered. In the mid-1960s, the membership reached over 1,600. It is now about 980. More than 250 of the sisters are between the ages of 50 and 59, while fewer than 25 are between 20 and 29. Three times as many are over 60 as are under 40. The average age is 55.

Not a lot of worry was expressed about the decrease of vocations. What is happening at Maryknoll reflects the condition of many—perhaps all—religious orders. But benefits have come also. Those joining now tend to be more mature, more educated and more apt to have professional skills. An example of the latter was a sister across the dining room who joined Maryknoll in 1978. She is a physician with three years residency in general surgery at a Miami hospital. She has already served in Central America and will return there shortly. When asked about her being a physician, she said that medicine happened to be her skill, but that every other sister in the order had a special skill as well.

The order had its share of organizational turmoil in the late 1960s, though the tension between conservatives and liberals trying to define "renewal" did not split Maryknoll as it did, say, the Glenmary Sisters in Appalachia. In Sister Melinda's life, a conflict in renewal came when she and two other sisters were thrown out of their Central American parish—by a Maryknoll priest who was pastor. "It was the old story of the clerics, of who's in control of this place," she recalled. "At that time, and I don't know to what degree today, women didn't have any juridical power within the church. The reasons for removing us were that I was seen as a heretic regarding the doctrine of grace and also because we treated the people as equals. It was made very clear that you don't do that."

Down the road from the motherhouse—which is a term from the old days, "center" being favored now—is the headquarters of the Maryknoll priests. The main building, an immense multi-winged structure of five stories built with upswept roofs in the style of Chinese architecture, dominates 100 acres of prime Westchester County real estate which was bought for pennies in 1911. Latin inscriptions over doorways recall an era of piety long gone but still respected by the priests.

For one thing, many of the oldtimers are here. "I'm 150 years old," joked Edward McGurkin, a witty man who still wears the Roman collar and looks almost like a visiting Anglican vicar. "I'm 75 years in age, 50 years a priest and 25 years a bishop."

The kindly prelate is revered at Maryknoll as the real article. In 1941, he was taken prisoner by the Japanese in Manchuria. His imprisonment lasted three years and eight months. He returned home briefly and then was assigned to Tanzania, where he was raised to the episcopacy. In 1975, in a startling move rarely seen in church politics, he voluntarily turned over his office to a native black priest. He was the first priest McGurkin had ordained in Africa.

The bishop, a tall man with rough, immense hands that tell of years of manual labor in the bush, is a reservoir of stories. One of them has a special poignancy in light of the charges being made that Maryknoll has gone Marxist: Years after when he was the rector again of that seminary in Manchuria, "the Communists came in and dispersed the sisters. They begin a persecution of the church that was to last a long time. The sisters went underground. I received a letter not long ago saying that the surviving sisters are now back together and living in the community. The political situation has relaxed a little, it seems. The faith has been kept. Christianity is strong in many parts of China."

The Maryknoll vicar general is Father John Halbert. Wearing an open shirt, a sweater and rumpled trousers that had the mark of community property about them, Halbert was elected to the No. 2 spot in the order after returning in 1978 from five years, in El Salvador. His first three months in Santa Ana were devoted to visiting the homes of the poor. "I was trying to find out what they needed," he recalled, "and how they saw life. Their need as they expressed it was for a home and work. We began a housing project for 1,200 families. They built it, they did all the work." In time, Halbert says, he aroused the wrath of the Salvadoran government. "I was taken in for questioning. The accusation was that I worked with the poor, that I said mass in their homes, that I taught in their homes and that I took care of a tubercular unit in a hospital that was in the parish. That was considered sedition." Some time later, when the priest went into a local jail to seek the release of a parish member, he was told by prisoners that Archbishop Romero, eventually to be murdered while saying mass, had just been on the radio defending him. When Romero was killed in March 1980, Halbert, then back in New York, went to his funeral in San Salvador.

Halbert was ordained in 1959. He recalls that in his seminary days the prevalent thinking centered on being priests first and missioners second. A few years later, the roles shifted: They were roughly equal. Today he believes the emphasis is on mission: "This is not to the detriment of the priesthood. It's a recognition of a variety of ministries. Twenty years ago, the priest, at least in our culture, was seen as the answer to everything. He stood as the educated one who could be trusted. Now we're finding that many others can do some of the work that priests were doing. At Maryknoll, we identify as closely as we can with the poor. God's saving grace is with the poor. The priests' work takes on the flavor of the needs of the local church."

A stronger feeling of resentment against the current attacks seemed to be present among the Maryknoll priests than among the sisters. "Haig and others made what we think are irresponsible statements that put our men and women in danger," said Halbert. The statements "were unfounded from their own reports based on the investigations of the U.S. government, even to the extent that there were private apologies to us by members of the administration who didn't want to be named. That's putting our men and women in jeopardy. It's tough enough to die for Jesus Christ, but I assuredly don't want to die for a stupid statement of a government official."

One of the major concerns of the Maryknoll Fathers is their missionary work in the United States. It is an educational effort that seeks to counteract a lack of interest in global poverty and what America—its citizens and its policy-makers—should be doing about it. Maryknoll currently has offices in 19 cities from which priests go into parishes, conduct seminars and write. In Washington, three Maryknoll priests run the order's Justice and Peace Office.

The director is Father Edward Killackey. He was born in Yonkers, N.Y., has a brother and uncle in Maryknoll and spent 18 of his 25 years in the priesthood in Tanzania, Kenya and Uganda. For a while, he was in the diocese of Bishop McGurkin. In a corridor outside the hearing room of the Senate Foreign Relations Committee on the day Sister Melinda was testifying, he told of his work visiting parishes and schools in Maryland, Virginia, the District of Columbia and North and South Carolina.

"There has been a gradual evolving in the responsibilities of missionary orders like Maryknoll," he began. "We are transnational, and that's part of our difficulty. We upset people because of it. We've brought, say, the charity and mercy of the American people—through medicine, hospitals, schools—to contries over- seas. Suddenly, because of the American presence and realities overseas or because of the level of injustice that may be maintained or sustained by us, we find ourselves moving from charity and mercy to charity, mercy and justice. We are seeing a growing militarization of human society. We are seeing poor people who have absolutely no participatory power in the decisions of their own lives. And ironically enough, the only place to which indigenous peoples overseas can come to exercise responsible participation is the Church. These people are the ones who told us to emphasize the social teachings of the Church to organize people to achieve human rights."

Fr. Killackey acknowledged that his own thinking has evolved. "I thought at one time that the problems of the world were cultural. I now find that they are economic. Economics is an export from this country, and to the realities you have in Chile, the Philippines, Taiwan, South Korea. We see patterns of economic aggression. It is an invasive presence. For Maryknoll, we have to respond to that."

This response, if examined closely, reveals nothing more than what Popes John XXIII and Paul VI were teaching in their encyclicals *Pacem in Terris* and *Populorum Progresso*. In the pages of Maryknoll magazine, the order's monthly that has a 1.3 million circulation and is an almost annual prize-winner in Catholic journalism circles, the thinking of these popes is reflected.

Some readers like it, some don't. Two recent letters-to-the-editor typify the split. "While I have long supported your mission endeavor," says the first, "I am increasingly distressed by your antagonistic and implied or explicit criticism of the U.S.A. Apart from being counterproductive, this attitude strikes me as negative and somewhat superficial. The modern world is of very recent origin and the ills in it were in many cases the fruit of very rapid growth, and many agencies in our society are struggling to ameliorate them. What about a more thoughtful, essentially charitable approach?"

A second reader says that "I am always surprised when some readers complain that you are too anticapitalist or put so much 'blame' on developed countries. Today in Nicaragua, El Salvador, Guatemala, the Church has sided with justice, cried out against brutality. What side do the developed countries take? ... I am glad to read Maryknoll because you share information about the people of the world, their struggles and cultures. A lot of this information is left out of pro-free enterprise newspapers."

One reason Maryknoll's leaders are not on the defensive about their current actions and philosophy is that a fair number of others are aggressively speaking out for them. Monsignor George Higgins, for decades the intellectual pillar of the U.S. Catholic Conference on issues of social justice, writes in the current issue of Maryknoll magazine that the Order's publishing house, "Orbis (Books) ranks near the very top of the list of Maryknoll's many enviable contributions to church and society."

Another defense comes from the influential National Catholic Reporter:

"The Maryknollers, bravely, with millions of other Christians, have taken the plunge into (an) extremely stormy and dangerous sea. They are striking out boldly, actively. Their experiences should not polarize the Catholic church. Rather they should mobilize us to intensify our own experiences of Christian witness, always paying special attention, as the Maryknollers do, to the poorest among us."

As he was preparing for Easter, Fr. Halbert said neither he nor many others at Maryknoll were overly concerned about the current controversies or what they might mean for the future. With the median age for priests at 53, "most of us," he said, "have 15 to 20 active years left. Then we'll start dying off. We'll really be in trouble. But it's not really important. If Maryknoll does its mission and we die, something else in the Church will pick it up. The sad thing would be not to do our work well. If we do well and we die, then that's God's plan."

# Whose Church Is It? 1983

We used to be Roman Catholics. Now, it is said, we are cultural Catholics, selective Catholics, a la carte Catholics. Polls, surveys and opinion samples have been documenting this. For me, it hasn't been enough. To see it regorged still again that this percentage agrees or disagrees with this or that teaching or those statistics show a decline in vocations, a rise in divorces or a leveling off of something else, is to look at numbers, not people.

I want to know what feelings are in our gut. Polls show trends, not inner reflections. They picture the surface—a pollscape—not the deep roilings that stir our hearts. With this in mind, I sent to about 20 friends a list of questions I asked them to answer in writing. I wanted personal feelings, so I went to personal friends. Some were women and men I have known since childhood. A few were college friends. Some were neighbors I see regularly. Others I had met only within the past year. I work with some, play with others. One is a board chairman of a rich corporation getting richer. Another opened a soup kitchen for the homeless 10 years ago and is still at it. Two are Jesuit priests, members of an order that ran the college I graduated from in 1960. Two were young women who recently earned degrees from Smith College and Penn State. One is my brother Denis.

In all, it is a circle of friends that is centrifugally pushing the church to take bolder risks of commitment. They are a gathering of people I care about with the best fraternal warmth I have. Each reminds me of the line that "a friend is someone who knows the song in your heart and sings it back when you have forgotten how it goes."

I would have liked to pose a hundred questions. I went with 10:

1. What does the church mean to you?

2. Is the church serving your spiritual needs? How? If not, why not?

3. Where do you see the church headed? Do you like what you see?

4. If you were the pope for one day, what decisions would you make?

5. How is your Catholicism different from what it was 10 years ago? Twenty years ago?

6. What in your daily life are you doing that you wouldn't be doing if you weren't a Catholic?

7. What should the church be doing more of? Less of?

8. What has been the worst mistake the church has made in your lifetime? And what was the best thing it did?

9. Who are the three living Catholics you most admire?

10. If you were arrested for being a Christian, would they have any evidence for a conviction?

These being questions for friends, there was candor and occasionally some humor in the replies. One woman—a psychiatric nurse, divorced, comely, an athlete who once gleefully outran me in the final 100 yards of a 10-mile footrace—confessed that the questions were "difficult for me because I have had so little to do with the church for so long. But I am still a Catholic, and I do have pretty strong feelings about it, particularly in the past." She wished me well with my survey and said brightly after sending me her answers, "Now you know what a truly rotten Catholic I am. I hope we can still be friends...."

Another prefaced her answers with the comment, "I am amazed how hard these questions were to answer because I hadn't really thought about my religion for so long.... Luckily I had developed a very strong base of Catholicism as I was growing up."

One theme dominated the answers: there is deep bitterness and even loathing for what the church has done to people in the name of Christ and conformity, but despite all of that, an allegiance is still there. I have never accepted the notion that you can be an ex-Catholic, and my informal survey confirms it. The only fallen-aways are the fallen-away atheists.

The joining of bitterness and allegiance was most startlingly noticeable in the answers of the nurse, who was anything but the "rotten Catholic" she thought she was. In reply to the first question, she wrote: "I am currently not a practicing Catholic but feel that being Catholic affects me a great deal. I have found the Catholic influence to have been quite negative for me, having attended Catholic schools in a particularly conservative parish in western Massachusetts. The teachings about sexuality were very destructive and served to fuel negative feelings about myself and natural healthy impulses. A lot of time I felt like a 'bad' person for what I considered 'sins of thought' without even acting out those feelings. I didn't receive much support from the church during these years and perceived it as a very restrictive force in my life."

At the same time this woman was getting the business in her Catholic school, she was also absorbing something positive. She answered the sixth question—the influence of Catholicism on one's daily life—by writing: "I think that my choice of a profession (nursing) was influenced by my Catholic education. I was impressed as a child by the inequalities in the world and my own responsibility to have some impact upon this. I find this to be the most positive aspect of my Catholicism, and it continues to this day. I become very moved by the Catholic support of the little guy in the world, most recently in Central America."

What this nurse in her early 40s remembers of the archaic negativity of her schooldays was also the experience of the Smith graduate. "One thing I wouldn't be doing if I weren't a Catholic," she writes, "would be feeling guilty all the time." Here again, though, there is an underside of brightness to the gloom. "If I weren't a Catholic, I would not pray to God so much." This is a young woman from Oil City, Pa., who went from there to Smith and then to Washington to work for the Appalachian Regional Commission. She did not know the other young woman—recently graduated from Penn State—who is from Pittsburgh and now works at *The Washington Post*, but a similarity in their answers came through.

"If I weren't a Catholic, I wouldn't be reciting the same prayers I do," said the Pittsburgh woman. Another similarity was in their choices of Catholics they most admired. Both said Pope John Paul II and Mother Teresa. The first choice, for one, was "my parents" and for the other "my mother, because she has faced some tough times and has never turned from God as many, many others would have." Both saw the church in the same way. For one it "is an indomitable shelter where I frequently receive 'cover' and assurance in my existence," and for the other, "the church means giving me a set of rules and values in an almost ruleless secular society."

Both young women are winsomely pretty and intellectually alive. They are critical of the church but with no rancor. One balanced her thought with self-criticism: "I don't think that the church does not so much serve my needs as I won't let it. I think that many parishes have made concerted efforts to reach out to different sectors of the Catholic population. Unfortunately, many people, including myself, turn back again and again to the rituals and basic teachings of the church instead of reaching out to find new ways to love and serve God."

The young woman from Pittsburgh said that "what general principles I have managed to retain from the doctrines I recited as a child—those beliefs that make up the Catholic faith—equally satisfy me. But that is because there has been no conflict of faith in the family I come from. I have no reason to rebel against the faith, though I rebel freely against other things in my life."

I was surprised that neither woman referred at all to the issue of women and the priesthood. This was on the minds of the men in the survey, however, and it was mentioned repeatedly. "Whether mass is celebrated by a man or a woman," wrote a professor of criminal law at George Washington University Law Center, "is for me an accidental matter which will not alter my commitment to the church." He believed the church's "worst mistake" is "the refusal to give a more positive and influential role to women."

The one dissent to a greater opening for women was from a businessman who believed that if Jesus wanted what many in the 1980s want for women, "he would have said it (back) then." This is a former Marine Corps captain who served in Vietnam, is married to a grade school teacher and the father of a young son. He wears a religious medal, begins and ends the day with prayers, gives money to the church, attends mass regularly and serves on the parish council.

His main resentment is that the church pays too much attention to what he sees as "minority issues": gays, Hispanics and women. In saying the church should "preach and teach (more) of Jesus Christ," he wrote that it has become "divorced from the spiritual" and is too much involved in "picnics, coffeehouses, fundraisers" and issues such as the draft, ERA, AIDS and programs to "satisfy the Spanish." He would like the church to "go back to where it was 50 years ago and do as it was doing then."

If we had a gob of stickum and were putting labels on people, I suppose my businessman friend would be called a conservative: not right-wing reactionary conservative but conserving conservative. Oddly—or odd if we remain only on the surface—the views of this man are not so different from those of a philosophy professor at Georgetown University who is an energetic booster of the "minority issues" such as women's ordination. The ex-Marine said that for him the church was "a conduit." The professor of philosophy had a similar feeling, though his answer, giving his calling, was exquisitely nuanced: "The church to me is not a matter of meaning so much as a life. In a strong sense it constituted much of my living and it continues to influence much of my living. I had no choice about being born of Catholic parents who were themselves utterly encultured into the faith.

"For them it didn't mean, it *was* (as the man said about the poem). For about my first seven years of life I was unconsciously as well as consciously strongly dyed by the great beauty of its liturgy and the solemnity of its concerns with what is really important about life—beauty, truth, forgiveness, evil, death, sickness. The Sermon on the Mount is still for me the greatest moral document ever given to humans and the church with all its scars—the bad popes, Galileo, the Inquisition, Jansenism—is still a living community of loving people bound in a common cause and backed by a rich tradition. It is to me at least vastly superior to any collection of media experts, technocrats, bureaucrats or corporate executives. The last best hope of the world is still, thank God, the church and not General Motors."

The philosophy professor, who is 64, married and the father of three grown children, spoke of his personal spiritual life. In comparison with 10 or 20 years ago, "I am less moved—almost unmoved—by 'fear of mortal sin' and the threat of hell. I find better reasons to do what I should do. I go to confession far less. Months and months go by. It takes a major retreat to get me into the box now. I am less concerned about missing mass for a cold, or even because of mild fatigue. But I remain convinced that regular common worship is a duty... I think of it now as a self-imposed duty.... I remain deeply influenced by my Catholic childhood and youth.

"I think that fidelity in marriage, my inability to think pornography an innocent diversion for a sufficiently liberal mind, my concern about the hungry and the poor, my need to examine my life—all of these flow from my being a Catholic. I do not argue for a minute that another person may have the same practice flowing from a different background."

Unless religion affects behavior, it is only religiosity. It is mere dabbling in God. Of the 10 questions I asked my friends to answer, the final one involved behavior: "If you were arrested for being a Christian, would they have enough evidence for a conviction?"

I received one firm yes—from a writer and teacher, 52, a graduate of a Jesuit college who has not spent a day in the past 25 years without directly easing someone's pain or cheering up another's spirits. He is no dabbler. "Yes," he answered about his pending conviction for being guilty of Christianity. "I don't pay taxes because I don't believe in killing people, and I think that was the central message of Christ—to love, not hate, my brother. So I am forbidden to kill or consort with and support those who do. Why is this so difficult a precept to follow? Why isn't every bishop and priest in America in jail for tax resistance? Why isn't every Catholic in jail for the same reason? It is utterly impossible to call yourself a Catholic or Christian or Jew or Moslem if you are taking up arms against your brother," he said.

Unsurprisingly for this person, who was a U.S. Army private in the Korean war, the church's biggest mistake is that it does "not make it a mortal sin for Catholics to pay taxes to a government that spends excessive amounts of its resources and manpower on war." With the same consistency that is beginning to emerge from some of the recent statements of Catholic bishops, he said that the stand of the church against abortion represents a worthy effort. "But to hold for life in the womb and then allow it to be killed on the battlefield makes a mockery of even that stand," he said.

One of the Catholics he most admires is Rose Kennedy. "She symbolizes the great truth for which the church has stood for centuries: that the vows of matrimony, even if you are married to a rake and philanderer who one day will embarrass you before the world, are to be taken seriously and great sanctity can result for those who live this way," he said.

Of the 20 replies, this one from a pacifist was the strongest. It has bold definitions and intense convictions. I would guess, too, that of th 20 people in my survey, he would have the outward appearances of being the most ordinary: a white, middle-aged male who works, is a reliable neighbor and minds his own business. Yet, it is radical business he is about: the total transforming of the church's and society's values. His efforts are credible because he has begun with himself.

His closest fellow traveler is another white, middle-aged male who also sered in the military but then became a pacifist. For a few years, he was a priest. He is now married and has four children. "Twenty years ago," he said in answer to the fifth question, "I sought out the church as a vehicle toward salvation. Ten years ago, I defected in hope of finding salvation. Now I have returned to the church in hope that, hand-in-hand, we can kick each other's rear and crank in the right direction," he said. Throughout the 1970s, this former priest did the priestly work of feeding people. He opened a soup kitchen, drew volunteers to his work and saw to it that nobody loafed around writing manifestos while people on the street needed to be fed or housed. Even now, he gives the quick, short answer that says it all. Catholicism's worst mistake: "Ignoring *Populorum Progressio*." It's best effort: "Ignoring *Humanae Vitae*."

Perhaps my questions were on the heavy side, but this friend was moved to lighten things up with his remark that "Christianity has given me a sense of humor—the hallmark of a good Christian."

The most introspective response came from a Jesuit priest. He lives in a rented house in my neighborhood and taught last year at a Catholic military high school. Among the high points of that year was organizing a "peace day" in which the students—most of them dressed in soldier suits—listened to "the other side." This year, he is working as a counselor among drug addicts. "Twenty years ago," he wrote, "my Catholicism was young, brash, showy. I wore a Jesuit habit on the streets of Jersey City like it was a black leather jacket.

"Ten years ago, my Catholicism was in jeans and boots, tracking across the country from Washington (graduate school at Catholic University where I found my strongest friendships in my life) to Wisconsin, from New York and Baltimore to the Great Smokies. This was the living out of 'my travels with Charley' fantasy . . . . My Catholicism thus was ecumenical and open to all the many faces and voices of America.

"Now, at 48, my Catholicism means corduroy and an occasional mismatched tie with an ancient jacket. No more smoking, no more ever-changing settings. Now it's lived in the same familiar surroundings. Now I want to stay home and talk, to open up more deeply. Now the job of counselor brings me to a point where the people who come are all in deep trouble, and I have fewer illusions about my ability to 'make things right,' but I can listen and occasionally see a gleam of light, pounce on it and hope my addicts see it, too."

From my conversations with this priest, I know that he is a man who asks much of himself. He has a delight in this, as though he is aware that that is one of the benefits of the unmarried priesthood: he can give of himself without worrying, or feeling guilty about, taking something from his wife and family. There is no uneasiness about helping people whose need is desperate while letting things slide at home because the demands from one's family don't appear to be critical but which often are. At mid-life, this priest relishes his freedom to serve. When asked what the church should be doing more of, he said that it must be "more demanding of its own members, over and above their religious and spiritual duties—like Mormons and Adventists—and maybe asking for more free-will giving, service and time."

The other Jesuit priest in my survey is younger by some ten years. He lives in community at a small liberal arts college in West Virginia. His views about where the Church is headed were uncannily similar to those of his brother Jesuit. "Under the current Pope," he wrote "the Church seems headed toward more internalization, more bureaucracy. I do not particularly like what I see, but I have no great fears that we all will become a 'Roman-Polish' Church. Somehow I have the feeling the Spirit will save us, despite ourselves. The Spirit might even surprise us—like having women bring about a new Pentecost by their refusal to play the game. Who knows?"

His fellow Jesuit had written: "the Church must begin moving, as it is in many places, toward "small groups, communities of Christian life that try to live concretely in a simple, open, non-violent way—in amazement at the beauty of the world and of life, open to the surprising and constant inrush of grace, the little stirrings of the Spirit."

In my Pope-for-a-day question, my friends put tiaras on their heads and took the best of Roman holidays. A woman who has devoted her life to ending the violence done to animals said that as the Holy Mother she would "guide the ark toward a vegetarian diet."

A lawyer who tries to emphasize simplicity in his life "would sell all the jewels and artifacts as necessary to take care of the hungry and homeless of the world. Then I would refocus the Church to an emphasis on seeing the God in everyone, instead of focusing on sin and heaven."

One of the Jesuits would "get out of the Vatican and maybe take up residence in the city." The other Jesuit would "involve women more in the life of Jesus's Church."

The wish lists were well-founded, but at the heart of many of them was a dissatisfaction with Pope John Paul II. The strongest reply to the question of where is the Church headed came from a person—a staff member of a California congressman—whose loyalty to Rome has been both deep and costly. He accused the Pope of being "more comfortable with the Council of Trent than Vatican II. His attitude toward women is, for the most part antidiluvian, and his attitude toward marriage is even more constricted. What most disturbs me is his selective politics. I can understand that, as a professional Pole, he is committed to the liberation of his native land from foreign domination, of course excluding Rome. But his restrictive, exclusivist attitude towards the struggle for social and economic justice in other lands has left me appalled. What about the God-given rights of people in the Philippines, in Central and South America, in southern Africa? Certainly they have the right to make a reality of the Gospel in their daily lives—with the assistance of, and direct involvement in, the political life of the country by both clergy and laity. How is it that Fr. Drinan or Sister Mansour can be prohibited from holding office in the U.S. but certain preferred prelates in countries as Colombia are allowed to be generals in the Army and the National Security Police? And what of the Vatican's tacit support for the continued escalation of the nuclear arms race? The Pope speaks out against at the UN, but then allows the bishops in western Europe to endorse the deployment of theater nuclear weapons."

Despite the criticisms, despite the pain that many of my friends endured or are enduring because of their allegiance to the Church, I sensed in each of the replies an exuberance of faith. The Church, whether it is being celebrated or dismissed, arouses feelings. It also rallies appreciation. No one had trouble listing the Catholics they most admired. Parents received the most votes. Mother Theresa was next. Others included Graham Greene, the Poor Clares, "my wife Mary Jane," Daniel Berrigan, Norman St. John Stevas, Bishop Cisco Claver, the Little Sisters of Jesus and "all anonymous Christians in today's world, from Central America, Appalachian hollers to office buildings and factories everywhere."

Anonymous Christians. I concur. I have not used the names of my friends I have been quoting here. If asked for my own list of admired Catholics, each would be on it.

# If St. Francis Came Back                                              *1981*

In this year's celebration of the 800th anniversary of the birth of Francis of Assisi, the Rev. John Roach, the president of the National Conference of Catholic Bishops, observed forcefully that the work of this heroic saint is unfinished. He said that "evils of the world at the time of Francis are similar to those of today, including the proliferation of weapons and greedy affluence in the face of widespread poverty."

But what if St. Francis had been born into our times, not the distant one of European feudalism? How would we in the late 20th century be receiving him and his values?

A hint of the answer can be found in Thomas Carlyle's remark: "If Jesus Christ were to come today, people would not even crucify him. They would ask him to dinner, and hear what he had to say, and make fun of it."

St. Francis in modern times would also get us laughing. We would immediately place him in our electronic funhouse, the talk show. Merv or Johnny would ask Francis for some babblewit on his charming ways with animals. Tell us, Francis, about the time you tamed that snarling wolf. And how about the birds: do they really stop chirping when you preach to them? We have five seconds before a commercial break: let's hear your newest birdcalls.

After the show an agent comes forward with a book proposal. I'm only 40, protests Francis, I haven't lived long enough to write my memoirs. "What memoirs?" asks the agent. "You're a thin guy. Let's go for the big money. I can see it now, number one on the best-seller list: "The St. Francis Diet Book: Love God and Eat What You Will.'"

When the agent goes off to phone a blockbuster publishing house, Francis is whisked to the airport. He is to be taken to a seminar convened by a learned institute. There, after being awarded the first annual Henry Kissinger Peace Prize, Francis is engaged in a panel discussion on Christian capitalism.

You don't understand, a scholar instructs the gaunt and unsmiling Francis: living with the poor and going hungry with them is a noble gesture, but the free-enterprise system is actually the real ally of the poor. Haven't you heard of trickle-down economics?

When Francis stares back in astonishment, he is told of President Reagan's recent economic nostrum to the Third World poor: just imitate the United States, and life will get better.

Another panel member, sensing that it is Francis' spiritual side that must be developed, quotes from one of the latest publications of the American Enterprise Institute: "Toward a Theology of the Corporation." It declares that, "If we look for signs of grace in the corporation, we may discern seven of them—a suitably sacramental number." Through these signs, which include creativity, liberty and social character, "corporations offer metaphors for grace, a kind of insight into God's ways in history."

Francis, looking properly awed by this Deepthink but clutching his worn rosary nevertheless, takes his turn. He asks his fellow panelists—all veterans of the seminars-on-heady-issues circuit— some modest questions. How many hours have you volunteered at the soup kitchens that Franciscan priests and brothers run in many cities? How many prisoners have you visited, how many illiterates have you taught to read? How many open sores of homeless people have you dressed?

When silence follows these questions, Francis explains that he isn't out to embarrass anyone. He tells of his own life and how little he has done. He was a rich man's son who liked silk clothing and the ways of the dandy. But after a year as a prisoner of war, he chose a life of pacifism and service to the poor. Of his conversion, he says: "That which seemed to me bitter was changed into sweetness of body and soul."

The panel moderator rings the bell and calls for a 10-minute break. Francis tears from his robe his "Hello, I'm Francis" lapel sticker and runs out the door, on his way back to the streets and alleys of the poor.

Giddy with his freedom, he laughs uproariously at a sudden thought: all those self-scourging ascetics of the Middle Ages who believed their hair shirts and fasts were hard penances! They had it easy. They should be around for the 20th century and the martyrdom of being laughed at by clowns and lectured to by pedants.

# The Pentagon's Convent                                    1980

St. Benedict, the early church father who has kept up the spirits of his followers these past 15 centuries with the inventiveness of his spiritual Rule, somehow neglected to leave behind any wise words about Behavior on the Barricades.

Not that its been needed much. But yesterday morning, with the sun rising over a fittingly contemplative Potomac, 43 Benedictine sisters gathered at an entrance to the Pentagon. They came to tell the desk people arriving for another day's toil in war preparation that no thanks, the Federation of Saint Scholastica, a group of 22 Benedictine communities in North America, prefers "to live without the protection of nuclear weapons."

Pentagon employes are well used to these rituals of buttonholing. A mixture of citizens—from harum-scarum blood spillers to ex-colonels who could stomach no more—has been showing up, almost time out of mind, to try to convince the operators of the military machine that a better way exists to end disputes among nations than war and weapons.

But this is the first time that the Pentagon has seen a movable convent on its doorstep. For emphasis, the sisters came on Monday and would remain through Saturday.

Taking a break from the handing out of leaflets that carried a quotation from St. Benedict—"Seek after peace and pursue it"— Sister Mary Lou Kownacki, a teacher at a Benedictine girls academy in Erie, Pa., and who helps out at the Pax Center in the same town, explained that in no way did she look down on the Pentagon workers who were passing by on the way to their desks.

"In fact," she said, "I'm keeping my eye out for my brother."

"Your brother?" she was asked. "He works here?"

"Uh-huh. A weapons analyst."

If God's Providence were all that it's said to be, the brother of Sister Mary Lou would have come bounding into view at this precise moment, ready to engage in a dialogue with his sister from the peaceable kingdom and let it be recorded publicly, the way the dialogues of Benedict and his sister Scholastica—a first-rate saint in her own right—were once collected.

But Ed Kownacki, either already inside analyzing weapons or perhaps stuck in a traffic jam at the mouth of the vast east parking lot, didn't appear. It may have been just as well, because not only do brothers and sisters tend to let the global discussions of war and peace drift into the fights and truces of the family's aunts, uncles, cousins and other brothers and sisters but also because Ed Kownacki had already articulated his views.

He wrote a letter earlier this year to Sister Mary Lou, and she reprinted it in "The Erie Christian Witness." For those who try to fathom the Pentagon mind by reading the speeches of Harold

Brown or by suffering through a day at the Senate Appropriations Committee listening to Sen. Ernest Hollings' (D-S.C.) thunderings for more money for weapons, Ed Kownacki's letters to his sister may be one of the most intelligible and candid documents we have.

"Do what you think is right," he counsels his sister about her plans to demonstrate at the Pentagon. "I don't take it as a personal affront. I agree with you that war is wrong and nuclear war especially an abomination. Most of the people I work with, if really pinned down, also agree to these premises. The main point of disagreement is what does an individual do about it."

Kownacki comes up with an analogy—"not perfect," he suggests, but one with "a lot of merit."

"Picture a school bus loaded with the kids moving down a littered (rocks, walls, ditches, etc.) hill. There are people standing around and they notice that the bus is out of control. There is no driver. What do they do? Most people do nothing; it doesn't concern them. A few start shouting, 'hey, the bus is out of control!' and then throw themselves in front of the bus to attract the attention of others, and maybe slow the bus down when it grinds them into the dirt. Still others jump on board the bus and try to steer it and apply the brakes. Which of the methods of bringing the bus under control is more effective?"

The letter ended with a question: "The average Pentagon employe, whether military or civilian, does not control the system. The American people through Congress do. Why pick on Pentagon employes?"

It was hard to get a sense that the Benedictine sisters, least of all Sister Mary Lou, who is an affable, unhardened woman, were picking on anyone. If anything, they were somewhat unschooled in the ways of confrontational protest. Not a one scowled. They handed their leaflets to people, as against ramming them down their throats. Many said good morning, especially to those who looked down-in-the-mouth. Politeness, not pushiness, was the order of the morning.

On the line next to Sister Mary Lou was Sister Mary Collins. In her mid-30s, she teaches at Villa Maria College, also in Erie. She hadn't come to the Pentagon, either, as an exercise in belittlement. Instead, she explained, the week-long vigil was part of a process that began about 10 years ago when she and others in the order began to think about expanding their vocation. "The women's orders in the church need to redefine pacifism. We have no religious order, male or female, that has maintained a pacifist tradition down the centuries."

Does this mean, she was asked, that she had scrapped the church's Theory of Just War? Yes, she said, it doesn't hold up.

And what about the withholding of taxes to a government that uses them to finance the arms race? "I don't happen to have a salary that's taxable." Sister Mary said, "but in my school—I teach courses on peace and justice—we are telling the students that tax resistance is a respectable alternative."

In the context of the church's religious orders, it may well be a collective miracle that this diverse a group of people has organized itself into a bond so firm that all 22 independent communities—in this case priories that have a membership of 2,200 women—are behind the Pentagon vigil.

"It's been a matter of internal education," Sister Mary Lou said. "Once we began shifting, we discovered that we had to explain to ourselves what we were doing. Most of us come from traditional Catholic families that give uncritical support to the government and believe in the just war theory. The fact that we are here this week—43 of us today and about 50 for the rest of the week—is a sign that we have been internally successful in our explanations to those in ours convents, schools and communities."

In the hour-and-a-half that the Benedictines were at the Pentagon yesterday morning, the only authoritarian moment was when a policeman ordered one of the sisters to move back from the 20-foot ledge above an underpass. "Don't want you to fall," he said.

Several of the sisters were surprised by the unexpected friendliness of the Pentagon workers. It was hard to get the juices going, one said, when everyone was smiling at you.

Another believed that that was the core of the problem: the public's sense of normalcy about the registration for the draft, the preparation for war, the presumed inevitability of a nuclear escalation or blowup. "We need to say to ourselves," Sister Mary said, "what's going on here?"

# Corpus Non Grata 1979

Holy Mother Church hoisted her skirts a bit high the other day when she stepped over a body that lay in her path. It was Carmine Galante, the New York gangster who hastily went from the underworld to the next world after a hunting accident in a Brooklyn restaurant.

The Roman Catholic Archdiocese of New York reviewed the criminal past of Galante and decided that this was one sinner who would have to meet his maker on his own. It would allow no requiem mass as a send-off. Canon lawyers cited a church law—written in the Middle Ages—that allows the hierarchy to deny a funeral mass to public sinners.

Little doubt exists that Galante had fallen into the ways of public sin. High in the ranks of the New York mob, this godfather had long been prospering in low-life rackets and violence. But some question does remain—protruding like the horns of Satan, perhaps, but still there to be faced—that, however mean a fellow Galante may have been, he was still worthy of a dollop of mercy in a requiem mass.

The archdiocese, understandably, didn't want to give scandal. Funeral masses for the seedy thugs of organized crime are an affront to all decent church-goers. But the affront was built into the religion long ago, in the scandal of Christianity's teaching that the Lord came to save sinners. The decent will do fine on their own.

Catholicism's early canon lawyers, idly speculating in the days of Bernard and Anselm on how many unangelic mobsters can fit on the head of pin, took the breadth out of that teaching. Some sinners are in, they ruled, and some, like Carmine Galante, are out.

The archdiocese stressed that it was issuing no decrees on the departed's spiritual state. It said that a few years ago another mobster—Carlo Gambino—did get a funeral mass. He had been a churchgoer, it seems, in the last years of his life. As they said before Vatican II, he had "gone back to the sacraments."

The choir of angels doubtlessly sang the highest notes of joy when Gambino turned pious. But for all anyone knows, Galante could have been on his way that bloody afternoon to Fr. Luigi to recite an act of contrition. As St. Ambrose of Milan wrote to

Emperor Theodosius about one of the repentant, "He now esteemed as a Father one whom he formerly repulsed as an enemy."

When the church lawyers of New York ruled the dead Galante *corpus non grata*, they were turning the church into a club. Since Galante didn't keep the rules, whether he kept the faith—far back in the shadows of his soul, it would seem—didn't matter. He was let in the club as a baptized infant, but 69 years and a foul lifetime later, the church's membership committee had turned choosy.

If all goes according to gangland lore, we are likely to hear soon that Galante had a hidden good side. Perhaps he had put orphans through college or gave gym equipment to the local boys' club. We know already that he was a devoted papa to his four daughters, all of whom, reporters noted, were in full sob at the funeral home.

I know something about the unrecorded largesse of syndicate chieftains. My aunt was a Carmelite nun who worked with the elderly poor in the Bronx for 30 years. Among those she put the touch on in the 1940s, including bishops and the upper-class Irish, was Frank Costello. He reigned then as the mightiest don outside of Sicily. Anything Sister Mary Stella needed for the old folks— clothes, food, linen, silverware—would come in truckloads, compliments of Costello.

Some of the more proper nuns in the convent chided my aunt for her ties to the underworld. But she said it was theologically proper: If God provides, let's not turn up our holy noses because Frank Costello delivers.

By most accounts, though not my aunt's, Costello was a repulsive character. So was the late Galante. But they were baptized Catholics, and that's that.

If the founder of the church hadn't had this unsettling habit of going among the repulsives himself—even taking Dismas the thief with him to heaven—it might be different. Snubbing a dead *capo* would make sense, except that if the church were only a club it would have faded away long ago. It's the Galante ilk, who represent the worst-case theory, who give the church its mission.

*Chapter 6*

# Writers
# and Words,
# Winners
# and Losers

We all more or less lied about the war. On
Armistice Day, four of us took an oath on the battlefield
that we would tell the truth the rest of our lives, that
we would begin telling the truth in time of preparation
for war, that we would do what was humanly possible
to prevent the recurrence of another such vast and
useless horror. Then we all went back to prosaic
reporting in America. —*George Seldes, 1918*

## Silencing Journalists 1981

Johnny Sullivan, a young free-lance journalist from Bogota, N.J.,
traveled to El Salvador in late December. He was on assignment
from Flynt Publications. Sullivan, a member of The Newspaper
Guild who had written for Forbes, Argosy and several newspapers,
checked into the Sheraton Hotel in San Salvador. That night he disappeared. He hasn't been heard from since.

Sullivan's family, including his father, who has been a photo-
engraver at the New York Daily News for 30 years, is frantic with

fear. "We phoned the U.S. Embassy in San Salvador," his sister Donna says. "They told us of a preliminary investigation. But it was superficial, and they knew it. When we pressed, they suggested we hire a private investigator."

The Sullivans, who refuse to let the U.S. government dismiss them so casually, fear the worst: that Johnny was abducted and murdered by the same forces that have already killed six other Americans since early December.

Until it is learned otherwise, it is easily possible that Johnny Sullivan is the latest casualty in the worldwide war against journalists. Rene Tamsen, a stringer in El Salvador for WHUR-FM of Washington, has been missing since October. The breadth of the violence ranges from outright murder to long-term imprisonment. In Nicaragua during the last days of the Somoza regime, Pedro Joaquin Chamorro, the editor of La Prensa, an opposition newspaper, was assassinated. In Singapore, Said Zahari has been imprisoned by the government since 1963. He has never been formally charged. When Laurie Nadel, who works for CBS News, recently wrote to the prime minister of Singapore about this case, she was told by return letter that Zahari has "remained in detention by his own volition."

Exact figures on journalists who have been killed, imprisoned, tortured or harassed are not available. The estimated number of writers jailed in 1978 is 600, with about 280 of those reporters, editors or publishers. In every part of the world, from Argentina to South Africa to Cuba and the Soviet Union, national security laws are routinely and brutally invoked against the media.

Each of the imprisoned journalists is a newsworthy story, with the theme of conscience, professional integrity and freedom of the press the major part of it. But there is a story about these stories, and it is not a bright one: the victimization of so many journalists seems to be of little concern to the American press.

In the course of a week, I read about 20 or 30 out-of-town newspapers. Editorials on imprisoned or disappeared journalists are rare. Occasionally a brief wire story appears on an editor sentenced in South America or a reporter seeking his freedom in Eastern Europe. Columnists seldom touch the subject. At the 1980 convention of the American Society of Newspaper Editors, a report from its International Communications Committee said nothing about imprisoned journalists.

Putting it mildly, this lack of interest is shameful. Here is one subject that ought to be a natural for the American press. At the last, feelings of fraternal compassion should be aroused. If journalists respond with little more than a collective shrug when violence is done to a John Sullivan, Said Zahari or Pedro Joaquin Chamorro, why should anyone else bother?

Some stirrings are appearing. Under the co-direction of Laurie Nadel and Michael Massing, the editor of The Columbia Journalism Review, the Committee to Protect Journalists is being formed. I was asked to join as a board member, and I did.

Our single goal is to help journalists who are denied either their human or professional rights. The group lets the juntas, dictators and impostors who rule much of the world know that they are being held accountable for their violence. Should American journalists of conscience, as well as the readers served by them, get behind the committee, much future suffering can be prevented.

We have the word of Jacobo Timerman, the Argentine newspaperman imprisoned for 30 months before his exile. He wrote in The Columbia Journalism Review of his time in prison:

"When some newspapers reported on our situation in distant places of this world, be it a small town or a large city, this news reached us.... It helped us live through that day, to not give up in the face of filth, starvation and despair.... The awareness saved many lives."

# The Media: Money Talks                                    *1983*

Big talkers in the Senate, moving faster than the speed of their booking agents, earned $1.7 million in speaking fees in 1981. Seventeen of th top 20 were Republicans, according to Common Cause. Robert Dole of Kansas was the leading money winner at $66,850. Others with a lot to say, and groups rich enough to pay for it, were Jake Garn of Utah ($48,000), Paul Laxalt of Nevada ($33,500) and Lowell Weicker of Connecticut ($32,150).

When these facts appeared in newspapers, a companion story was needed: How much are the big talkers in the news business earning in honoraria?

The senators are stoop laborers compared with many in the media. They are limited to $2,000 a speech, but journalists, from television anchormen to prominent syndicated columnists, earn fees as high as $15,000 per lecture. At the cash register for much of this is the Washington Speakers Bureau. It reports that "a good print columnist can easily earn much more" than Dole's humble $66,850. With the bureau's stable sending horses to the fast track for between 20 and 60 lectures a year, incomes of a quarter- to a half-million dollars are possible. The Senate stipend of $2,000 barely covers warmup jokes.

With money talking, talking for money means that the public trust is at stake. The credibility of the media would be enhanced if fees were a matter of public record, as well as other sources of outside income for those in the news business. Media figures hot in the marketplace are not public employes as senators are, but they are in positions to shape the discussion of public policy. The larger, richer and more influential the media become, the more they have a duty to maintain their integrity.

The issue in public disclosure of speaking fees, whether for politicians or journalists, isn't conflict of interest. It is independence, coupled with the candor that creates public trust. Citizens want laws to be made by politicians free of ties to special interests, and they want the news to be reported and commented on by unbiased journalists. According to Common Cause, $977,000 of the $1.7 million paid to senators in 1981 came from business groups. It is much the same with the media. "A tremendous amount" of speaking dates, reports the Washington Speakers Bureau, "are with trade associations."

If a columnist takes $100,000 a year for burbling to business groups about the glories of free enterprise and produces pieces saying the regulatory agencies are too powerful, shouldn't the readers know he is receiving that sum? What about his colleague who dispenses $7,500 worth of wisdom in 30-minute speeches to defense contractors and uses his column for pedantries on behalf of greater weapons spending?

These journalists can be assumed to be as honest as St. Francis sharing crumbs with the birds. But the public, because it is the object of the columnists' attempts at persuasion, should be informed of how the crumbs are gathered by the lecture circuit regulars. Nothing more threatening than the ethics of Las Vegas are needed: I trust you, mother, but cut the cards.

If we trust the senators but ask for financial disclosure, it isn't too much to apply the same standard to the powerful media. Nothing grubby is ever part of the lecture contract, either for politicians or press. The wealthy trade association knows it can't purchase votes or viewpoints. It does know that it can try to buy the speaker's sustained attention. Before and after the lecture, and during the Q&A, he is in the company of the association's leaders who in the spirit of friendship may describe the woes of earning an honest buck in these miserable times.

As he is paid a fee, how can the lecturer not also pay attention? And perhaps be sympathetic. A few days ago, I paid attention to an audience of 300 military officers at the Industrial College of the Armed Forces at Ft. McNair in Washington. I am a busboy at the lecture banquet and received $100 for my unagented talk. For that sum, I gave my military friends exposure to the priceless thinking of Gandhi, King, Tolstoy and peacemaking bishops. Throughout the morning, I was in the position of hearing the war college's view that military might is needed in America's hour of peril. I liked and respected the intelligent men who told me this, though nothing they said is about to prompt me to write in favor of the MX missile or any other weapon, cherished at the war college.

Whether I do or not is not the main point. Press accountability is. It demands that the reader know that for many in the news business "reliable sources" can also include reliable sources of income.

## Late Honors For George Seldes                    *1982*

NEW YORK—Amends, of a sort, were being made. George Seldes, the 91-year-old reporter who wrote his first story for the Pittsburgh Leader in 1909 and whose latest article appeared recently in the Nation, looked over the lectern as the audience of 300 rose spontaneously to applaud him.

Seldes, entering a spry 10th decade with legs, heart and mind in spunkier shape than many men half his age, had just received a George Polk award. It is one of journalism's major honors, named for the courageous CBS newsman murdered, it is thought, by right-wing assassins in Greece in 1948.

At the awards luncheon, the citation of the Polk committee caught a little of the uniqueness of Seldes: "By mutual agreement, he belonged not to the journalism establishment, nor was he tethered to any political philosophy. With a gimlet eye ever fixed upon transgressors, he soared above the conventions of his time—a lone eagle, unafraid and indestructible. He is 91 now, and still a pretty tough bird."

And rare bird, the committee might have added. Seldes was a tireless muckraker for most of his career, practicing the art that today is called—now that newspapering is a proper calling—investigative reporting. The muckfields when Seldes started out were no deeper or thicker than today's. They differed because fewer publishers or editors assigned reporters to rake them.

When he wearied of bucking his bosses, Seldes began his own weekly newsletter. He called it "In fact," offered a hard surface of press criticism, bubbled by Seldes' bluntness. He ran exposes on newspapers that would not offend tobacco companies by printing the bad news—emerging in the 1940s—about cigarettes and lung cancer. He attacked columnists who were secretly paid by special interests. He reported press campaigns against unions. He editorialized against publishers who suppressed or ignored the news.

At its peak, "In fact" had 176,000 subscribers. Many of its stories came from newspeople who couldn't get their copy into their own papers. During the "In fact" decade, reactionary newspaper owners dealt with Seldes by redbaiting him. Had they sent reporters to interview him, they would have learned that in 1923 Trotsky bounced Seldes—then a Chicago Tribune reporter—from Russia.

After the awards luncheon, I spent the rest of the afternoon with Seldes. We took the Fifth Avenue bus from downtown to the apartment of his nephew. Not only is there not a trace of physical slowdown in Seldes but spiritually he is free of any worldweary cynicism.

Seldes, who was widowed three years ago, lives alone. He rises at six and writes daily.

During my afternoon with Seldes, I suppressed my urges for hero-worshipping well enough. For one thing, he would have none of it. And for another, his message to younger journalists—which has to be every last one of us—is not to waste time praising his zeal. Do better: share it.

# Save The Progressive                                        *1983*

Small-magazine publishing, the poorhouse of American journalism, imposes nickel-and-dime restraints on what are often journals of priceless value. Few magazines better exemplify this than The Progressive, the monthly that for nearly 75 years has kept its radicalism unmellowed, its ideals unwatered—and its books unbalanced. Every year but one it has had a deficit. The current debts are so severe that publication may soon cease. As much as $200,000 must be raised.

If the money does come, it won't be from wine-and-cheese fundraisers staged by liberals summering in the Hamptons and looking for a cause, or from foundations that dabble in the bankrolling of literary respectability. The support will come from readers who will send in hard cash to guarantee the flow of hard truth.

The Progressive, founded by Robert M. LaFollette Sr., a U.S. senator from Wisconsin from 1906 to 1925, delivers each month to its 50,000 subscribers choice cuts of investigative reporting, defenses of the poor and minorities, and exposes of militarism. For years, its pages were air vents for the fresh lyricism of Hal Borland's nature writing. For wryness, few essayists in America match Milton Mayer.

The special pain of the magazine's current fix and possible collapse is that its circulation has never been higher. Nor have the costs of publication, from paper and ink to mailings. Postal rates have increased more than 100 percent in the past five years.

Bare-bones budgets and voluntary poverty are the normal Franciscan way for most small magazines. The Progressive is different because its small size has never limited the size of its influence. Its articles are regularly picked up as reprints by the wealthy mass-circulation media. One of its recent pieces—on sweatshops that employ and exploit undocumented workers—was the basis for a network television documentary.

Articles from The Progressive are anthologized in dozens of high school and college textbooks. If the censors of the right want to ban such threats to children's minds as books by Studs Terkel and Kurt Vonnegut, they should really get worked up and assign full-time vigilantes to rid the school libraries of all traces of The Progressive.

The magazine's acceptability is based in part on its origins in Midwest radicalism. It speaks more from a tradition than from an ideology. The early Populists who looked to The Progressive 70 years ago to oppose corporate excesses have given way to the populists of the 1980s who are now regrouping to battle the same powers.

The Progressive, which is published in Madison, Wis., deserves to be saved if only because of the service it provides younger, developing writers. Unknowns who write articles of substance are printed: a big name who comes in with fluff is not. Some 200 unsolicited articles are considered every month. One or two are printed, which isn't a bad average.

The current editor is Erwin Knoll, a former Washington reporter who left the capital 10 years ago when a trade-off in lower pay for higher satisfaction proved irresistible. For a man who may be unemployed in a few months, Knoll sounded on the phone the other day as defiantly cranky as if he had money and friends to burn.

He was asked to comment on some of the stormy and unpopular articles The Progressive has run of late, from ones that defended the free-speech rights of Nazis and Klansmen to others that criticized the left for its inconsistency in opposing every threat to life except abortion. "We aren't here to stroke our readers," Knoll said, calming not at all, "but to provoke them into testing their own assumptions and reassessing their own positions."

Knoll has an appetite for provoking more than his friends. He wrote recently that at The Progressive "we make no pretense of 'objectivity,' at least in the sense that the mass media like to use that word.... We believe subscribers are better served when our opinions are readily apparent than when they are carefully hidden and, as is often the case in "objectivity" publications, injected by sly subterfuge."

That's another reason for rallying behind The Progressive in its crisis. It has yet to be caught printing a subterfuge, sly or otherwise.

# The Media and Abortion                    1979

In the last few years, or at least since the Supreme Court's 1973 decision on abortion, I have met few opponents of abortion who think the media have been fair to their side.

John T. Noonan, a University of California law professor and one of the most intellectually respectable voices in the pro-life movement, has documented a strong case against the media. In articles and books—the most recent work is "A Private Choice: Abortion in America in the Seventies"—he has detailed many of the distortions and omissions.

"The pro-life movement," he says, "fights against a news blackout of what is good on its side. It fights against the media propagating everything that can help the other side. It fights against a journalism which is either indifferent or hostile."

I'm troubled by Noonan's charges, because for some time I have had far different perceptions. If anything, public opinion appears to be turning against the abortion ethic—and the laws supporting it— precisely because the pro-life message has been getting through as never before.

A major turnaround occurred in March 1975 when Newsweek ran on its cover a color photograph of a 16-week old fetus. Fingers, toes, physical features and even blood veins were graphically clear. Previously, this was the picture that many people found ghastly and repulsive as it was waved on placards by marching right-to-lifers. But now it waved on Newsweek's cover.

The fetus wasn't a lifeless tissue after all. The startling photograph, given sudden respectability from an unexpected source, couldn't help but stir those who hadn't really thought that much about abortion. It was a moment to stop and reflect: Perhaps it isn't so simple an issue, to be neatly summarized in the slogans of pro-abortionists.

If the Newsweek cover was a breakthrough, so also was a piece a year later in Good Housekeeping. Dr. Bernard Nathanson wrote "Second Thoughts on Abortion from the Doctor Who Led The Crusade For It." Nathanson was saying in a mass-circulation magazine what he had written earlier in The New England Journal of Medicine: "I am deeply troubled by my own increasing certainty that I had in fact presided over 60,000 deaths ... We are taking life, and the deliberate taking of life, even of a special order and under special circumstances, is an inexpressibly serious matter."

This week, Doubleday is publishing "Aborting America." At Notre Dame University's conference on abortion last week Nathanson told of his years of moral struggle that have led him to believe "abortion on request is wrong."

Articles along these same lines—by writers re-examining old positions and exploring new feelings—have been appearing regularly in the past two or three years.

Linda Bird Francke's op-ed column in The New York Times, which led to her book "The Ambivalence of Abortion," was memorable. Last year's Chicago Sun-Times exposes on the abortion mills of Chicago was journalism at its most powerful. In the current issue of Harper's an essay called "Of Two Minds About Abortion" describes abortion foes as anything but fanatics.

What's striking about these new media probings is where the articles appeared: from Good Housekeeping to the Chicago Sun-Times. In the minds of many in the pro-life movement, these publications are among the media that are considered the "indifferent and hostile enemy."

This doesn't mean tomorrow's headlines in the major papers will announce "Abortion Is Wrong" or that Henry Hyde will be given a testimonial at the next NOW convention. It means only that a lot of citizens are taking second and third looks at an issue that a few years ago they were prepared to give only one glance.

What may have once been seen as unfair media coverage may now be understood as having been *unknowing* media coverage. In the early 1970s, the moral and legal complexities of abortion caught much of the media off guard, much the way energy issues had the press slipping and stumbling in the late 1970s.

What Prof. Noonan laments about the media on abortion—the "distortions, the omissions [and] exaggerations" is echoed in strikingly similar words by Steven Rattner of The New York Times about the media on energy: "There's a staggering amount of misinformation and misconception and misunderstanding."

If more and more examples can be found of a new awareness in the secular media to the moral and social questions of abortion, it is still regrettable that the pro-life movement has had to take as allies such figures as William F. Buckley, George Will and Nick Thimmesch. These columnists are only marginally aligned with the pro-life position. I get the impression their being against abortion is merely an excuse to dump on what they see as liberalism. Little in the rest of their writing—though I confess I have less and less interest in keeping up with their one-note journalism—suggests they are as equally passionate about the pro-life position in housing, unemployment, welfare, prison reform, arms control, hunger or the environment.

That is one of the ironies. It hasn't been a Buckley or Will that has been a force in possibly changing the minds of the undecideds, but the Nathansons in Good Housekeeping and the reporters in the Sun-Times.

Even then, recognizing the improvements and the positive contributions of the media may come hard to some. I notice in Prof. Noonan's book a chapter is devoted to criticizing the media for their failures. The analysis is well done. Later on, though, Noonan cites a number of examples—from The Washington Post, NBC television—of coverage that he found worthy. He says if the growth of the anti-abortion movement "continues to be fairly reported, the curtailment of the abortion liberty is certain."

That's a guess, but what's odd in this is that Noonan offers his praise not in the chapter on the media but in a remote footnote—on the last page of the book in the next to last paragraph. It wasn't exactly equal time in giving the media their due, after so angrily giving them the business.

# Hobnobbery Journalism                                    1983

Edifying loyalty is displayed by Ronald Reagan when he phones George Will, his friend, favored columnist and former debating coach. Reagan sought to console Will for the criticism—ranging from scathing attacks to modest eyebrow-raising—he has been taking for helping the president prepare for an October 1980 debate and then, with a quick hat change, appearing on television after the event to praise his man as "a thoroughbred."

As Reagan and Will stick together through thick and thick, loyalty of another kind is the issue: loyalty to journalistic standards. Instead of keeping an arm's length from the Reagan campaign—in the name of professional detachment—Will linked to it arm in arm. Readers assumed he was an observer, not a participant. A few of them may also have assumed that Will, the dutiful Republican, had read and understood Orwell's advice: "Whatever else he does in the service of his party, a person should never write for it. He should make it very clear that his writing is a thing apart."

In a column last Sunday explaining the upbeat side of service to Reagan, Will justified his contributions at the coaching session as an occasion for career enhancement: "It was a valuable chance to see certain gears and pulleys of the political backstage. I recommend the experience to some persons who today seem to have strange assumptions about how politicians at the highest levels of our life go about their craft."

One wonders how this recommendation would go over with some journalists at the highest levels of their craft—say, I. F. Stone or Mike Royko.

Stone's long and exemplary career, as well as the ruthless steel of his integrity, resulted from avoiding insider journalism ever available backstage and working hard to cleave through the abundant guff and fakery offered frontstage. To Stone, examining the public statements of presidents, and not their private whisperings over lunch to a pet columnist, was the best and only way of serving the reader. It can't be done both ways. Hobnobbery journalism serves the elected public figure, not the readers and not the columnists who practice it, regardless of how it satisfies a Will's craving to suck at the roots of power. Call him George Shill.

Royko, as admirably independent as Stone, didn't need to look at the backstage "gears and pulley" of the Mayor Daley machine to conclude that Chicago politics were gutter-level. It's Royko to whom we owe a debt for saying as long ago as last July that a cockeyed pattern of chumminess marked the Reagan-Will relationship. At that time, Will had shifted roles from coaching to speech-writing. He wrote a speech that Reagan eventually used, in parts, before Parliament in London.

When called to account—and not called as widely or as loudly as now—Will had only a few rebels like Royko to deal with. Accordingly, he was high-handed and combative: "...It's a sign of the times that I can't do [the president] a favor like this without people blubbering about it. I have yet had anyone intelligently explain the ethics part of this. By asking me about ethics, you are moralizing. Who are you to moralize? Whoever said that journalism is value neutral? I have a right to do what I want."

From this assertion of journalistic self-righteousness, the bluntness of a year ago has been replaced by a tone of disingenuousness. The coach-speechwriter-friend now says he would decline an invitation to participate in coaching Reagan. "Some of the questions now being raised seem to me to have merit," Will wrote last Sunday. Second, "it makes so many people anxious." In other words, the blubbering moralizers can't control their anxieties. Thus Will, harassed by the unsophisticated ruck, will yield to its deficiencies and say no should his leader summon again.

Nowhere in Will's account of his adventures in near-the-throne journalism is there an expression of apology. Squirms at having been found out but no regrets. He borrows the tone that Reagan first tried when seeking to explain away the stolen briefing book: much ado about nothing, it's a laugher. Minus, for once, quotes from Disraeli and Yogi Berra, Will says in mock horror of his recent lunches with two Democratic candidates: "I wonder if something I said constituted 'advice' or 'coaching.'" The joke falls flat.

The further fall is Will's drop in credibility. The reader's trust has been eroded. Supporting a politician in a column is different from helping him privately as an adviser. Viewpoints aren't the issue. Clarity of vision is. To ignore that—"I have a right to do what I want"—is to disdain the right of the readers to be leveled with. It betrays the fund of believability that countless newspaper people, most of them far less known or paid than the fortunate Will, have built up over the decades. It isn't a fund to be trifled with.

Will came to his syndicated column in 1974 unrooted in either reportorial or editorial writing experience. He apparently didn't know one of the basics: "When a commentator has a direct personal interest in an issue, it behooves him to say so." The quote is from an April 1982 column by Will on an issue other than presidential palhood. Is what he should have announced to readers in 1980 when friend Reagan came calling. Instead, Will welcomed Reagan into his Chevy Chase salon. They then began trading off each other, with the unknowing public cut out of the deal.

# The Appallment of Zizzy Zedonks              *1981*

A three-sentence, quick-to-the-point letter came the other day from Michael Gartner, the editor of the Des Moines Register and Tribune. Mr. Gartner, a man who keeps his disposition sunny and his readers happy through his avocation of word-watching, is emphatically antimonkey—as when a writer in the jungle of the newsroom dares to monkey around with the language.

Mr. Gartner caught me swinging among the vines. "Appallment?" he asked, referring to a word—one of my allotted 770 twice a week—that I used in a recent column. "You have invented a word, and it's a lousy one. Please don't use it again, or it will appear in some dictionary."

Word-watcher Gartner's quarrel is not with me. The inventor is Robert Penn Warren, the poet and linguistic stylist who used appallment in a poem published last summer. I wouldn't claim even to be the second user of the word, the universe (or at least my universe) being so filled with both Robert Penn Warren readers and word gourmets hot to taste some fresh-cooked vocabulary.

When I phoned Mr. Warren, who lives in Fairfield, Conn., he was delighted to talk about appallment: "If you're writing and a word is needed, you create it. This is a word that ought to exist. I've invented several other words. Appallment is my latest."

Had the creativeness of Mr. Warren been put to work a bit sooner, he and we might have seen appallment in "The Second Barnhart Dictionary of New English." It was published a few weeks back by a group of unabridged spirits whose impatience with standard dictionaries led to the explosion in 1973 of "The First Barnhart Dictionary of English."

The current volume, they explain, "is the outgrowth of files so burgeoning with new words and new meanings and new applications of old words to fit new situations that we are publishing this material three years ahead of our scheduled time for a second book."

With the suggestion that all people with the nerves and refinements of Michael Gartner now leave the room, I pass along a few of the once free-roaming words the Barnhart boys have lassoed in the New Lingo Corral: blissout, deradicalize, supercrat (a powerful bureaucrat), slamdunk, futuristics, wasteplex (an industrial complex for recycling wastes), wimp, zit, oracy (the ability to express yourself orally), beautility (an object of beauty and utility), maladapt, maladept, earthlubber (all of us except John Glenn, Neil Armstrong and the other travelers to outer space), petropower (what the sheiks have) and tube (what a lot of people, whom we can now call back into the room, think the language is rapidly going down).

The Barnhart editors report that both of their volumes contain 10,000 words that the standard dictionaries ignore. Some of these entries, reeking of the fumey headlinese of Variety, are likely to flunk the test of time, and quickly. They will be seen as temporary adornments, or what the Barnhart dictionary calls add-ons.

I don't think, for example, that zizzy will survive its babyhood, despite its purebred lineage. It first appeared, as best the moles on the Barnhart research team can tell, in the New Yorker in 1976: "If you can accept the silly, zizzy obviousness (of a Mel Brooks comedy), it can make you laugh helplessly." Later that year, Alec Guinness was quoted in the Times of London: "My wife said I should wear a dark suit but I did risk a particularly zizzy tie."

Despite the New Yorker and Sir Alec, the better bet for longevity, at least among the z words, is zedonk. This is the animal produced when a male zebra mates with a female donkey, a blissout that first hit the barnyards in the mid-1970s.

Zedonks, unlike words which need the care and feeding of oracists to survive, shouldn't be scorned for what they have done to the language. They are well short of the jackass' crime—as in jackassery, defined unlaughingly as far back as 1967 in Webster's Seventh New Collegiate as "a stupid and foolish act."

Whatever crimes and appallments word inventors may be indicted for, the jackasserication of the language isn't one of them. Those who think it's time for a back-to-basics movement may be the ones most in need of Barnhart's Second. In it they will learn that the meaning of basics in back-to-basics is an Americanism first uttered in the 1950s. It probably came out of the mouth of a farmer in Iowa. Or maybe an editor.

# Is There Anyone Who Isn't Shy? 1972

Among the anemic adjectives we insist on bleeding dry on the table of lifeless language, few are more worn out than shy. Articles regularly appear on people of power and money that try to tell us about "the real person," the private pulse of their dazzling life that only the writer can hear thumping. Inevitably, the description includes shyness as a major personality trait. It is always deep-down shy, the inner skin that never sheds. Don't be fooled by the big talk of headlines or the small talk of gossips—so and so, if you only knew him, is really a shy person.

In only the last few weeks, we've been told by columnist Jack Anderson that "the real Nixon is a warm, rather shy, basically decent human being." The Washington Star quoted a friend of John Mitchell: "He is basically a shy man." The New Yorker reported that John D. Rockefeller III "was a very shy, sensitive, and rather unaggressive boy." Life magazine tailed actor Jon Voight and found him a "shy, ornery, funny, serious, quicksilver man."

Should you tire and run from the newspapers and magazines— fine therapy for any occasion—chances are that shy will follow you. In "The O'Hara Generation," a book of John O'Hara's stories, one character "looked at my shyly, as she always did." Another: "When she finished singing she stood shyly smiling in the momentary total silence." Still another of O'Hara's people: "We were newlyweds but I was shy and wanted separate rooms." Turn from O'Hara to a worthy biography of poet Elizabeth Bishop and there she was at Vassar: "it is probable that her intelligence and shyness . . . made her seem inaccessible to many of her contemporaries."

If the articles, stories and books about our citizens, from presidents to poets, are believed, it appears that from sea to sea there isn't anyone who isn't shiningly shy. Could it be true? Or are our writers using the word as a crutch, a way of hobbling along to conclusions and insights that might otherwise be crippling by their weight? It is not easy to write about another person, at least not easy to get past the do-not-disturb sign that all of us place at the door of our minds to keep out the useless curious. The writer can't tell his readers that he was blocked at the gate, much less that his subject would not come forth with the intimacies the writer set out to find. So shy is used. The tangled complexity of another human being is thus reduced to a code word, a black or white when what is really present is a kaleidoscope of grays. The complexity is never defined—how can it be, short of 50,000 or 100,000 words?—but in place of this reward the reader is given shyness as a door prize. "I'm no dummy," says the writer or speaker who depends on shy. "I've studied my subject. He's deep, he's got a lot down there and I've seen it. So here's my report: It's shyness." Actually, the word is a tip off that no depth was seen at all. Shyness is the door of the emotional house, not the house within. The writer was too lazy to go around to a back window and get in that way, so he settles for a description of the door.

We deserve better. As an adjective—the word is only three letters and it turns up a lot in Scrabble (worth six points, 12 on a double word square)—shy is almost meaningless. But as an emotional illness, it has a precise pathology. The person who is abnormally withdrawn suffers a serious affliction. Children may refuse to go to school, an adult may sweat profusely before entering a room of strangers, if she enters at all; another may suffer averted-gaze shyness, an inability to look at another face to face. In a recent report, "Helping the Shy Child," Newsweek told of a California clinical psychologist who has been "interested in treating the shy child, since he seems so docile and obedient, may suffer unnoticed by his parents and teachers." The treatment that worked involved a method of reinforcing sociable behavior—rewarding the child when he mixes with other children, or confronts groups rather than retreats from them.

One possible reason that shyness is among our best selling words is that, unlike the psychologist, few see it as an illness. Three years ago, Parents' magazine, a journal of "child rearing and family health," ran a story "In Defense Of Shyness." Don't worry about it Moms and Dads, if the young one isn't a budding leader: "A certain amount of shyness in children is normal and just about inevitable." Taking the argument further, Seventeen magazine tells about "Making Shyness Work For You." Sure you're a shy teen, says Seventeen. "First of all, everything is new. You have suddenly come into a world of fresh experiences: first date, first job, first invitation to an adult party, first long trip alone ... or any number of firsts." Where are all these supposedly shy kids? The high school teachers would like to know. Many report that the last few years have produced students of uncommon brazenness and defiance. If anyone is withdrawn and reserved, it is the teacher, looking on at student behavior like a ferryboat captain going back and forth between islands of astonishment and dismay.

One reason writers depend on shy is that many indeed prefer being seen as shy—not pathological shy but social gracefulness shy: I'm a sensitive soul, the world is much too tough for me, so *I'll prove my tenderness by tucking in my head, like the shy turtle I am*. Most of those who send advance billing that they are shy are usually the ones who dominate the evening's conversation, food and loose singles. Shy? Within 10 minutes you know enough about them to wish that you were shy—too shy ever to have left home that evening to sit next to them.

Just as easily uncovered is the brash one who acts that way because he wants you to think its a cover, a chess maneuver to put the world out of position and make impossible any counter moves of fact. The Irish playwright George Moore wrote about this one: "Within the oftentimes bombastic and truculent appearance that I present to the world, trembles a heart shy as a wren in the hedgerow or a mouse along the wainscotting."

In truth, none of us is a wren, mouse or even turtle. We are human beings, machines of vast complexity who persist in functioning even though much else on the planet has been reduced to simple formulas and still simpler slogans. Perhaps that's why we use shy so much. Everything else is simplified, let's work on people now. Make them simple, too. Let's make us all shy, and start from there.

A fine thought, but it is doomed to be a false start. Leave our presidents and poets alone. They are complex, as we are, and nothing else makes the times so alive.

# Nothing Is News                                              *1979*

J. D. Salinger, the author of "Catcher in the Rye" in the 1950s, turned 60 the other day. No one save his family and dogs knows how he celebrated. Since the fame of his book about Holden Caulfield, Salinger has been the National Carthusian Hermit.

He has a mean fence around his hillside home in Cornish, N.H., declines all interviews, babblechats on no talk shows, poses for no pictures and does nothing tangibly useful, like produce another book that would lead to requests for interviews, babbling and posing.

The ursine ways of Salinger's long hibernation have become a challenge that many in the media can't resist. What manner of a mortal is it who hasn't opened the door in 20 years to a reporter and looks content to be mum 20 more years? How is it possible for a famous person to possess so much self-control that he doesn't want a press agent or 10 minutes of network gab with Merv or Johnny? If that's the galling way he wants to play, think the media, we'll get him another way: confer celebrity for his passionate refusal to be a celebrity.

Reporters have been tracking to the north woods for two decades in hopes of catching just a syllable from Salinger's lips. Another head-hunter tried a few days ago, and produced 2,000 words to report that he had no news. So that became the news.

The Salinger case isn't the only example of an irritating celebrity who becomes an anticelebrity. Christina Onassis is also out of view. The Associated Press won't stand for it. Filing from Moscow, it reported that the recently married heiress refuses all interviews: She "succeeds in keeping out of sight and out of the headlines." By saying that the young lady is out of the headlines, AP put her exactly there. One American newspaper, running the story on page two, blared: "Onassis Still Staying Out of Limelight."

The same week that Christina wasn't cooperating in Moscow, The New York Times devoted 8 inches of space to William Shawn, described as "the best-known least-known man in America." Shawn, the editor of The New Yorker magazine, had placed a brief memo on the office wall saying that he would continue to serve in his job. Rumors of retirement had been spreading. To The Times, apparently, news about William Shawn is so precious a commodity that even when he doesn't do something about doing nothing, i.e., retirement, the world should still be told.

Americans have developed so feverish an appetite for heeding what should go heedless that a giant exposure industry works mightily to feed us. Celebrity is measured by media exposure, not personal accomplishment. Mark Twain said that once you get a reputation as an early riser, you can sleep till noon. For the exposure industry, it is much the same: Get a reputation for being famous and it will keep you famous because of your reputation.

The industry's output has entered its peak season. All styles of personalities have come to Washington to take up their chores in Congress. A newspaper story the other day told of the newly elected Sen. William Cohen (R-Maine). Spread over three pages, the piece acknowledged that the subject's political career was lackluster: "Little legislation is associated with his name." But so what? At 38, Cohen has boyish looks, sandy-colored hair, "a perfect grin" and strides around his modernly decorated house with "panther-like grace." Mrs. Cohen, who has "hazel eyes," likes nature. Being from Maine, she adores trees. Together, the story called the Cohens "the Golden Couple."

As though not to ruin all this by suggesting that these celebrities had defiled the art form by actually seeking publicity, we are assured that Sen. Cohen is "shy" and Mrs. Cohen is a "very private person."

Of course they are. The exposure industry knows that the public retains some standards. Publicizing crass showoffs might suggest a character defect in the celebs, as though they are applause junkies and the media happily supply the fix. That would be unpleasant. If anyone is going to have defects, let it be the recluses like Salinger or Christina Onassis. It's all right to be shy and private like the Golden Couple, but don't get emphatic about it.

If you do, and word gets out that you don't want the nation to know that you strike like panther or are dippy about trees, it will be trouble. We are a people who insist on being in the know, with it, tuned in, on the inside. Keep on snubbing America, J. D. Salinger. We'll get you yet.

*Chapter 17*

# Column Left

The struggle is always between the individual and his sacred right to express himself and the power structure that seeks conformity, suppression and obedience. — *William O. Douglas*

## The Mugging of Liberalism                    1978

Liberalism, we are told, is dying. The latest brain scan of the comatose patient bleeps with the election defeats of five Senate liberals. It is being said and preached that voters have finally wised up to free-spending liberals who created big government by big taxes; liberals throwing money at problems have turned liberalism into a sorry problem itself.

Whether the attacks are coming from without—the New Right pushing the old wrongs by popping up one Jack-in-the-box Kemp or another—or from within, as when liberals hunker and call themselves "realistic progressives," liberalism isn't dying. It's being mugged.

As with all attacks from the shadows and from behind, the victim has little chance for self-defense. The Washington Star, claiming that "voters are undoubtedly reacting against liberalism," twins that hazy statement with the other standby, that liberalism's "central dogma is that money solves problems, and the more money the better the solution."

The dogmatists, the evidence suggests, are not the liberals but the conservatives. Barry Goldwater, Carl Curtis, John Tower, John Rhodes and others on the right have been the foaming big spenders.

Their voting records are gaudy pompons raised high to cheer-lead programs and bills for weapons, unexamined military schemes, useless public-works projects and Federal subsidies for failing corporations. If someone in a nervous Pentagon announces that the Russians are getting pesky, throw money at the problem by spending a few billion for more bombs or planes. If agribusiness needs more water, throw money at the problem by building a Federal dam. If an industry finds that free enterprise is a bit unpleasant, raid the Federal treasury for a corporate dole.

To rest their weary arms turned sore from all this money-throwing, conservatives sit back and attack those underfunded liberal programs that feed hungry children, educate the illiterate, clean the filthy air and water, restore neighborhoods or keep open the libraries. When citizens demand an end to government waste, whip them into a fever to cut back funds for people programs, while diverting their eyes from wasteful he-man programs for weapons, dams and power plants. Make America strong but leave its people weak.

After recognizing the falsity of the charges that liberals are the big spenders—most liberal-inspired social programs, from Head Start to legal services, are so underfunded as to serve less than 25 per cent of the eligible citizens—it is crucial to understand that the current mugging is not necessarily fatal. While laid up, liberals need to renew their strength by accepting as still robustly true Franklin Roosevelt's thought in 1938: "Government has the definite duty to use all its power and resources to meet new social problems with new social controls."

If liberals are wavering by voting against programs for the poor and the victimized, or are joining the blind by siding against big government without distinguishing what part of the bigness is the actual curse, then perhaps they have forgotten the tradition of political compassion and fairness from which they spring.

To forget this tradition is to kiss off the buoyant record of liberalism, and perhaps even be ashamed of it. Breast-beating liberals are intent on public confession. When Sam Brown, the head of Action, discussed in The Wall Street Journal the big national programs of the past, he judged "that the liberals have been wrong" in their approach. Now that he wears suits and combs his hair, Brown also keeps himself presentable by adopting the fashionable pose of the antiliberal liberal. Dump on your own kind. Take rank and separate yourself from foot-soldier liberals of the past fifteen years in Congress like Don Fraser, Phillip Burton or Ben Rosenthal. Denounce as wrongheaded their struggles to create government programs for food stamps, housing and education, or to protect the powerless from land abuse, price fixing or consumer fraud.

When liberals put their heft together and passed a few humane programs, the government could at least be respected for its instinct. People were hurting and the government made a moral commitment to help. If these programs are now seen as failures by upstarts fresh off the barricades, they have failed because too little money backed them, not too much. The social programs of the '60s were too small, not too big.

Today, with some liberals getting anemia and others confusing their blood type, it is fashionable also to argue that no one knows anymore exactly how to define a liberal. But that is really the easiest of tasks. My own definition of liberalism has less to do with specific words than with specific behavior.

Consider yourself a sane and healthy liberal if you are one who:

• Subscribes to The Progressive, Commonweal or The Nation.

• Reads the Mobil propaganda ads for comic relief.

• Kicks yourself for swallowing Jimmy Carter's campaign guff that he would cut the defense budget.

• Exults in the continuing protest of Dan and Phil Berrigan against the madness of nuclear buildups.

• Enrolls your child at birth in the ADA.

• Sends Allard Lowenstein a check when he finds a new Congressional district to run in.

• Is not fooled by Strom Thurmond's putting his children into public school.

• Wonders how the country would be today if we had heeded George McGovern's warnings about Nixon in 1972.

In the gene pool of my politics, I was born of two liberals, educated by others and expect to die and spend a bracing hereafter in the company of fine liberal saints like Phil Hart, Paul Douglas and Robert Kennedy. Here on earth, meanwhile, I join the work of other liberals who are trying to make the streets safe from the intellectual muggers of the New Right. A further task is to clear the sidewalks of the Old Right. Toward that goal, we need a Federal program for a convoy of wheelchairs for the Goldwaters, Curtises and other rightist big spenders in their political dotage.

With these two groups brushed from underfoot, we can move ahead to deal with inflation, waste, unemployment and rampant militarism. Perhaps we can also recapture our generous instinct.

# An Undefeated Loser                          1980

When the final results of the election are announced, a safe bet is that more people will have voted for David McReynolds than for Jimmy Carter or Ronald Reagan.

David McReynolds? He is the presidential candidate of the Socialist Party. A longtime staff member of the War Resisters League and a man whose work in the civil rights, labor and anti-war movements was as unsung as it was effective, McReynolds is the rarity this year because he is someone you *vote for*. He will get no lesser-evil votes: if you are against Carter but are more against Reagan, you vote for Carter. However many positive votes McReynolds receives—and there will be few because, regrettably, the Socialist Party is on the ballot in only 10 states—will reflect the deep feelings of citizens for the ideals of American socialism.

When I am in polite society and can take no more polite talk about Carter, Reagan or the third least evil, Anderson, I mention McReynolds' name. No one has heard of him, of course. But when I ask if anyone remembers Norman Thomas, everyone brightens and says yes. What a giant of socialism was Norman Thomas, all agree. Then come the ah yesses. Ah yes, what an inspiration was Norman Thomas. Ah yes, he was way ahead of his time. Ah yes, a stalwart true to his radical principles.

Well, David McReynolds is carrying on the causes that Norman Thomas fought for in six presidential campaigns and in thousands of speeches and rallies in between. He is not another Norman Thomas, just as Thomas was not Eugene Debs. On his own, McReynolds is the candidate of an energetic party that goes back to 1901, created at that time, among other reasons, because less than 4 percent of the American labor force was organized.

The need for Socialist leaders like Debs, Thomas and McReynolds has been constant—even though we honor them posthumously. We are a country founded by radicals and revolutionaries, yet our mongrel heritage gives us the shakes. We are at ease with radicalism only after the passing of time has sanitized its reformist messiness. Socialists who came before McReynolds were dismissed as dangerous firebrands when they fought for such far-out proposals as the five-day work week, a minimum wage, low-cost public housing, health insurance for the elderly and unemployment insurance.

Now it is McReynolds' turn to be kissed off as irrelevant. He calls for "the unconditional dismantling of all nuclear weapons." His democratic socialism seeks "a genuine social ownership of the basic means of production." In the current issue of The Progressive, McReynolds argues that "capitalism is a deepening socioeconomic disaster which cannot provide full employment, cannot house all of us decently, cannot assure us of adequate medical care, cannot reverse urban decay. Capitalism is a luxury most people cannot afford."

Among the nation's leftists, McReynolds is one of the most seasoned. His civil disobedience in the peace and civil rights movements was such a threat to the established way that its head-busters arrested him more than a dozen times. What he was saying from southern jails in 1968 is still starkly true: "The real problem—unemployment—isn't going away. Integration without jobs is meaningless."

McReynolds' campaign budget is about $35,000, a sum that is about one-tenth what Jimmy Carter has spent only in legal moves to thwart John Anderson. With no big money behind him, McReynolds has been all but ignored by big media.

About a month ago, he thought that God's favor might be turning to him, or at least the gods of public television. He reports that a film crew, gathering material for a PBS program on minor candidates, taped him for about an hour during a campaign stop in Wisconsin. But when the show was aired, it was all Ed Clark and Barry Commoner. These two provided enough farfetchedness for one evening, without a Socialist wildly talking about taming the greed for private profit, demilitarizing America or getting jobs and homes for all of the poor.

In the print media, it isn't much better. The patter of Barbara Bush and Keke Anderson rates more coverage than the visions McReynolds is holding up before us.

McReynolds, who is a pacifist and has a Catholic nun as his running mate, gets the question all the minor candidates face: why vote for a sure loser? His answer has the bite that marked the thinking of Thomas and Debs: "If you want to build a new political structure, the only way you can really waste your vote is by giving it to the existing Establishment .... Is there no point at which we say no? ... Is there not a point where finally we realize that our only hope of being relevant within history is to risk being irrelevant at this moment in time?"

The risk is not so great. As the record shows, American politics has needed only a few decades to catch up with many of the standard Socialist positions. Today, with the public frustrated by the piddlingness of Carter and Reagan proposals, the fruition of the ideas of McReynolds and his time-honored party may not be as far down the road as we think.

# Why Do The Militarists Hide? 1981

Some of the nation's 2.5 million Vietnam-era veterans are angry because, unlike the returned hostages, they were greeted with no parades or public honors. "We were heros, too," they are saying, "and instead of being appreciated we came home to the national cold shoulder."

This is a weak argument. Collectively, how could the nation have pretended that this was a proud moment in its history? Too many citizens came to realize that Vietnam was a mistake and that little about it was worth celebrating.

This may embitter many Vietnam veterans. But instead of pressing to be recognized as heros, which can never be, a much stronger and perhaps irrefutable argument should be advanced: the policy-makers who boosted the irresponsible war have been iresponsibily ignoring the needs of the young men they once sent off to fight.

This is a wrong worth trying to right, and forget the low-priority gripe that no homecoming parades were staged.

Where have they been these past years, the strategists in the Pentagon and the White House, the flag-wavers in Congress who voted for larger and larger military budgets, the captains of defense and munition industries? Most are silent. Almost none has reached out to Vietnam veteran groups that have been pushing Congress and private foundations for desperately needed funds. If they talk about the Vietnam War at all, it is in their self-serving memoirs.

Advocacy groups like the Vietnam Veterans of America aren't demanding a lot of the former policy-makers. They aren't after donations, much less guilt money. They want no denunciations of American militarism. A few have become articulate denunciators themselves of the hard-line military policies that are again surging. They seek no more than a modest display of public support that suggests some basic decency and consistency: let the policy-makers of the Vietnam War champion the veterans with just a little of the vigor they once put into the championing of the war.

Veterans groups have approached the powerful for help. Robert Muller of the VVA has asked a number of former officials to align themselves with his group. A stronger coalition would be created, he believes. "A lot of these people," says Muller, "don't even have the politeness to respond. They've forgotten us so quickly."

The sorriest part of all this is how large numbers of the veterans have had to go it alone in grubbing for help. Rates for depression, suicide, alcholism, anxiety and insomnia were, and are, high for Vietnam veterans. As many as 1.7 million veterans were once seen as needing readjustment counseling. In 1969, Max Cleland, who lost his legs and an arm in combat, told a Senate committee that help was needed fast for veterans with psychological problems. Ten years later, Cleland, by then head of the Veterans Administration, went before the same committee with the same plea.

Last year, after a decade of denials, a small program of less than $20 million for psychological counseling was approved. But the spirit in which Congress gave the money—here are a few pennies, now go away and don't bother us—symbolized the begrudging attitude that has been the unspoken policy.

Cleland himself has done well in his four years at the VA. With good cheer, he kept the issues of Vietnam veterans before the public consciousness. But he was frustrated at almost every turn. Along with advocates like Muller and a few Vietnam vererans in Congress, he felt the pain of seeing one Congress after another, since 1969, beat back the modest bill for psychological counseling.

It is likely to be the same—or worse—in the Agent Orange dispute. A few million dollars for some distrubed vets is one thing, it is being said, but billions would be needed to settle the claims of the thousands of veterans whose bodiesand childrens' bodies may have been deformed by exposure to Agent Orange. The word that veterans are now getting is the standard one: more evidence of linkage is needed. In other words, more veterans need to die young and more of their children to be born with defects.

Meanwhile, the leaders who once needed soldiers to carry out their grand designs for foreign policy triumphs are busy with new projects. Robert McNamara is into population control, David Packard thrives as a defense contractor, Barry Goldwater enjoys new respectability, and Henry Kissinger is a Nobel laureate. But until they link arms with the veterans who are hurting and work to ease their pains, they stand accused of desertion. They flee the obvious: the war is over, but the war's damage is not.

# The Era of "Good Americans"           1980

For a number of years, talk of an impending World War III was heard mostly from a few pacifists seeking to jolt the complacent into an awareness that the arms race was out of control and leading to nuclear devastation.

But then, beginning a few months ago, people calling themselves "national security experts" co-opted the World War III specter. With the Soviets in Afghanistan and détente dead, they argued, only a massive increase of money for weapons will get America ready to fight World War III.

Now, it seems, both groups are wrong. In "The Real War," Richard Nixon writes that "World War III has begun, and we are losing it..." This view is echoed by Michael Novak in the current Notre Dame magazine. He hails the World War III theories of Alexander Solzhenitsyn and states that "we are already at war, have been at war all our lives and have not by any means been doing all we ought to do. We have flagrantly misperceived our situation."

One effect of these war whoops is to push those who think World War III is still avoidable further and further into the fringes of the discussion. It is even to silence them altogether, because now the debate is controlled by those who do not see the next conflagration as the insanity that it was previously thought to be.

A second effect of the rising military fever is that propaganda for the weapons industry assumes a tone that is rational and calm. For half an hour on public television the other evening, Ben Wattenberg, in the pose of a journalist offering facts and asking questions, made a baldly one-sided pitch for more and more weapons. As it has been doing for years, the Wattenberg brow, in almost a permanent twitch, again furrowed over Russia's having more tanks and aircraft that the United States. They are spending more and getting stronger, he said, while America is spending less and getting weaker.

To give his journalist pose credence, Wattenberg went aboard the USS Forestal. It's "a remarkable floating city," he reported, before floating himself into a rhapsody about the fighter planes—"functional, beautiful and almost alive"—that were filmed swooshing off the deck behind Ben the Patriot.

The program, which couldn't have been more pleasing to its sponsors—Dow Chemical, Conoco and the LTV Corp.—was little more than a repetition of the already shopworn. As Wattenberg surely knew, Defense Secretary Harold Brown recently said that the "we v. they" comparisons "can be extraordinarily misleading when it comes to making judgments about the adequacy of our forces."

If Brown is read out of the debate, even more dismissible are those who have been persistently pointing out that the problem with the military lobby is its enchantment with high cost and fancy weapons and its dislike for cost-effectiveness. Reliable analysis of the harmful effects of extravagant military spending is left for low-circulation journals like The Progressive. Last month in a lead editorial, "On the Road to Recession," it said that "high levels of military spending have contributed to a marked decline in civilian research and development, and have thus weakened the competitive position of American export industries. And because military contracting is heavily concentrated among the largest firms, the military dollar enhances their market power and permits them to increase prices even in a declining economy."

Whether World War III is about to begin or already has, Congress appears eager to pay for it. "Without so much as a drumroll,"

George C. Wilson wrote in The Post last week, "Congress is about to launch the American military's biggest peacetime buildup." The five-year total would be about $1 trillion. The military share of the federal budget will go from 23.6 percent in 1980 to 26.1 percent in 1985. The cost per American would average out to about $520 a year, or more than $2,000 for a family of four.

The truly chilling aspect of this new surge in the militarization of America is that it is occurring with little dissent or controversy. A few peace groups, to their credit, keep on picketing the Pentagon, and an occasional faculty member publicly critizes his school's cheerful acceptance of Defense Department R&D money.

"Good Germans" is the phrase historians use to describe a people who silently go along with their government's grand plans for military adventures. If the madness of World War III really is upon us, perhaps this is the era of Good Americans.

# A Friendly President? 1982

"You are such a friendly man," Ronald Reagan says he was told by the President of Colombia at an airport farewell. During the Latin American trip, the Reagan friendliness—the charm, the homeyness—couldn't have failed to impress every dignitary on the four-nation, five-day whirl.

Why shouldn't it be? Here at home, we too cherish Reagan's friendliness. Its force is that of a relaxant that much of the public seems to need like a drug to ease the tensions being worsened by the president's policies.

In our relaxed state, public anger is not easily rallied against Reagan's policy decisions that continue to set new records for deficits, bankruptcies and military spending. His warm support during the Latin American trip for the dictator of Guatemala who is exterminating peasants in sieges of mass slaughter was no help to the poor who may be on tomorrow's death list.

After elected a run of presidents who turned out to be personally unlikable men—Johnson, Nixon, Carter—voters are grateful for a respite. It's as though now that we have a truly charming leader, we can't bear to discern the damage of his policies from the friendliness of his manner.

Discernment would be easier if the socalled friendliness were examined for an authenticity greater than mere smiles and story-telling. The president wasn't such a charmer when he stayed away from the dedication of the Vietnam Veterans Memorial down the street from the White House. The commander in chief who called the war a "noble cause" gave the surviving troops a noble cold shoulder.

That was one of several recent insults. The supporters of the nuclear freeze were told by the president that they had been infiltrated by foreign agents. Reagan explained that his lips had to be sealed about the agents' identity. This was the second alarm about foreign agents up to no good. Earlier this year, Reagan told of Libyan hit squads on the prowl in America. Reagan backed off from supplying more information that that, except to say that Muammar Qaddafi "knows" the terrorists were here.

The Libyan rascals were never found. Presumably, they donned wigs and went to New England town meetings to undermine America by infiltrating the freeze movement.

For someone given to friendliness, Reagan doesn't appear to be surrounded by similarly amiable spirits. When explaining the now-scotched scheme to tax the unemployment benefits of the jobless, Edwin Meese said that "when unemployment benefits end, most people find jobs very quickly after that."

A few days before the nation was given the Meese Law of Human Motivation, the U.S. Conference of Mayors held an emergency meeting in Washington. It told of unprecedented waves of homeless people turning to city halls for help to survive the winter. The mayors, saying that their budgets were overloaded and that private charities were swamped, concluded that the desperation requires federal help from Washington.

A few days later, Reagan, discussing the problems of cities in a speech, gave the answer. He not only ignored the issue of home-lessness but lectured the assembled mayors in Los Angeles that they had better shape up on their own: "You . . . must call on all your imagination and creativity to find new, local answers for today's urban problems."

Few think ill of Reagan for these insults and slights. If Jimmy Carter were still president and did what Reagan is doing, he would be loathed for meanness. As it was, Carter insulted far fewer groups but was still tagged as mean-spirited. Eventually, the voters decided he should pay for it.

No similar resentment about Reagan appears to be rising. Reagan can say, "I bleed for the unemployed," but then bloody programs that help a few of the poor get by, and the difference between words and action is not seen as a character flaw.

For citizens to be disgusted with their choice of Reagan is to admit that they fell for the con of friendliness. It's a hard admission, although every time the president puts down another group he is making it easier.

# Tax Form for Pacifists                                      *1979*

Many of those who see their government as a wanton spender on weapons and military programs are having uneasy moments—they have been sending in their income tax returns.

It is the one time of the year when those citizens realize the hollowness of denouncing increases in the defense budget, or damning "the wicked Pentagon." Citizens are paying for both, and through the Internal Revenue Service, this is collection time.

It isn't a proud moment for those taxpayers who resent a government that uses nearly a third of its revenue for military purposes. The complicity is obvious. The flow of money from citizens to the government to the military programs is kept secure when obedience becomes the national virtue at tax time.

Signs have been appearing, though, that a growing number of people prefer a different kind of obedience—one directed at conscience, not the IRS. In Congress, the World Peace Tax Fund bill has been introduced, with 28 cosponsors in the House and two in the Senate. That isn't a large number, but each session the bill keeps coming back with a few more supporters.

The bill would bring to the federal income-tax return a measure of startling simplicity. A space would be provided for the citizen to state his conscientious objection to war and to designate that his percentage of military taxes go instead to the World Peace Tax Fund.

It would be a trust fund within the government to sponsor such peace projects as retraining workers displaced by cutdowns in arms spending. Research into disarmament would be expanded.

Tampering with the military budget is already too daring an act for many in Congress without crashing off the edge by empowering individuals to do the tampering themselves. But as a legal alternative, the appeal of the bill is that it is pro-conscience as much as it is anti-military. Whenever weapons-spending bills come before Congress, the arms lobby inevitably tells of its polls about the lack of political support for cutting the defense budget. But the one reliable poll is the income-tax return: Why not ask citizens about war fever as they are being hit in the wallet to pay for it?

Without doubt, large numbers are happy to pay for more nuclear bombs, missiles or aircraft carriers. If the consciences of those citizens are respected, why shouldn't a means be provided for those who think the other way? Officials at the National Council for a World Peace Tax Fund estimate that some 8 million people would request that none of their tax dollars be spent for the military.

Without this kind of legislative relief, conscientious objectors are left with three options: violate their moral values by financing the military, violate the Internal Revenue Code by not paying, or earn so little income that is is not taxable.

Traditionally, courts have had little patience with tax resisters. Often judges mistakenly see those citizens as evaders, when actually they are pacifists who want to put their money where their convictions are.

According to William Samuel of the council, cases of conscientious tax resistance have not only been increasing in recent years, but they have also been going on to higher courts of appeal. Next month in Richmond, the 4th U.S. Circuit Court of Appeals will hear arguments from three citizens claiming First and Ninth amendment rights not to pay taxes for military spending.

While Congress and the courts mull over the issue, a few individuals are acting on their own. Only blocks from the White House, Edward Guinan's Collective Impressions Printshop has been refusing for the past two years to send its federal withholding tax to the IRS. Instead, this corporation submits the money to the Arms Control and Disarmament Agency.

The defiance of these pacifists unloosens only the smallest of screws in America's vast military machine. The arms-control agency politely returns the checks and eventually the IRS seizes the group's bank account. But it doesn't seize its moral integrity, or squash the option for dissent that is so crucial to keep alive.

# Antiabortion Liberals                                    *1984*

Obstetricians and gynecologists are arguing among themselves aout the question of whether a human fetus suffers pain as it is killed. The debate was prompted by Ronald Reagan, who continues to be a courageous opponent of abortion. The president told religious broadcasters that "medical-science doctors confirm that when the lives of the unborn are snuffed out, they often feel pain— pain that is long and agonizing."

Like psychiatrists at an insanity trial, two groups of physicians have looked at the evidence and reached opposite conclusions. Reagan was disputed by a physician from the American College of Obstetricians and Gynecologists, which supports the abortion option. Then 26 physicians led by the head of the American Association of Pro-Life Obstetricians and Gynecologists wrote to the president to tell him that "in drawing attention to the capability of the human fetus to feel pain, you stand on firmly established ground."

The pain dispute now brings the medical community into the ever-raging abortion war, with the battlefield already crowded with judges, politicians, ethicians, feminists and other combatants. Peace is not only nowhere in view, but the obstetricians and gynecologists appear at a moment when those on the same side are taking aim at each other.

In December, Cardinal Joseph Bernardin of Chicago broadened the definition of pro-life by saying that there should be "a seamless garment" of opposition to all threats to life, including nuclear war and capital punishment.

For years, the Catholic hierarchy was uneasy about the criticism that they were single-issue capers. That was never true, but the perception persisted. All doubts have now been dispelled. A right-wing faction, sniffing a sellout by Bernardin, is now upset. Stormily, it says no—opposition to abortion can't be compromised by making it just another "life" issue. It must stand alone as the preeminent issue.

The No Compromise theory is vented in the current issue of Human Life Review by Prof. James Hitchcock of St. Louis University.

He suspects darkly that the bishops, through Bernardin, are

weary of the abortion issue and see it as an "albatross." Their new policy will have the effect of "dissipating" pro-life "intensity."

The reactionary right prefers the selective approach. It is Ronald Reagan's method as well. If only a portion of his well-directed fervor against abortion were marshaled against the pain that children feel after they are born—because of inadequate health care, housing and feeding—he could claim to be authentically pro-life.

Selectivity works the other way, as well. Sen. Robert Packwood (R-Ore.) is Mr. Abortion in Congress. He speaks with the single-issue zealotry that is the mark of his opponents, the hard-right faction of the antiabortionists. He takes pride in being the only senator in 1977 to vote against Joseph Califano as secretary of Health, Education, and Welfare "because of his political opposition to abortion." He voted against Margaret Heckler as secretary of Health and Human Services "because of her adamant opposition to a woman's right to choose abortion." He depicts Sen. Jesse Helms (R-N.C.) as an enemy of women's rights.

Packwood, in a fundraising letter for himself, says "the right-to-lifers are already planning a massive nationwide campaign to defeat me in my next election." Packwood, claiming that "I am target Number One," asks for "Americans of good conscience" to send money to his "Emergency Campaign Fund."

The senator's fears of defeat by marauding "right-to-lifers" would be more founded if in fact the opposition to him was a conservative monolith. It isn't. Congress has a fair number of liberals and moderates whose votes against abortion put them in the company of what Packwood screamingly calls "right-wing powers." These include the senator's fellow Oregonian, Mark Hatfield.

In the House, such liberals as David Bonior (D-Mich.), Mary Rose Oakar (D-Ohio) and James Oberstar (D-Minn.) oppose abortion. In four votes in the last four months of 1983, they took identical positions with Rep. Henry Hyde (R-Ill.), the House's most militant opponent of abortion.

Antiabortion liberals are as much "Americans of good conscience" as Packwood believes his potential supporters are. By ignoring the subtle and shifting coalitions that now exist in the abortion debate, the senator, as well as the conservatives now attacking the bishops, guarantees that shouting at each other will continue to be the form of dialogue.

# Pumping With Purpose and Poetry          *1978*

I don't think of myself as a patriot, mainly because most of the current, self-proclaimed breed links America's greatness with its power to push around the rest of the world.

But President Carter has me thinking that perhaps I am having a few patriotic moments that go beyond cheering on Uncle Sam the Global Bully.

Carter has called on citizens to avoid using their cars for 15 miles a week. We're in a fix, he said, and voluntary gas rationing would keep the nation secure against the fuel shortage.

The presidnet's do-your-bit message stirred me to begin seeing my bicycle as a free-wheeling means of contributing to the national good. Although I had been biking 10 miles between home and office for the past 10 years, weather and legs permitting, I never had reason to think that national interests were coming before my own interests. It was enough that my daily 10 provided a trinity of personal benefits: exercise, a slower pace and the pleasure of denying the oil industry a few coins.

Perhaps I should be more of the sophisticate, but I admit that in these past months behind the handlebars I have enjoyed feelings of patriotism. I am even something of a superpatriot: The president asked for 15 miles a week, and I'm donating 50.

Troubles have come, though, like potholes on the bike trail. The first of them is in the danger of admitting to anyone that I took seriously Carter's call for getting out of our cars. We have developed such a harsh fundamentalism in our distrust of the government that even a president's mild plea for personal involvement in voluntary conservation is greeted with jeers or snickers.

Let him first give up his limousine, we think, then we'll leave our cars home and car-pool, bike or take the bus to work. And what about those secret gas pumps beneath the Capitol for Tip O'Neill and the big shots in Congress? Why no gas lines for them? Why should we do anything when the government won't level with us about what is surely a hoked-up fuel shortage?

The questions aren't asked in hope of securing answers. They are blankets meant to provide cover for the cynic, the person for whom the sharpest pain is to be duped. Amid America's immense wealth and power, the fear of being snookered—whether by Big Oil or Big

Brother—is the new and uneasy sensation. Barnum said there is a sucker born every minute, to which we fretfully add: yes, and another one to fleece him.

To get out of cars for 15 miles a week would be accepting the humiliation that some anonymous fleecer has gotten the best of us. Worse, it would be an admission that you aren't important. When J. William Middendorf, a former secretary of the Navy, installed a 4,000-gallon gas tank in his front yard in McLean, Va., he explained that he was no commoner: "I find myself in a situation where I have to get places. I'm in constant demand from a business, social and political point of view." With his home tank filled, Mr. Constant Demand has seven years' worth of gas to make his high-blown rounds.

Should I see Middendorf along the avenues of Washington—him guzzling gas and me guzzling fumes—I'll likely feel more like a chump than a patriot. There goes a real American, I will think. No one is suckering him. If it is bad form to do what the president asks, it is worse to admit that you are willing to make a sacrifice for the common good.

In the produce section of the supermarket, I once stooped over to gather up some apples that had fallen to the floor. A fellow shopper berated me. "Don't do that," she said. "Now I can't tell which are the bruised apples."

I've been waiting for another call from the president that asks citizens to sacrifice for the common good. Some stirring speeches wouldn't be so bad. But he appears to have dropped the idea, as though he himself has a tin ear for any bugle call to patriotism.

Meanwhile, I've noticed traffic is back to its old heaviness. Fewer patriots are on the bike lanes. But the ones who are can still pump with purpose.

To my brother and sister cyclists—I offer the suggestion that we have loftier things to discuss than who are our worst menaces—car owners to gas hoarders. We should put our feet on the pedals and heads in the clouds and ask: who better praises us—the novelists or poets?

The question is current. James E. Starrs, a law professor at George Washington University and a cyclist who common-wheeled across America three times, has written "The Noiseless Tenor: The Bicycle in Literature."

If he has covered every transcontinental inch of our country in three coast-to-coast journies, Starrs also appears to have gone over every line of prose and poetry written about the bicycle. Novelists who have written about what William Saroyan called "the noblest invention of mankind" range from Ernest Hemingway, Henry Miller and Stephen Crane in America to Vladimir Nabokov, D. H. Lawrence and Samuel Beckett abroad.

All would co-sign the testimony proclaimed in wide-hearted fervor by a character in "The Red and the Green" by Iris Murdoch: "The bicycle is the most civilized conveyance known to man. Other forms of transport grow daily more nightmarish. Only the bicycle remains pure in heart."

For Henry Miller, the bicycle was "my best friend." For Saroyan, "as I rode my bike, music began to happen to me." Bicycling literary couples, whom Starrs calls "head over wheels in love," included Jean-Paul Sartre and Simone de Beauvoir, and Will and Ariel Durant. When Henry Adams' wife died, and the grief would not go away, he learned to bicycle at 50 "as new means of life. Nothing else offered itself." Leo Tolstoy, at 67 and mourning the death of his 7-year-old son, Vanichka, became a cyclist. He found joy again.

The novelists are stirring, but after several hundred carefree miles of thinking about it, I favor the poets as the more lyrical singers of the bicycle. Poetry is the language of graceful metaphors, the bicycle a metaphor for graceful motion. The pairing is natural.

W. H. Auden, Dylan Thomas and Kenneth Rexroth have produced bikish verse. In "Bicycle Rider," Eugene McCarthy of Minnesota wrote a poem to his daughter, Mary, that could be addressed by any parent to a child:

*Teeth bare to the wind*
*Knuckle-white grip on handle bars*
*You push the pedals of no return,*
*Let loose new motion and speed,*
*The earth turns with the muliplied*
*Force of your wheels.*
*Do not look back.*
*Feet light on the brake*
*Ride the bicycle of your will*
*Down the spine of the world,*
  *Ahead of your time, into life.*
  *I will not say Go slow.*

In the ten years I have been commuting, I have seen cyclists break traffic laws, scare pedestrians and forget the poetry of it all. I would be more joyful about my liberation, except that I know that to sound too happy about my 10 miles of daily commuting is to risk the rage of car owners, enfumed as they already are in surliness. In my merrier days, I would tell car addicts that I saved large sums by commuting. The figures were simple: 10 miles a day, 50 miles a week times 50 weeks is 2,500 miles a year. Multiplied by the 25 cents a mile, which with all expenses included is what it costs to drive a car, that comes out to $625 a year.

I have had no harsh words from envious car owners, but knowing the nature of the beast I am aware that their emotions must come out somewhere. On the road, I fear. I've had beer cans thrown at me, dodged spit over the years and been sideswiped by everything from military convoys to mopeds. For some reason, chauffeurs for Arab diplomats are the severest threats. Perhaps the oil sheiks order them to attack cyclists, fearful that this craziness might spread.

When I ride through traffic jams, I am cautious not to look too carefree or happy. Even though I pass by and miss being beer-canned or spit on, the cyclist behind me may catch the wrath of the entrapped driver. I have made one sociological discovery about traffic jams: the greater the horsepower at the command of the driver, the hotter the seething when a cyclist whizzes past. The truly apoplectic are those in foreign cars, equipped with $300 wind-catches in the back. All that wind to be caught, and traffic is backed up for three miles.

According to a five-year-old Department of Transportation figure, I am one of America's 470,000 bicycle commuters. We save oil for the country, and time and money for ourselves. What we don't do is convince Presidents to create a transportation policy that works as well as the bicycle itself.

Until the powerful get out of their own cars and head for work on three-speeds, they won't be using their power—neither that of their office nor of their legs.

# Chapter 8

# Animal Rights and Human Wrongs

Love all God's creation, the whole and every grain of sand of it ... Love animals. God has given them the rudiments of thought and joy untroubled. Do not trouble their joy, don't harass them, don't deprive them of their happiness, don't work against God's intent. Man, do not pride yourself on superiority to animals; they are without sin, and you, with your greatness, defile the earth by your appearance on it, and leave the traces of your foulness after you—alas, it is true of almost everyone of us!

—*Fyodor Dostoyevsky*
*The Brother Karamazov*

## Agnes, A Sacred Cow
*1972*

GREENWICH, Conn.—Spring came late to the back country of this upper-rung town, filled with rich men perched atop golden corporate ladders. Only in early May were the skunk cabbages opening to size and only in mid-May were the dogwoods breaking and entering in the gentle thievery of beauty. Spring came late for Greenwich but it didn't come at all for our family cow Agnes. She died at winter's end. A six-year-old Jersey and a defender of a needed faith, Agnes was a loser to milk fever, a common ailment among family cows. Agnes suffered little, as doctors like to tell grieving survivors, but in her case dropping dead quickly was a final act of spontaneity, a trait she acquired early on.

I was this sacred cow's guardian for six years—I would say owner, but does anyone ever own another life?—the last three years by proxy. My wife and I received Agnes as a wedding present, from a group of farming friends who doubtlessly feared to themselves that stable Agnes would outlast a potentially unstable marriage. They were wrong twice, but among the candle snuffers, tea sets, linens and other wedding gifts long ago worn out or thrown out, Agnes had a class of her own.

The first grass of her cud was from the pasture of a horse farm on the outer mail route of Oakton, Va., where we lived then. Agnes, only a calf and not long off the teat, shared six acres with four horses, eating and playing among these high-standers like Susanna among the elders. For a few days, the horses could do nothing but look the gift cow in the mouth, but they found only firm and clean teeth, ones far superior to their own. It is seldom reported in the newspapers anymore—the big events crush in, editors explain— but cows only have bottom front teeth, no uppers. This makes the chewing better because the grass is ground down slower. But self-defense is harder. A neighbor's dog, an ungreat Dane whose skin was constantly twitching away fleas, learned early that Agnes, unlike the horses, could not return bites. After this loathesome mutt terrorized the rabbits and cats, it regularly came over for some nipping at Agnes' ankle, in the hard bone above the fetlock. I saw this meanness many times, often reflecting on the obvious irony: here was Agnes, the noble daughter of a spirited bull, being hassled by a spiritless bully. The mischief stopped one day, when one of the horses galloped over and in barnyard justice seldom seen elsewhere anymore, gave the Dane an unmelancholy kick with a hind hoof. The officious mutt never bothered Agnes again; even better, the growing calf knew that the horses, friendly with the earth, were now friendly with her.

As with people, you can learn much about a cow by her style of eating. Agnes could feed anytime in her lush pasture but she had a special flair for bounding across-field when I called her for a quart of molasses grain. She threw her tail high up, dividing the sea of grass like the blade of an oar, then chased an imaginary self down the hill and catching up only in the final dash to the fence where I waited. I had a special call for Agnes—"Come onnnn"—and this sprint of high leaps was her special answer, a style of motion that initiated what Emily Dickinson once called "a transport of cordiality."

Once she arrived at the fence, Agnes remained cordial. To show thanks for the molasses—and also to get more the next time—she developed a habit of licking my shoes. She savored it better if I was barefoot; her rough tongue, full of grab, played at my toes like a hand going over the keys of a worn piano, proving that music is felt long before it is heard. Cows are not instinctively amiable; only after months of my jumping inside the fence—to read a magazine, or perhaps a novel urged on me as "a must"—did Agnes relax enough to sit down and chew. In time, I unlocked the fence and let her roam free, one less caged animal for us to be guilty for. The land was good for wandering, but Agnes, obedient to her parole conditions, learned to follow me. Many mornings, I drove off only to see her trotting behind, the tail up high.

We moved to the city when Agnes turned three. The new neighborhood was crammed with animals in Agnes' weight division—an Afghan hound, a sheepdog, an English setter—so I anticipated no problem in bringing her along. But a city official said no, cattle aren't allowed in Washington. But pets are, I argued, explaining Agnes didn't represent a ranching operation. The no stuck, and the city took another loss, and as usual, a self-inflicted one.

A friend in Greenwich, my brother Justin, looking from behind the town's nets of gold for still more treasure, said he would happily take Agnes. He had four acres of land and old boots that could take endless lickings. In a place loaded with registered Republicans—Connecticut's junior senator lived only a mile away—Agnes fit in because she was a registered Jersey. Any pure-bred affiliation will do, lest any rabble break through the town's wallfront. Apparently taking government to the people, a high-up Nixon administration official who grew up in Greenwich, recently returned to his hometown to warn: "Don't for one moment think that Greenwich can't become an opulent slum in 50 years or a Bowery in 250 years. Those options are very much alive."

Agnes in no way pushed Greenwich toward slumminess, but occasionally she did disturb the town's chary peace. In heat one month, she spent a few nights awake issuing loud calls to an imaginary mate. Others were kept awake, too. An agent of the local humane society called on Justin to say that a neighbor was complaining and that this neighbor believed Agnes' cries were caused by beatings. Word went back to the complainer that Agnes' condition was a natural one. On a later visit to Greenwich, I learned by discreet investigation that the complainer was an 80-year-old widowed dowager who kept on her estate three gelding horses, four spayed dogs and two neutered cats; evidently, surrounded by this sexlessness, she had lost contact with the rhythmic realities of a mating call.

Agnes bore two calves and shared her ample udders with two other young ones. She took to the adopted beasts—a Hereford and an Angus—as though her own, a rare gesture among Jerseys who are usually stingy with their milk of animal kindness.

My last visit to Agnes was full of her old tenderness—going for my boots, muzzling close in search of a friendly pat, resting in the pasture of a long sit. Her new grassland had many apple trees, and Agnes moved among them like pillars at a grand hotel. Justin reported that Agnes fattened on the apples but, unlike Eve, she became giddy, not sinful, from eating them. The juice made her light. When Agnes died, my brother had the sense to bury her not on a lone hill, by a pond or some other impractical sight, but among the roots of the apple trees. A reincarnationist, he believed Agnes would appear every year in the fruit. Perhaps: we'll know more late this summer when the apples come in. If they are luscious and sweet, so much the better. But for now, the blossoms bloom brightly and are a wonder. That's a good enough reminder of Agnes. She was a wonder too.

# A Crow in a Back Hollow                                    1974

HAMPSHIRE COUNTY, W. Va.—It came noiselessly. In slow wingbeats that rode the air in sweeps of grace, the crow soared in between the peaks of rounded hills deep back in a mountain hollow that few people but legions of birds know about. The crow flapped slowly between sprees of gliding, exerting power in its wingtips to stay high on the updraft of wind. The sun reflected off the largness of the bird's back; the blue and black tints played their colors against the sheen of the extended wing feathers, shining to an orange in one angled moment. The bird banked and let its wings out in a wide stretch; it was not a stiff-arm, the way hawks fly, but an arc that cupped the air and floated the body of the bird like a bubble. At the end of the wings, separate feathers moved like fingers, catching and fondling the wind as though it was a touchable surface.

Suddenly the crow stiffened. Its blackness hung in heavy hulk over the woodland. Lowering its legs beneath its body, its claws opened in military poise. Loud calls stammered from its opened beak. The crow, forgetting its flight pattern, circled, dropping its head and looking in hard vision at a scene below in an open meadow of fieldgrass. Its wits now at work more than its wings, it eased low in a soft deadfall. It was renting air space now, making payments of time before dropping to the ground.

It came in and made the kill quickly—violent jerkings of the head, stabbings of the beak and quick pecks into the body of a small meadow rodent. The crow, about 21 inches long, seemed to swell in size, its predator ego in touch with ancestral instincts that grow large. Squeals came from the grass but the crow snatched at the sounds by tearing still again into the trapped body. The crow jumped off the ground in a hop-dance, laying off the mouse for the moment. But only a moment. With a few final thrusts of the beak, and a gripping of the claws, the crow had its prey.

At the edge of Fitzpatrick's meadow, the crow feasted in a world apart. In late April, when the messages of nature are sent and received with no butting in from man, few parts of the wildlife community better illustrate the annual resurrections of growth than the crow. Despair is often heard that the planet is doomed, that exploitation and mongering have ruined the earth beyond repair and that time runs out. But the crow suggests otherwise. Its population today is said to be larger than when the English settled in New England in the 1620s. In the 350 years since, we have driven out large numbers of animals—the plains wolf, the sea mink, the eastern elk—and destroyed almost to extinction such mighty creatures as the blue whale, the timber wolf and the bald eagle, but the simple crow has not only survived, it has flourished. Our bulldozers, hunting rifles and real estate deals have not been able to harm the life energy of this amazing creation.

The crow's good fortune may come from the fact that man has never found a way to make money from killing it—which accounts for the vanishings of whales, wolves and polar bears—but a stronger reason is the crow's reliance on a virtue that man blindly insists is unimportant: a communal spirit of staying with each other. Crows warn each other of danger, they share the good news of a new-found food source and they pool their intelligence into a common fund of local knowledge.

Stories are told of hunters shooting into a flock of crows, only to have some of the crows break ranks and swoop in to attack the hunters. Never ones for a fair fight, the hunters slink off and go pick on such weaker species as the dove, the symbol of peace.

A debate goes on as to whether the crow is harmful or helpful to man. But even to put the issue in those terms is getting it wrong immediately. The question is less what crows do to us but what they do to nature. They serve it. If they do anything to us while going about the obligations of this service then it is because we have withdrawn from our obligations, and the crash is caused by this selfish looking away. Crows rob the nests of other birds, hauling away eggs and young, but robbery is a word of human invention that has nothing to do with nature, ever balancing itself. An instinctual reason exists that allows the crow to dominate the wren, because the wren is dominating another being, and all of it together becoming a transcendence more noble than any chapter headings we devise to sort out the confusion.

We are confused because we aren't sure what time it is. Historians insist that men have been performing large deeds for thousands of years, but in the middle of a West Virginia hollow, with a crow taking its protein, the scale of time is different: if the entire life of the planet is matched to a span of one year, human beings have been here for only about one hour. Only an enlightened few have learned what the crows have understood long before we came: that sharing the wealth is better than hoarding it and that intelligence is a better means to survival than hostility.

Perhaps it is too much to lay all this onto the crow, but as a symbol of what is most enduring in nature it epitomizes Walt Whitman's belief in "Specimen Days": "After you have exhausted what there is in business, politics, conviviality and so on—have found that none of these finally satisfy, or permanently wear—what remains? Nature remains: to bring out from their torpid recesses the affinities of a man or woman with the open air—the sun by day and the stars of heaven by night."

After it finished its meal, the crow in Fitzpatrick's field lingered. It killed its victim for a meal, not an ideology, so it had no shame to remain on the scene. It rustled in the grass, walking a few feet, bobbing its head. When a wind swept through the field, the crow decided to take it. It lowered its body in a backward crouch and bent its tail into the ground. From that, it pushed up and flapped in strong motions, sweeping away in the same route in which it came.

Lately scientists have been trying to prove that life exists on other planets. Perhaps. But they ought to come to Hampshire County, because the big discovery here among the hearty crows is that there is life on this planet.


# Saving a Whale                                    1981

FIRE ISLAND, N.Y.—As drafts of steamy breath wafted up from the blowhole of Physty, a beached 25,000-pound, sperm whale who was in its sixth day of sick leave, caring hands caressed the mammal's immense snout, Physty—pronounced "feisty" and taken from physeter macrocephalus, the Greek term for sperm whale— lay ill in the shallow waters of a boat basin at the western tip of this barrier island that protects the southern shore of Long Island.

After the mammal had been towed in, some marine veterinarians, whale lovers and citizens with secret reverence for God's largest creature convened as an amateur lifesaving crew. This was a moment not to be missed. Here was one whale, blessed by Jonah for sure, whose meeting with man would be through the laying on of hands, not the bloodying of harpoons. Although sperms are the best known of whales—Moby Dick was one—they are still creatures of leviathan mystery. Herman Melville wrote that the sperm "lives not complete in any literature. Far above all other hunted whales, his is an unwritten life."

On the afternoon I stopped by to catch Physty's rescue attempt, hope itself seemed to be drowning. The medicine—penicillin, injected with seven-inch needles and 100 times the dosage for a human being—was not taking. The whale floated motionless, listing on its left side. Among the several hundred spectators lining the dock, a sense emerged that this whale watch was becoming a death watch.

Despite that, the scientists were grateful: First, no other beached whale in America had ever been kept alive this long and, second, a fair amount of new information had been gathered.

One of the gatherers was Richard Ellis, the world-known artist who paints whales and travels the earth—Patagonia, Newfoundland, Hawaii, Japan—to dive into oceans to observe them close-up. Ellis, wearing a red diving suit, hovered over Physty and regularly placed his ear on the mammal's immense head.

He was taking soundings. The sperm whale has a highly developed internal sonar system known as echo-location. At times, Ellis reported a few days later, "the sounds were so strong that they literally popped my hands off the whale. This is important because we are still trying to learn about their biology to determine what we should do to protect them ... All we've known about sperms in the past has been how to kill them."

With the outlook bleak and everyone far out to sea on how to cure a sick whale, no one was ready for Physty's sudden and amazing recovery. But even as plans were being made for an autopsy, the giant cetacean regained its health. After nine days, Physty, with a brain more complex than man's and perhaps a tougher spirit as well, returned to the open seas of the Atlantic.

Unless this sociable, intelligent and peaceful creature beaches itself again, this is a man-and-whale story that ends happily. Most others are the opposite. According to Save the Whales, a Washington group, "every day 50 whales die, their backs blown open by 150-lb. harpoons fired by cannons from high-speed catcher boats." Japanese whalers, subsidized by their government, are the high sea's most fanatic killers. "There are cheap, plentiful substitutes for all whale products," reports Save the Whales. "Several whale species have already been driven to the brink of extinction."

For a time in the early 1970s, the United States made some halting progress in becoming a world leader against the slaughter of whales. At home, the Marine Mammal Protection Act was enacted. Eight kinds of whales were put on the endangered species list. Abroad, Americans tried —with no success—to get the International Whaling Commission to impose a 10-year moratorium on all commercial whaling.

But now, the United States has backed off. At a recent meeting in India of 67 nations that had signed a 1973 treaty to protect endangered species, West Germany proposed to ban whale products from the international market. The U.S. delegation, along with the Soviet Union, objected.

As Physty eased out to sea after its miraculous recovery, an ominous question was raised: Was this gentle creature saved only to be blown apart one day by harpoonists?

# The Only Cats in 'The Club'                          1983

Abigail, somewhere between seventh heaven and cloud nine, was at it again. I didn't mean to catch her in the act, but when I walked into the room, I couldn't have known she would be there drinking. Abigail has a problem, and here she was in the middle of a few strong sips.

It's not what she drinks—only water—but where: out of a flower vase on a desk top in a senator's office in the new $137 million Hart Senate Office Building. And it's not that Abigail isn't entitled to her water. The problem of Abigail, a 7-year-old Manx cat owned by Sen. John Melcher (D-Mont.), is one of adjustment.

It's the Hart building: a cool-sleek, glassy, uncozy, structure into which Melcher and 49 other senators and entourages are now unpacking their moving crates.

Abigail was carried last week from her living quarters of six years, the homey Melcher office in the Russell building. With her was Emily, her gray-coated sister, also a tailless Manx. They are the nation's most exalted office cats. The American Cat Fancy Association gives no best-of-breed ratings for office cats. But if it did, Abigail and Emily would be at the top. They are the only cats in the world's most exclusive club, the U.S. Senate.

Abigail and Emily, as most of the club members like to say of themselves, have humble origins. Melcher, a good man and a cat lover since boyhood, found the pair in 1976 in the Missoula, Mont., animal shelter. He was moving up in the world at the time—from the House to the Senate—and thought that going from a shelter in Missoula to his Washington office would be a rise for the constituent cats too.

No Oversight Committee on Relocation Traumas has yet been appointed to learn what mental pressures the 50 senators are enduring in their new quarters. It was a move few wanted to make from the cozier offices of the Russell and Dirksen buildings. If the current edginess of Abigail and Emily tells us anything about the effects on the nerves and the psyche of being exiled to Hart, an oversight committee, and perhaps a presidential task force, should be appointed immediately.

Between Abigail—named after First Lady Adams—and Emily—as in Dickinson, the poet—Emily appears to be more mentally troubled.

A year ago when I interviewed her master in his office in the Russell building, Emily exuded friendliness and charm. When I sat, she jumped on my lap. I petted her satiny coat and she purred. Then, conferring a still higher honor on me, she sprung to my shoulder on the way to the headrest atop the armchair. There she remained during the interview, as content as the feline in Keats's "Sonnet to Mrs. Reynolds' Cat."

Last week, Emily's old self had vanished. She avoided me. Purrless and wary, she kept her silence and distance. In the new office, with unpacked boxes against one wall and an unhung mirror resting against the base of another, she was showing the tiger in her genes and the jungle in her blood.

"Don't you remember me, Emily?" I asked. She all but raised her back, as though I were the lowest of Washington's humanity—a fat cat lobbyist.

Abigail appears to be in mental turmoil, too. Scaling a secretary's desk to drink out of a vase between the Rolodex and pencil box is the least of it. Last year, she couldn't get enough of ankle-rubbing. The other day, she lurked under a desk and could bring herself only to rub the lower drawer of a cold file cabinet. She meowed several times. These were plaintive meows, as if to say, "I'm going to the dogs in this joint, take me back to Russell—or Missoula."

The happiness of their Russell years was unbounded. They could mouse and roach—pleasures not to be found in lifeless too-scrubbed Hart. For hobnobbing with the greats of the republic, they pawed down the corridor to the neighboring offices of Sen. Robert Byrd of West Virginia. All that's next door now is some fellow from Alabama who's less known than Garfield.

John Melcher understands the angst of his cats. In time, he says, they will adjust well. He is the only veterinarian in Congress and knows of these things.

I won't argue with him about Abigail and Emily. But with the cats belonging as much to the nation as to the senator, I have sought a second medical opinion on the case. Dr. Walter F. Burghardt Jr., a leading veterinary psychologist who provides therapy for cats at $45 an hour, says that many of his patients do indeed suffer mental problems caused by moves. He has professionally treated angry, anxious and emotionally shattered cats. Burghardt did not believe prolonged therapy is needed for Emily and Abigail. Some special care will probably bring them around, he said.

In the Hart building, where a roof-top tennis court will be available to ease the relocation pains of the senators, why not some perks for the cats? Start them off with a bowl of goldfish. If that doesn't cheer them, bring in a tub of salmon.

# Not a Crank Cause                                          *1984*

Rep. Tom Lantos (D-Calif.) has no trouble uttering the graphic phrase to explain his reasons for supporting legislation to ban animal leghold traps. "Steel-jaw leghold traps brutalize their victims in the most agonizing way imaginable," he told his colleagues on April 9. "Trapped animals break their bones, crush their teeth, and even chew off their own limbs in their frenzy to escape the metal jaws."

Two days before, Lantos addressed some 2,000 animal rights activists who came to Washington to protest the jaws of death used by the trapping and fur industries. "It is high time that our society ...recognized the rights of our animal friends," Lantos said, "so they will be free of unnecessary pain and torture and suffering."

That would appear to be all that's needed to say on the issue, save a mailing or two from the Fund for Animals to raise money to send out another mailing. The legislation has 115 cosponsors in the House. Not much political courage is needed to sign up. More than 50 other countries have already banned the traps.

The kind of bravery needed is what Lantos or few other members of Congress appear to have: a consistent animal-rights position.

Lantos talks about "humane alternative traps" that are available. In other words, kill them gently. That's acceptable. Grisly killing is not. The congressman speaks of "unnecessary pain and torture." Presumably he favors "necessary" pain and torture. Lantos protests the leghold traps as "one of the most appalling atrocities" man commits against animals. What about the routine atrocities, the kind needed to get annually about 5 billion mammals and birds and uncounted fish to the flesh-savoring mouths of America's non-vegetarians?

Animals deserve better than selective protection. Beasts in the wild caught in leg traps are said to total 17 million a year. Almost that number of cows, calves, chickens, pigs and sheep are slaughtered daily. Banning leghold traps would be progress, but of a minor kind. Only the method of killing, not the reason, would be outlawed. Animals would still be victims of economic, scientific or recreational exploitation.

Congress is nowhere close either to recognizing full animal rights or to staying the human hands that kill animals, kindly or cruelly. Perceptibly, though, the animal-rights movement is growing as a national force.

It is a movement no longer limited to such citizens as placard-carrying anti-vivisectionists or sentimentalists worrying about stray dogs left out in the rain. The strength of the new understanding can be judged by the intellectual depth of its philosophers, who are making the moral case that the animals being eaten, hunted and experimented on by man are individuals with rights that demand respect.

The most prominent of these philosophers is Tom Regan, a philosophy professor at North Carolina State. Regan is a scholar who can as easily demolish the views of the 17th century's Descartes, who wrongly dismissed animals as "thoughtless brutes," as he can examine the institutional violence behind rodeos or the Pentagon's wound labs. When Regan is asked, "Where's the beef?" he answers that in the world of Wendy's and Big Macs the corpses of cows are "symptoms of our culture's throwaway attitude toward animals, as if these sensitive creatures are commodities or things."

Regan is the author of "The Case for Animal Rights" (University of California Press). If newspaper sports sections were turned one day a year into philosophy sections, Regan would combine the coolness of Jack Nicklaus and the power of Mike Schmidt. His book, at once scholarly and stylishly written, advances the moral theories needed to counter the imbalance between animal rights and human wrongs. The movement, Regan writes, "is not for the faint of heart. Success requires nothing less than a revolution in our culture's thought and action."

Regan does the important job of refocusing the argument. The question is no longer why citizens such as him are so seemingly eccentric as to defend all animals but why other people are so extreme as to justify attacking any animal.

# Chapter 9

# Life's Games

**S**port is not a test but a therapy; not a trial but a reward; not a question but an answer.

—*George Sheehan*

## Meeting At The Wall 1979

Coming to the 20-mile mark, the questions, like my running, began to get rough.

"Dad, what does it feel like? Are you hitting the wall now? How come you're slowing down, Dad? Look at that guy—he must be 60, and he just passed you. And now a lady is coming up behind you. Dad, I mean you've really got to get it moving."

The flow of commentary was coming from Jimmy McCarthy, my 10-year-old. Jimmy met me on his bicycle a little past the halfway point in November's Marine Corps Marathon in Washington. Now, he was wheeling along in merry spirits, having seen about 6,000 of us start off about two hours earlier, everyone cheering everyone else.

As all the books on parenting tell us, we are supposed to raise our kids to talk frankly with adults. Now here was mine, in the sweet candor of youth, asking me what it's like to hit the wall. It wasn't one of the grander moments in father-son dialogue. Look at me, I thought, not only am I hurtling headlong into the cursed wall, but I have this young inquisitor demanding a blow-by-blow account.

But an electron or two were still jumping in my exhausted brain—enough for me to realize that I had brought this interrogation on myself. I had asked for it. I remembered all the times I had talked about The Wall to Jimmy and his two younger brothers. How raptly they listened. In the living room after a fine suppoer, they'd be warm and content in their pajamas, listening eagerly for what I had to say. I'd rise to the occasion: "Boys, it's really amazing what I do in those marathons," I'd say. "I've yet to be done in."

I'd tell them about conquering the wall at Heartbreak Hill, in New York, Beltsville, Satyr Hill in Balitmore and in last year's Marine Corps, too. I'd end these dramatic tales with the same rousing line: When you talk to the other kids in school, tell 'em about Iron Legs, your dad who runs through walls.

So here was Jimmy next to me at 20 miles. He had come to see for himself. He had listened to me for so long that he knew the questions to ask: Do the cramps in your calves hurt more than your dizziness? Why don't you throw water over your head at the next sto, the way Bill Rodgers does?

The 20-mile mark in the Marine Corps Marathon comes near the bend at Hains Point, which juts into the Potomac River. The real retort I had for Jimmy at this point was: You want to be heaved into the river head first or feet first? But I didn't ask it. I was hobbling along at a turtle's pace. Talking would use up too much energy. I had wasted it already by going out too fast—five miles in 37 minutes, ten miles in 76. At 20 miles, I was deep in debt, with nearly all my energy spent. Even a 12-minute mile meant giving it my gutmost.

And all the while, Jimmy was taking it in. Ambulances were beginning to come by for the lame and halt, and I probably would have piled in except for this 75-pound boy on his bike, who, in some way, was carrying me along. I have heard of one marathoner psychologically hauling another along—one runner's emotions acting as jumper cables recharging the fading will power of another. And now it was happening to me. Jimmy's only ten, I thought, and already I'm depending on him for energy, for life.

The thought was melancholy. Poets and philosophers talk of life's circles: how fathers pick up their babies from the cradle and then, when the children are parents, they pick up their dying fathers from the sick-bed to nurse them in their last days.

Here were the final miles of the marathon and I was being nursed along. Jimmy knew by now that all the kick had left me. I told him I would try to break four hours. That would be great he said, although I knew he knew better. He remembered that I had done last year's Marine Corps in 3:26. But compared to this year's conditions, that was almost a cakewalk. The temperature then was around 50°. This year's 75° made this run more like a death march.

As for the often devastating impact of the wall, Jimmy began to experience it himself in that last mile. He said his legs were killing him. He'd never bicycled more than five miles before, but now, coming up the hill at the finish line, he had doubled that distance. This was his marathon as well. By the end, we were pulling each other in.

The agony has passed now. How quickly the memory and the muscles forget the tough parts of a marathon. I'm already back to gathering my sons around me for some new tales of the wall. But now, with hubris in check, I'm also doing some listening. Jimmy is telling the real story, not the heroic one. The old man is mortal. His legs aren't iron, they're flesh. And one day they'll need nursing.

# Summer From the Mound                                    *1981*

Major League baseball players have plenty of skills, but they lack one: being able to ruin my summer because they are on strike. I'll go further. The strike is helping my summer. In the forced decline of spectatorship, a few of us have taken to the playing fields ourselves, or at least, in my case, to the bench behind the first base line.

I've become a manager. Some neighborhood boys in a 10- to 12-year-old league, apparently unable to get Edward Bennett Williams to release Earl Weaver from the Orioles, invited me to take charge. I should have checked first with Williams, because the kids, lawyer-like, now have me contractually bound to drive them to their away games. Could it have been that having access to a station wagon was the managerial talent they most admired in me?

As the chauffeur-manager, my first discovery was that my nine players wanted to take their pre-game calisthenics in the car—exercising their lungs, leaping over seats to get next to the window and jumping to conclusions that I was a weakling because I obeyed the speed limit.

When we arrived at the other team's field, the subject of speed again came up. Their pitcher had it. We gaped at his fast ball as he warmed up.

Tall and long-armed, he threw hard and low. He reminded me of the way Ewell (The Whip) Blackwell—an underballer—used to pitch and the way Sandy Koufax used to think. Said the latter: "Pitching is... the art of instilling fear."

This kid on the mound was a born instiller. Gazing at him, one of my players whispered to me, "I don't wanna bat." It's all right, I answered, we have a helmet for you. "I still don't want to bat." Just then, the pitcher, like a sonar man picking up shock waves of fear and wanting the thrill of hearing louder bleeps, reared back and sent in a pitch that sailed over the catcher's head by five feet. It went into my player's imagination by another five.

The wild pitch brought to mind the comment of Early Wynn, the old Cleveland Indian pitcher of such competitive terror that in one game he dusted back his own son: "I've got a right to knock down anyone holding a bat."

I held back on my Early Wynn stories. Tell you what, I told my lad, I'll put you up ninth: That way, Koufax II out there on the mound will have eight kids before you to terrify. By then, he'll be bored scaring people.

That seemed to offer some comfort. Then, as the bumper stickers advise, I gave the kid a hug. It helped his confidence. He was ready to play.

Now I was a chauffeur-manager-psychologist. I was also in the company of my favorite contemporary manager, Tom Lasorda of the Los Angeles, nee Brooklyn, Dodgers.

At spring training in Vero Beach a few years ago, Tom addressed himself to the cosmic baseball question of managerial displays of affection: "It's been said you shouldn't hug your players. I've been reading the rule book for years and I have yet to find a clause that reads you can't hug your players. It also has been said that a manager shouldn't eat with his players, or go visit them in their homes. I do both. We are told, too, to be sparing in our praise so that the players will feel we're sincere. I praise everyone. Like my pop said, show me a law in the United States that says I can't tell everyone he's great."

In the style of Pop Lasorda, I wanted to tell my players that they were great—except that in this game they weren't. Only the batting helmets were having a good day. When we fell back by 10 runs, then

12, perhaps I should have become a stomper and shouter and looked for a water cooler to kick. Or an umpire to bait.

But the demon of the fanatical Little League parent isn't in me. I may be fired by the squad for publicly admitting this, but I don't know our win-loss record this season. I don't know who has the most hits or the least errors. During the games, I forget the score.

I assume that if the kids wanted a computer, instead of a chauffeur-manager-psychologist, they would have picked one up, maybe in a trade. All they have in me is someone who likes their company.

Baseball, I want them to know, is a social sport. With the wretched example before them of Major League owners and players snarling at each other over money, this is a truth that may, like Koufax II's fireball, be going right past them.

# Why No Nicknames? *1981*

VERO BEACH, Fla.—Like a poacher looking for a piece of safe earth, I try to find a seat close to the playing fields. It is an hour before the spring training game at Holman Field between the Los Angeles Dodgers and the Minnesota Twins. The outfield grass, greener than I had imagined before breaking free last week from my northern city, is rimmed by palm trees. Infielders are playing pepper behind home plate, schooling each other in the basics. A coach, his belly hanging over his belt like loose freight, pops fungoes to outfielders. Behind them are pitchers running wind sprints, unshackling winter for themselves and us.

It's almost all I could ask for: the air busy with baseball and the Dodgers, birds flown to Los Angeles but banded still with Brooklyn, taking me back to boyhood days at Ebbets Field and "dem Bums."

But not all the way back. Something is missing, and if I hadn't had a few words with Walter "Smokey" Alston, the former Dodger manager and still one of baseball's true gentlemen, I might not have figured out what was awry. In the press behind home plate we talked about Pee Wee Reese, Cookie Lavagetto, Dixie Walker, Duke Snider.

Nicknames, I thought. The old Dodgers had them, even their manager Smokey. But the new ones don't. They're Steve, Ron,

Rick, Doug, Bill, Dave. It's the same for every team. A lot of Mikes, Petes, Gregs, Scotts and Jeffs are on the rosters, but no Pee Wees, Cookies or Dukes.

Even stars with no first names—Nolan Ryan, Ferguson Jenkins, Carlton Fisk—have never picked up dugout monikers. A generation ago fellows with ill-fitting first names made it almost a display of manliness to walk onto the field with a nickname. We had Enos "Country" Slaughter, Elwin "Preacher" Roe, Sal "The Barber" Maglie, Stan "The Man" Musial. They sounded like Mafia hit men. Brothers were paired in the public's consciousness by their nicknames: Dizzy Dean and Daffy Dean. Today the rowdy Dean boys would be stuck with what they were given at baptism: Jay and Paul.

When the Pee Wees and Dizzies dominated the game baseball was a subculture with its own dialect. Announcers, not needing a color-commentator to pep up the play-by-play action, had a ready fund of entertainment in the nicknames. Mel Allen, calling it a game for the Yankees, often took long stretches of air time talking about Yogi, Scooter, Snuffy, King Kong and Whitey, and never using the last names. Sportscasters had nicknames too, like Red Barber who opened his broadcasts for the Dodgers by drawling "here's the old redhead up in the catbird seat."

If nicknames have gone the way of baggy uniforms and spitballs, the loss means that blandness stalks the basepaths. Big money is one factor. How's a scamp known as Yogi or The Brat going to command the respect of an owner at contract time when demanding a million dollars for the next three seasons? It's better to be Carlton, Ferguson or Nolan.

With the nicknameless preoccupied with self-decorum, it means they also have less time for dugout clowning or off-field capers that lead to people being called Leo the Lip. The situation was assessed a few years ago by Lefty Gomez: "When I first signed with the Yankees, the regulars wouldn't talk to you until you were with the team three or four years. Nowadays, the rookies get $100,000 to sign and they don't talk to the regulars."

Some straight-named players perform so well that even playing field excellence doesn't get their juices going. Last year George Brett of the Kansas City Royals hit .390 and was the Most Valuable Player in the American League. But according to Jamie Quirk, a teammate, the slugger didn't feel as though he had fully arrived until he did a Seven-Up commercial. Quirk told Baseball magazine that Brett had done a Life-buoy commercial, "But when he got Seven-Up, he realized he was there.... Ask anybody: [George is] twice the player Dave Parker and Mike Schmidt are, but when he got the Seven-Up commercial he felt he had reached their level."

At Dodger Town, a sparkling operation complete with Jackie Robinson Avenue, I enjoy the game. But as I watch the athletes I am looking also for the boys of summers past, Dodgers like Smokey, Pee Wee and Duke. They are here too, and just the memory of their nicknames adds immeasurably to the color.

# Sports Should be Tougher                        1981

WASHINGTON—America's athletes were at it again last weekend: muscling their way to such feats of excellence that the bindings of records books were stretched once more.

In Orlando, Andy Bean won the Bay Hill Golf Classic with a course record 266, which was 18 under par and included a 62, another record. Tom Watson, who has set money records for the past three years, finished second. At the U.S. Indoor Track Championships in New York, a high jump record of 7 feet 7¾ inches was set by Jeff Woodard. A pole vaulter soared 18 feet 4½ inches, a meet record.

Even when records aren't being set, amazing performances have become commonplace on the American sports scene. Every star is a superstar.

How astonishing is all of this. And how boring.

The problem is that as the athletes get better, their sports don't get tougher. In pro basketball, the 24-second rule was introduced a few years ago. But this was less a difficulty for the players than an opportunity to shoot more. In golf, architects added extra yardage to the new courses they designed. But in 1977 Al Geiberger shot his record 59 on an exceedingly long layout of 7,249 yards.

The changes weren't enough. When records become meaningless, great performances have little greatness to them. Toughening is in order. To advance the cause, as well as decrease the number of times I yawn when another basketball player scores 40 points or golfer shoots a 62, here are five sports in need of radical changes.

• Basketball. Raise the baskets two feet and decrease the size of the hoop two inches. Slam-dunking is how gorillas would play basketball if we let them out of the zoos. Stuffing a basketball isn't the same as shooting it. By raising the basket from 10 feet to 12 feet, King Kong dunking would be eliminated. By reducing the rim size from 18 inches to 16 inches, the game would be returned to players with a sharp eye. If these two measures fail, take away the back-board. The game is basketball, not basket-backboard ball.

• Baseball. Aside from permanently muzzling George Stein-brenner, the owner and meddlier-in-chief of the New York Yankees, the major improvement needed on the diamond is a quick-ening of pace. A simple tinkering would achieve this: Instead of four balls and three strikes, let it be three balls and two strikes. In addition, the batter would be allowed only one foul ball. On the second foul, he is out.

• Tennis. Raise the net two inches. The Borgs, McEnroes and Everts have splendid long games and resounding power strokes. But can they dink and bloop? I don't know, nor does anyone else. We've never seen them try. Tennis should be a game of finesse, not strength. By raising the net two inches, the dominance of the booming serve and scorching volley would be tempered. I would rather watch players who can dink on their feet instead of uncoil from their toes. Why shouldn't a great blooper ever win Wimbledon?

• Golf. Limit the players to seven clubs, not 14. Artistry in golf requires the skilled use of the same club for three or four different shots. Today's pros have been spoiled. They have pitching wedges and sand wedges. With dexterity, they would need only a nine iron. A seven iron can be punched with a closed faced for 120 yards or swung with a wide arch and open face for 160 yards.

Why seven clubs? That's all the legendary Freddie McLeod carried when he won the 1908 U.S. Open. I once asked Mr. McLeod, who died a few years ago at age 94, about his seven club talent. He replied that "Golf required a little more skill in my day."

• Football. Narrow the goalposts by half and put them 10 yards back. Scoring by means of kicking has reduced the importance of running and passing, which are the essence of football. Too many coaches play for field position. To go for the three-point field goal, not the six-point touchdown. They are soccer coaches.

The purpose in altering the way these, and other, sports are played is to ensure that excellence remains excellence. If records are set every weekend, how can the fans be given special moments? Dr. Arnold Beisser, a Los Angeles psychiatrist writes in "The Madness in Sports," that "high quality play has become so routine that the fans' threshold for excitement has risen. Although Americans watch sports more, they obtain a narrower range of satisfaction and enjoy them less."

Dr. Beisser and I aren't the only ones yawning, are we?

# Cardiopulmonary Wonders, Orthopedic Wrecks                                    *1982*

In the slow circles that I run in, I know of almost no one who doesn't have an injury story. It's gotten so bad that I never ask a fellow runner, "How are you feeling?" Instead of a conversation, I'll get back a medical report. I'll hear more about a runner's last visit to his doctor than his last race.

Even deliberately avoiding the medical reports, I still get them. One friend trained throughout the spring and summer for the New York Marathon but withdrew a week before with a knee injury. Another friend prepared with equal diligence for the Marine Corps Marathon. On race day, she was home and barely able to walk. Her sciatic nerve was painfully pinching.

I have my own injury stories, not a one of which could be told in less than 10,000 words. But I can summarize my pains with a brief statement that summarizes what I think is happening to many, many others: we are cardiopulmonary wonders but orthopedic wrecks.

Eight or nine years ago, when the running boom hit and thousands of us went with the mighty flow, the major health debate was on the benefits that running provides the heart. A marathon, one school of thought said, was as close to an absolute guarantee against a coronary as we could get, short of a warranty signed by God in heaven. Another group advanced the idea that while not enough evidence was in to make that kind of a claim it could be safely said that runnning does increase the fitness of the heart and lungs. Still a third argument was pushed by the negativists: running is bad for the cardiovascular system. These were the sedentary who took their scientific evidence from the obituary pages: another 35-

year-old jogger dies during his morning run. See that? What further proof is needed—running is bad for the ticker.

In looking back, I wish the debate had been on bones and joints, not ventricles and auricles. By not paying enough attention to the orthopedic hazards of running, the experts created an atmosphere of false safety. I know that blaming the experts is better than blaming myself. But now that I have a bum left knee, an aching right hip and a sore left foot, I wish that the profusion of articles now in the running magazines about knees, hips and feet had appeared years ago.

Not that I would have been smart enough to pay attention and do only two marathons a year instead of four or five. But I believe that my level of risk-consciousness would have been raised at least a little. I remember being told by a colleague—a non-runner—that the skeletal system wasn't made for the excessive punishment of distance running. But since the debate back then was on the benefits to the heart, I thought this was a side issue not worth even thinking about.

Alas, I am thinking about it now. Not with regrets for the numberless miles I've put in, and certainly not with any sense of disappointment for such thrills as running in Boston. But I'm wondering if perhaps I may have overdone it. And if I overdid it, how many others did too?

Quite a lot, I'd say. In this year's Marine Corps Marathon, which is the nation's largest after New York, approximately 6,400 of the 9,500 entrants were first-time marathoners. As Len Shapiro of the *Washington Post* pointed out, that means that only 3,100 of the some 9,500 who ran the year before, or had run a marathon elsewhere, were back for another run.

That's a significant drop-off. Short of specific information based on questionnaires, it is hard not to assume that a large number of the people who didn't run were injured, like my sciatic nerve friend. Shapiro recently wrote a "where-are-they-now" piece about his running companions of three and four years ago. A few are injured so badly that they no longer run at all, he reported. The others have dropped out of the marathon scene. Shapiro wrote of himself: "Once, training for the marathon consumed me. I bought all the books, read all the magazines, kept my daily mileage totals in the official Jim Fixx calendar, experimented with bee pollen and loaded up on carbohydrates every chance I could. These days, I'm happy to run four miles three or four times a week, a six miler on Saturday morning, with a little tennis here, a little YMCA basketball there."

As the born-again runners are tapering off in both their mileage and their enthusiasm, so are the bluebloods of the sport. Frank Shorter says, "Instead of 120 miles a week, I'm doing 90, but all things considered, it seems enough."

No doubt non-marathoners will be making much of how the distance runners were suckered into the sport by the prospects of the cardiopulmonary benefits, and never dreamed that as the heart was strengthening the knees were weakening. But one compensating fact is indisputable: joints that work at 80 percent capacity for athletes are not half as disastrous as hearts and lungs that work at 40 percent for loungers.

It is still something to be proud of that at some point in your life you decided to carry things a bit further than your conservative self and the conservative world thought was good for you.

Of course, 26 miles is going too far. But "man is a maximizer," says George Sheehan, who ran his best marathon (3:01) in the 1979 Marine Corps at age 60. I did the first mile with him—a sprightly 6:30, after which I watched George bound off. He was running in the spirit of what he's written: Man "is ripe for excesses and exuberances. When life becomes a celebration, we are likely to over-celebrate."

# Press Run                                                          1981

At the edge of the running world is the reading world. Although both follow separate paths, not long ago I had a heart-warming experience which revealed how closely they can sometimes track together.

It began when I wrote about the late Clarence DeMar's autobiography, a splendid—and at times enchanting—book in which the legendary runner wrote of his career in the 1920s and 1930s. DeMar was then winning seven Bostons and was hailed as the world's greatest marathoner. I called Marathon a "jewel" and a "rare prize" and ended with a modest suggestion: "Any publisher who wants to provide a public service (and no doubt sell a few copies in the bargain) has a rare opportunity to reprint something worthwhile in this little classic."

Copies of *Marathon* are still unavailable, but if my mail is any indi-
cation, they won't be for long. One letter came from a Deborah
Yamaoto of Redwood City, California, who wrote to tell me about
"Uncle Clarence." Mrs. Yamamoto's maiden name is DeMar, and
she explained that she was "one of many relatives of Clarence
DeMar." I read two sentences in her letter with some amazement:
"My uncle, Dr. Edgar, has the 'family' copy of Clarence's book and
we are very interested in seeing it reprinted. In fact, my uncle has
made attempts in the past to have the book published (but) with no
luck."

Then there was the letter from L. M. Passudetti of New Hyde
Park, New York, which gave me a gasp of another kind. I quote it in
full: "I have a copy of the DeMar book in good condition, which I
would be willing to sell for $75. It is just as you describe in your
article and this copy is clean and tight. If you want the book please
send me a check and I'll mail it immediately."

As much as I admired the business acumen of Mr. Passudetti, I
was saving up for a pair of new running shoes at the time and
needed my $75 for that. As it turned out, though, he would get his
cash from another source: Alfred Rosa, a co-publisher of The New
England Press. But more about Professor Rosa later.

One of the fascinating twists in all this is that the original
publisher of *Marathon* had no copy of the book either. In 1937, John
Hooper, as the owner of the Stephen Daye Press in Brattleboro,
Vermont, published 3,000 copies of DeMar's work. He had, he says,
"the darndest time getting rid of them."

Mr. Hooper is now 75 and writes a retirement column called
'Hooper's Pasture' for a weekly newspaper in Vermont. In a recent
piece, he wrote of his long-ago publishing venture:

"Clarence DeMar had retired and was living in nearby Keene,
New Hampshire. I persuaded him to finish a book about his
marathon years and experiences. I was sure that thousands (such as
those who stand on the highways each year to watch the Boston
Marathon) would buy it.

"But they didn't. Not many people were that much interested in
marathons—and it is a pity."

If the original publication of the book sparked any interest at all, it
was from librarians. They apparently bought copies and put them
on the back shelves, waiting for posterity to show up at the front

desks. Peter H. Stevens, the director of the acquisition division at the library of the University of Washington in Seattle, wrote to me about the Online Computer Library Center (OCLC). It is similar to an automated card catalog containing more than seven million titles. Two thousand libraries participate. Mr. Stevens enclosed a printout from OCLC which listed several libraries holding the DeMar classic. These included the Cincinnati public library, the Jacksonville, Florida public library, and the University of Texas at Lemar library.

Another librarian—Fred Mansfield of the University of Illinois at Urbana-Champaign—wrote to say: "I am sending a copy of your column to the "Books on Demand" program of University Microfilms International; this program clears copyrights and prepares master microfilm negatives for out-of-print titles, which are reproduced either in xerox format or in positive microfilm as orders are received by the company. This program makes it possible to make out-of-print titles available."

As it turns out, xerox or microfilm facsimilies for library special orders may not be necessary. It looks like DeMar's 1937 book is going to be published in a new edition. Which brings us back to Alfred Rosa, who wrote me a pleasant letter not long after my column appeared. As co-publisher of the The New England Press, a small publishing house in Shelburne, Vermont, which offers a modest list of about a dozen titles a year, he wanted to discuss the prospects of republishing *Marathon*. Rosa's full-time work is teaching English at the University of Vermont. Publishing, apparently, is an avocation that gives him relief from the tortures of freshmen who write too little and faculty who talk too much.

Professor Rosa explained that he wanted to take a try at *Marathon*. He asked what I thought of the book's prospects. After glancing at the shelf in my office that sags with the weight of about 25 books on running, I wrote back to the professor saying that the market, like the starting fields for marathons, was packed but that plenty of room was left in the front row for quality. The reality of the competition was no surprise to the professor, but the new—and cheering—information I had for him was that my column had evoked a fairly strong response from readers. An audience was out there. Finally, it seems the professor, in fruitless searching, could not locate a copy of the book, which he needed to give to his printer for duplication. So I put him in touch—you guessed it—with the scalper, uh, gracious gentleman from New York, for which he was grateful.

I am delighted that DeMar's classic will soon be available for the reading and running public. Being just a newspaperman and not a forecaster, I make no predictions that the reprinting of *Marathon* will be a success, much less a blockbuster. I can only predict that just as there is a lively interest in the book after 44 years, runners 44 years from now will also be eager to learn about DeMar and his era.

# Index